Bringing Learning

Bringing Learning to Life:
The Learning Revolution, The Economy and The Individual

Edited by

David C.A. Bradshaw

 The Falmer Press

(A member of the Taylor & Francis Group)
London • Washington, D.C.

UK The Falmer Press, 4 John Street, London WC1N 2ET
USA The Falmer Press, Taylor & Francis Inc., 1900 Frost Road, Suite 101, Bristol, PA 19007

First published in 1995

A catalogue record for this book is available from the British Library

Library of Congress Cataloging-in-Publication Data are available on request

ISBN 0 7507 0394 6 cased
ISBN 0 7507 0395 4 paper

Jacket design by Caroline Archer

Typeset in 10.5/12pt Bembo by
Graphicraft Typesetters Ltd., Hong Kong.

Printed in Great Britain by Burgess Science Press, Basingstoke on paper which has a specified pH value on final paper manufacture of not less than 7.5 and is therefore 'acid free'.

Contents

Preface   vii

Chapter 1   Introduction   1
David Bradshaw

Chapter 2   Learning Does Pay   18
Sir Christopher Ball

Chapter 3   Education and Training: An Historical Perspective   33
Jon Ainger and Roy Harrison

Chapter 4   Lifelong Learning: A Brave and Proper Vision   47
Naomi Sargant

Chapter 5   Human Learning Potential   65
Ken Richardson

Chapter 6   Learning Theory: Harnessing the Strength of a Neglected Resource   79
David Bradshaw

Chapter 7   Curriculum and Curriculum Process for a Changing World and an Uncertain Future   93
Anne Jones

Chapter 8   A Learning in Organizations Model   111
Alan Jones

Chapter 9   Towards the Virtual Library: Deconstruction and Reconstruction of Learning Resources in Higher Education   131
Alasdair Paterson

Chapter 10   Structures and Funding   140
Tony Cann

Chapter 11   Learning: A Qualified Success?   152
John Hillier

Contents

Chapter 12   Towards a Strategy for Lifelong Guidance to
               Support Lifelong Learning and Work   162
               A G Watts and Stephen McNair

Chapter 13   A Strategy to Achieve Lifelong Learning   177
               Tony Webb

               Notes on Contributors   191

               Index   194

Preface

In 1990–92 Sir Christopher Ball directed a project to examine ways of increasing participation in post-compulsory education and training in Britain. Based at the Royal Society for the encouragement of Arts, Manufacturers and Commerce (RSA), its findings appeared in an Interim Report *Learning Pays* in 1991 and a final Summary Report, Recommendations and Action Plan, *Profitable Learning*, in January 1992. Widely discussed at regional and national seminars and conferences, the project raised issues which could, in the nature of such documents, be treated only in summary. But as we considered the comments of the many contributors to the discussion we agreed that some further publication was desirable. As the project's Deputy Director, I agreed to bring together a collection of papers on some of the issues we had found especially significant and to which responses are needed from the managers of the nation's learning and from government. National life has moved on and the weight and detail of evidence in favour of the conclusions of the two reports has increased. There has been action too: some by government and agencies such as NACETT, some by other leadership organizations — notably the Confederation of British Industry (CBI) and the Training and Enterprise Council (TEC) movement — and much within companies and institutions of learning. But more remains to be done. This book is published in the hope that it will help in that process.

Some of the contributors to this book were closely involved in the RSA project, others accepted invitations to contribute later. But I thank them all for their cooperation in producing the chapters which follow.

David Bradshaw
Sheffield
June 1994

'In a time of drastic change it is the learner who inherits the future. The learned usually find themselves equipped to live in a world that no longer exists.'

Eric Hoffer (1902–83)

Reflections on the Human Condition

Chapter 1

Introduction

David Bradshaw

National Aspirations

Our national aspirations outrun our means. We want a high standard of living for our people, with high disposable incomes, high quality medical and social care, varied and rich cultural opportunities, vigorous intellectual life, and we want to remain influential in global politics. All depend on a strong and growing economy. But we have been in economic decline for many decades and have to improve to stand still and improve yet again to advance. Other problems include inner city decay, environmental deterioration, crime, drug misuse and the emerging underclass of the jobless or homeless. These too relate to the economy in part. The problems intertwine and there are no single solve-all solutions to any of them; they need multi-dimensional and integrated action. So although this book focuses on the connections between learning, especially of those who have left school (including those who left some time ago) and the economy, it does so in the awareness of other problems that confront us and the understanding that they connect one with another. It also recognizes two other circles of action. One is that learning supports many activities other than the economic, and the other that while the economy cannot improve without better learning it also needs action on other fronts to secure it. This book also acknowledges what has been achieved in the last decade and a half (especially in Jon Ainger and Roy Harrison's chapter on recent reforms). But its main concern is to examine some of the key areas where further change is needed.

The Economic Context

Economics is an inexact science, but there is strong consensus on some issues. One is the view that it is convenient but misleading to write of a national economy because companies and individuals perform within a global economy, with multi-national companies operating in dozens of countries world wide. Companies move production from one country to another to take advantage of lower labour costs and other more favourable circumstances and servicing can move around too. So it is possible, for example, for a British-based company to manufacture in Hungary and to have its accounts kept on computers in India. Money flows round the world at the flick of a switch.

Companies are helped (or otherwise) by national laws, the clarity and strength of government strategy, the availability of capital and the terms on which it is lent, current habits of investment, its people's commitment to learning and the quality of provision for it. Within national boundaries these constrain or support companies and individuals in similar ways forming the conditions for what Michael Porter calls 'the competitive advantage of nations' (Porter, 1990). So the appearance of a national economy remains while trade is world wide and the economy is global. Ends and means interlock: improvements in transport and educational provision serve individual desires, but are needed for economic change and growth. Health care, seen primarily as a basic human right, has economic consequences significant enough for most employers to take account of it.

National shares of the global economy change as rates of growth in one country and another fluctuate. By growing faster than western economies Japan became a super economy in three decades. Similarly the 'seven tigers' of South East Asia (Hong Kong, Indonesia, Malaysia, Singapore, South Korea, Taiwan and Thailand) are becoming ever stronger through exceptional growth.

Many sectors make up a nation's contribution to the global economy, all of them in a state of change. And the features which distinguish the rich, the poor, the emerging and the declining are their share of high value-added activities and those things which support them. Worker-intensive production of low value-added products produces jobs, but only a relatively small contribution to the general wealth in circulation, while a few workers may add substantial value by applying a high level of skill. For example highly skilled people using modern technology produce more steel in the city of Sheffield than ever before. But the number of people is much smaller than it used to be. The emphasis has also changed to special products, many of them 'designed' for specific markets to detailed specifications and the highest quality. Goods and services for 'niche' markets are one of the growth points in the economy. Highly specialized problem-solving activities such as research, consultancies and financial service management are another. They are all very highly skilled.

But economic change has a down side. No skill almost invariably means no job. Automation and changes in working practices can suddenly reduce demand for some skills or even make them redundant. Shop floor workers in manufacturing and office workers doing routine tasks have suffered particularly heavily from this, but computers are displacing middle managers in many companies as well. The result is not just unemployment but structural instability in the employment market.

A fundamental question emerges from this scenario — what are the essentials of learning that support a growing and dynamic economy? 'What knowledge is most worth?' asked Herbert Spencer a century and more ago (Spencer, 1861) when addressing similar issues. We have never answered the question satisfactorily in Britain and we urgently need an answer for our own times.

Available Work and its Dependence on Learning

Robert Reich, political economist and US Secretary of Labour since 1993, sees work in the first decades of the twenty-first century as falling into three broad categories:

> routine production
> interperson services
> symbolic-analytical services. (There is no fourth category for the unskilled.)

Routine production services include the work of manual workers in heavy industry, the production of consumer durables and new production work like filling computer circuit boards. It includes those who key in records of credit card purchases, update medical records, and fill the low level supervisory roles that go with them. Although new jobs are created in this sector, mainly out of the computer revolution, the proportion of people working in routine production has fallen and, because of the movement of high volume work to other countries (in textiles and clothing manufacture, for example), the decline will probably continue.

Interperson services serve other people directly. The list of jobs is vast and includes waiters and waitresses, hotel workers, cashiers, nursing home aides, child care workers, attendants and orderlies, taxi drivers, hair dressers, flight attendants and security guards. They need skills, but they need personal qualities too. For, in addition to the punctuality and reliability of routine workers, person-to-person servers 'must be pleasant in demeanour. They must smile, radiate charm and confidence even if they are feeling miserable or even bad tempered' (Reich, 1991, pp. 176–7). The numbers of them grow rapidly.

Symbolic-Analytic Services include most of the technical and professional servicing of manufacturing, research science and the new problem-identifying, problem-solving and strategic-brokering activities. These workers trade in symbols — in words, diagrams and graphic representations. Typical job titles show their range and give an inkling of their scope:

- design/civil/biotechnical/software/sound/surface **engineers;**
- management information/computer hardware (or software) **managers;**

- financial/tax/energy/architectural/armament/public relations/agricultural **consultants;**
- strategic/financial/**planners;**
- corporate headhunters; and systems analysts. (Reich, 1991, pp. 174–8).

Their support workers, the technicians, assistants and implementers must be highly skilled too.

Common threads run through all three categories and examples: every job today adds value; every job needs skills; the skills have to be learned; the skills change and must be updated or replaced. These categories of work are very broad and some of them are stated in very general terms. The examples which follow give meaning to the generalized descriptions and illustrate some of the features of today's connections between employment and work.

Routine Production Services

The motor car is a powerful symbol of twentieth-century achievement. The work to produce it is a good example of Reich's first category of work and the Nissan factory at Sunderland illustrates many of the features now seen as significant in production industries. The factory is new and in some areas is equipped with the most advanced machinery available, yet Nissan's success is seen in its people more than in the sophistication of its technology. The key is to find the fine balance between the prescribed elements of the work and the motivation of the individual to pursue the best. And this aim is directed not only at meeting today's exacting standards but finding improvements, however small, that will make tomorrow's production even better. The human side rests on a secure and supportive environment where mistakes are seen as the consequence of inadequate training or management. The firm encourages interest in the whole process of the plant and progress of the company, and information about its performance is published to all workers who respond by studying the latest bulletins and discussing them. Praise for success is plentiful (Wille, 1990).

The work at Nissan is divided between automated (or robotized) and hand processing, at every stage in the manufacturing process. The division is made on the pragmatic basis of what produces the best results. State of the art presses in the body pressing shop for example are operated by teams (a team of six workers to two presses) who change the dies, check for quality and make adjustments. Body construction is highly robotized, but in final assembly the processes are largely manual. However the part played by the workers is crucial at every stage. Their training identifies the precise specification of the tasks, its quality elements, time factors, the ability to train others and to trouble-shoot; but at no stage can any task be so tightly defined as to remove scope for personal commitment, so that motivation to do the job well is essential.

All the processes depend on learning. Workers are selected for their potential, identified at a testing centre, and can begin work at different ages and with widely different backgrounds. Some are in late teenage and may be joining Nissan through a Youth Training scheme; others may be in their mid-thirties after other employment experience. Initial selection assesses both attitude and technical aptitude, and responsibility for preparing them for their work is placed as close as possible to the point of delivery and rests with the production supervisors supported by a central training unit. The traditional division of 'training on-the-job' and 'education off-the-job' has been modified in favour of learning 'near-the-job' in a shop-skill school. In the case of learning to operate robots, however, they are too complicated and expensive for this approach to be practicable, so this takes place further away in a centre for practical training. These essential skills are developed within the threefold context of flexibility, teamwork and quality. Brief meetings at the beginning of each working day decide plans and special points for the day. Out of them come targets for the teams to which every member feels personal commitment.

Behavioural skills are introduced to everyone at every level of work and the Nissan College has been established to cover non-technical training. An open-learning centre is available during working hours and provides opportunities for staff to learn a variety of things systematically. The emphasis is on self-direction and the choice of learning package is up to the individual. Computer skills are one of the most popular areas for self-development. And self-development has a two-fold outcome. The worker possesses new skills both for themselves as well as for the company.

Inter-person Services

The work of the office, school or hotel cleaner (or one working in other situations) is a good example of service work. Once a considerable source of part-time and essentially low-skilled employment, the work is now often contracted out to specialist companies and has become essentially knowledge-based using specialist equipment and cleaning agents whose operations and qualities must be understood. Cleaners need knowledge, skills, willingness to go on learning and, in many situations, sensitivity to other people.

The work of a twenty-four strong team in a college where some of the students are resident and where there is a high quality conference facility shows how this happens in practice. The accommodation includes teaching rooms, offices, student study bedrooms, the conference suite and its bedrooms. The college has recently refurbished much of the accommodation and the conference facilities are of good hotel standard. Cleaning staff work for four hours per day with just a little opportunity for overtime to take care of especially demanding conferences. Newly appointed staff are first helped to feel part of the whole organization. Pride in work done and a sense of looking after the people who live and work in the college is a long standing tradition. This grows with discussion of the college's plans, its vision of quality and the special requirements of groups visiting for conferences. Awareness of safety has to be strong with conformity to the Control of Substances Hazardous to Health (COSHH) regulations and to other government and European Union health and safety rules. Knowledge of the materials cleaned and the machinery and agents used is fundamental. One of the work manuals lists six schedules of processes to cover seventeen different floor types. Each schedule has its own processes and specified cleaning agents and the finishes are laid down according to use. The products are designed for specific materials and surfaces, but can cause damage if used on the wrong fabrics and finishes.

Newly appointed staff are expected to acquire National Vocational Qualifications (NVQs) and established staff are encouraged to do so. The complete NVQ qualification includes assessment of communication skills, health and safety, public relations and teamwork. Cleaners work individually but are allocated to areas in pairs. Previously new staff used to be placed with experienced ones to learn the routines; now such continuity is avoided where possible so as to encourage changes of attitude and practices. Supervision also has to be of a different order with an eye for continuous improvement, the introduction of updated practice, close attention to time management and to recurrent training needs.

Symbolic-analytical Services

Reich's symbolic analyst is illustrated by a researcher working for the British Broadcasting Corporation (BBC) in the the specialized field of Spectrum Engineering. His job is to make maximum use of the radio frequencies allotted to the Corporation and to provide perfect sound on radio and perfect pictures and sound on television. Starting from the basic facts of electrical transmission and reception, he has to take account of the way signals affect and interfere with one another and also their behaviour with the physical environment. This includes hills, woodland, individual large trees, the sea, the built environment and all varieties of weather conditions. So he has to know enough about topography, architecture and building science and meteorology to know what might bear on the current schedule of problems to solve. Yesterday's perfect solution may be ruined by subsequent development and become today's pressing problem:

Canary Wharf's great tower of metal and metalled glass, for example, casts a ghost reflection onto transmissions from the Crystal Palace transmitter, affecting the television reception of 100,000 people. The development of wind farms can also affect television reception both in their immediate vicinity and, on some occasions, much further afield.

As the atmosphere is ever more crowded with radio signals, much of the researcher's work is collaborative, working with other spectrum engineers representing the users of personal communications like fixed or mobile telephones, police, radio amateurs, radar users and many others. And since radio wavelengths know no boundaries, much of the collaboration is international.

Most of the work is done in the office rather than on the ground as computers draw on information stored in data banks and calculate the interaction of the many forces involved. Only when the computer has produced a solution is it tested by physical experiment. Just as the researcher's work requires interaction with other specialisms, so those in turn interact with him in a series of overlapping circles. So the implications for television reception have now become part of the knowledge context for planners, architects, structural engineers and building scientists, for they too are symbolic analysts.

More than twenty years of learning have developed the range of intellectual and practical capability needed in the researcher's work. He learned the theory and practical skills of electrical engineering by full-time study at college and he used them in his first job of measuring signal strengths and improving transmissions to defined areas where reception was poor. But his present work is far removed from this. He is adept at using computers, the skills learned by practical experience ('I bought a computer, set it up and used it referring where necessary to the manual') and from working with colleagues. These have included junior engineers, graduate trainees or vacation students who bring in and pass on expertise from their recent university or college studies. Job hierarchies are irrelevant; he learns from wherever the best information is available. Knowledge of the context, the skills of analysing it, synthesizing the combinations of facts needed to solve the problems of the job, and in knowing where the detailed information can be found is less precisely definable and he learned these mainly from colleagues and on the job. Finally, he both leads a team and has to work with teams of people from many other countries. He learned his skills as a manager and team worker on short full-time courses, through experience gained by membership of various committees and by constructive appraisal from immediately senior staff.

Learning is continuous. There are some seminars to attend and others to contribute to, but most of the learning comes from the process of problem solving, by discussing options for action with colleagues and making decisions at meetings. Published research papers, the long accepted means of sharing research findings, are of limited use since they

7

appear months or even years later than the research they report. It is the technical notes, unpublished research reports and papers for committees that represent the growing body of formalized knowledge.

Several general principles can be inferred from this example: effectiveness depends on a combination of formalized instruction (college plus in-house), arrangements for keeping up to date (by means of news letters and circulation of correspondence, for example) and an ability to recognize the relevant. The balance struck between these learning sources is essentially personal (though not atypical) and so is the way it is taken into use. But the effectiveness of the learning makes a general point; it is not the memorization of facts but the perception of relevance and the will to grasp, master and apply with imagination that counts.

General Trends

Many sub-categories can be proposed within Reich's definition. But however it is classified and defined, the work is done by people, and the twenty-four million workers in Britain are people first and workers second. As learners too, it is easy to categorize — by subject preference or learning style, for example — but they remain individuals with lives to live, ambitions to pursue and personal ideas of what learning means to them. This book has a clear focus, but it has a defined context which includes the individuality of people too. Many employers recognize this and emphasize that the learning they encourage is for the worker as a person as well as an employee.

General trends run through all three categories. One is a growth in 'flatter hierarchies' and teamwork with a need to understand whole work processes rather than self-contained bits of them (Handy, 1994). The growth of small businesses where all functions are performed by very few people has a similar effect. The general change towards a smaller core of well-defined responsibilities and a rather larger undefined area where the employee relies on his or (increasingly) her initiative represents another. Then there is the increase in the numbers of people who work from home. In the case of people who process information, they actually work *at* home most of the time spending perhaps a day a week at the office to meet with colleagues for formal meetings, for informal discussion or for updating. Some of this is decision making, but some of it constitutes necessary learning. Workers like sales representatives and repair technicians who must travel to their clients also work increasingly from home and keep in touch with their base through mobile telephone (Girling, 1994). The other well-established and well reported trend is towards multiple careers in a working lifetime. Only breadth of background, flexibility of attitude and the skills of learning will enable people to make these transitions.

From the Needs of Employment to Changes in Education

We have still some way to go to take account of these trends. Sharp differences remain between the realities of employment and the practices of education. Employment is about getting the job done, education emphasizes the acquisition of knowledge — much of it divorced from its applications. Yet we have long known that children who are uninterested and uninvolved while being taught factual material as a class often become deeply engaged when involved in a group problem-solving exercise. The long separation of theory and practice, education and training, classroom-based and work-based learning obscures the way relevant learning frequently involves elements from both 'sides' of these distinctions. The assumption that we predictably transfer learning to new situations is also misplaced as, although the conditions for transfer are not fully understood, some studies show transfer as context bound, others that only some transfer takes place. Memorized knowledge may be capable of recall but not of application. (There is a striking example on page 68.) In any classroom across the whole field from primary school to university there is an essential distinction between questions which get a correct answer and questions which stimulate thought. Japanese teachers 'consider questions to be poor if they elicit immediate answers, because this indicates that students [are] not challenged to think' (Berryman and Bailey, 1992, pp. 45–64).

In much work, the emphasis is less on knowledge than on intellectual skills brought to bear upon knowledge. Abstraction, analysis, creating new syntheses are what counts. We have made some progress with developing core skills (often called transferable skills in higher education) but made less progress in ensuring breadth of conceptual understanding. Such skills are applied to information so that awareness of the spectrum of human knowledge, and understanding of its major conceptual frameworks is needed too. For decades some educationists have questioned the specialization of knowledge in the curriculum. Some have seen it as a reflection in the classroom of the nineteenth-century division of labour in the factory (Heyck, 1984). The national curriculum has done something to alleviate early narrowing of the curriculum during compulsory schooling, but the limited number of 'A' levels regarded as a suitable education for 16–18-year-olds and the single honours degree system in the universities can place us at a disadvantage when it comes to drawing upon a wide range of concepts at later stages.

The learning described within this discussion is controlled by the learner. Choosing from taught courses, private study and well-managed learning on the job they draw on a range of opportunities. They have learned how to learn. This is one of the most frequently stated aims of education for the present time, but specific strategies to develop the capacity, are less well developed. Study skills help for formal situations. Other skills are needed for informal learning.

David Bradshaw

People who work from home or with flexible job descriptions do so with little supervision. Both this and the growth of teamwork suggests that experience of this kind of responsibility is needed in the education process. Higher education in particular has a long tradition of encouraging individual excellence and discouraging working together. There are now many attempts to develop pairs, trios and larger teams to work jointly on assignments but such opportunities are still for a minority of students; they need to become more general.

An excellent example of methods of learning which meet these needs comes from the Department of Mechanical and Process Engineering at the University of Sheffield. The introduction to the course for students joining the department emphasizes their individual responsibility for their own learning and the way the course will help them become learning engineers equipped to 'learn for life'. Staff explain the objectives of all courses and the department's teaching and learning strategy during freshers' week where the key elements are:

- students will be helped to discover and use their preferred learning style;
- the taught course will include lectures, practicals in laboratories and workshops, seminars and tutorials; not all will help each student equally and they must find and make use of the ones which help most;
- much work will be done in tutorial/project groups of four;
- lecturing activities are designed on a 1:2 ratio; one hour of lecture assumes a further two hours of self-organized learning;
- most of the practical work will be solving problems. In some cases variants on the results of the same experiment are pooled and discussed by a group totalling twenty to thirty. In others, the work of a group of four students will be considered as two of the group present their findings to a group of twenty and the other two answer questions;
- basic teaching is provided on note-taking, organizing private study, making presentations, working in teams and time-management.

Two examples of the practical work are:

- 'Examine the flow control valve fitted to the cold water inlet of a domestic washing machine. How does it work? How is it manufactured? (A visit to the manufacturers shows this.) Write a report and make an oral presentation to your group.' (This will be a group of four in year one, later on the audience will increase to twenty.)
- 'Here is a piece of machinery (e.g., a gear box) from which one

part has been taken out. Design the missing part using engineering knowledge and a CAD system. Justify your solution to the group.'

There are far reaching implications for learning in these changes. There is an implicit need for a commitment from individual people to education throughout life. The concomitant is provision radically different in form and content than anything we have known before. So the discussion, while emphasizing the connection between learning and work, broadens to include the principles for an educational system for the twenty-first century which apply across the whole field, from nursery to adult learning. And most of them have been spelt out by the National Commission on Education whose report *Learning to Succeed* (The National Commission on Education, 1993) provides a clear vision, with seven goals. These are so important that they are reproduced in full:

The Commission's Vision

1 In all countries *knowledge and applied intelligence* have become central to economic success and personal and social well being.
2 In the United Kingdom much higher achievement in education and training is needed to match world standards.
3 Everyone must want to learn and have ample opportunity and encouragement to do so.
4 All children must achieve a good grasp of literacy and basic skills early on in life.
5 The full range of people's abilities must be recognized and their development rewarded.
6 High quality learning depends above all on the knowledge, skill, effort and example of teachers and trainers.
7 It is the role of education *both* to interpret and pass on the values of society *and* to stimulate people to think for themselves and to change the world around them.

And the Commission's goals are:

1 High quality nursery education must be available for all 3- and 4-year-olds.
2 There must be courses and qualifications to bring out the best in every pupil.
3 Every pupil in every lesson has the right to good teaching and adequate support facilities.
4 Everyone must be entitled to learn throughout life and be encouraged in practice to do so.
5 The management of education and training must be integrated, and those with a stake in them must have this recognized.

6   There must be greater public and private investment in education and training to achieve a better return.
7   Achievement must constantly rise and progress be open for all to examine.

In *Learning Pays* (Ball, 1991), Sir Christopher Ball proposed a simple model to describe lifelong learning:

Stage	Age	Attitude	Attainment
Foundation	Up to 16	Habit of learning	National Curriculum
Formation	14–21	Workplace readiness	Most to NVQ 3, 4 or 5
Continuation	18 and beyond	Independent learning	All to NVQ 3, 4 or 5

Securing continuity from one stage to another is not easy. There is structural weakness between foundation and formation where, for some, education remains school based while for others it is in college either full-time or part-time. Despite recent reforms, curriculum and qualifications lack integration at the same point. Learning to Succeed (The National Commission on Education, 1993) provides deep analysis and wide-ranging solutions to these problems, and John Hillier addresses some of the issues in his chapter on assessment and qualifications. Integrating learning away from the workplace (through a course at college for example) with learning in the workplace is also difficult to achieve. This is discussed more fully in Chapter 6 'Learning Theory: Harnessing the Strength of a Neglected Resource' in this book.

Learning and Unemployment

Work confers dignity and identity. It brings self-respect. It is difficult to envisage British society without this regard. The concentration of unemployment in particular localities, the large numbers of school leavers without work (for whatever reason), serves to deprive whole communities of these positive qualities. It is tragic that as the crippling effects of class differences are disappearing a new underclass is emerging along with the disasters of urban decay, poverty and the crime which grows with them.

Numerous causes contribute to present levels of unemployment and future patterns are impossible to predict; there may not be an equilibrium for many years and where it will form is unpredictable. Further jobs are being lost as information technology takes over from people, and work moves to where it can be done more cheaply. But new jobs are also being created and the Policy Studies Institute (PSI) is confident that more will follow. The PSI see the growth areas in 'a strong continuing increase in the numbers in scientific, engineering, managerial, technical, entrepreneurial and other professional occupations; smaller increases in office and personal services and in skilled manual occupations' (Northcott *et al.*, 1991, p. 145). But achieving transfer from declining areas to those of growth is proving extremely difficult. Moreover some, perhaps many, of the new jobs will be part time.

But even if we cannot deliver full employment, we can deliver 100 per cent employability. The key National Training and Education Targets (NTETS) are foundation target 4 ('Education and training . . . to develop self-reliance, flexibility and breadth') and lifelong target 3 ('50 per cent of the work force qualified to at least NVQ 3 (or equivalent)'). These are more precise and less susceptible to fudge than general aspirations towards high quality. But anything less will sell the unemployed short. It will require some radical changes in provision to secure them. In Chapter 4, Naomi Sargant examines some of the issues of adult learners, including attitudes towards the unemployed in her chapter 'Lifelong Learning: A Brave and Proper Vision'.

The capacity of people to learn is not in doubt, but it will be a large-scale task to win the commitment of those who have only ever experienced failure at school and unemployment after it. Part of the task is to provide better guidance with realistic assessment of new prospects (are vacancies in areas of growth or is decline just round the corner?) and freedom from the distortions of institutional self-interest. These judgments are increasingly difficult to make. The relief of returning to work — any work — can obscure the need to prepare for the next move. Helping people to take long-term views is part of the task. Tony Watts and Stephen McNair consider these matters in their chapter 'Towards a Strategy for Lifelong Guidance to Support Lifelong Learning and Work'.

The Wider Agenda for Learning

The main focus of this book is the essential connections between employment and post-school learning. But learning has much to contribute to advancing towards solving other national problems. The tasks include:

- strengthening the ability to contribute to the democratic process;
- working to solve the problems of the threatened environment;
- overcoming urban decay and deprivation;
- recognizing and benefiting from ethnic variety;
- improving health;
- supporting cultural and leisure activities.

This short and incomplete list is in no order of priority. The integrated insight and skill of many professions is needed to make progress in any of these and all of them have a learning dimension. But no matter how long the agenda, learning is individual and individuals have their own priorities for living.

In 1972, UNESCO received a report from its Commission on the Development of Education. Its underlying assumptions remain valid and include 'the aim of development is the complete fulfilment of man, in all the richness of his personality, the complexity of his forms of expression and his various commitments — as individual, member of a family and a community, citizen and producer, inventor of techniques and creative dreamer' (Faure, 1972). Today we would expect the inclusion of women to be explicit, even though the context shows that this was intended. But the economic imperative continues to dominate and, along with other widely shared objectives, to overshadow other purposes. 'It is we', writes Charles Handy, 'we individual men and women, who should be the measure of all things, not made-to-measure for something else. It is easy to lose ourselves in efficiency, to treat that efficiency as an end in itself and not a means to other ends' (Handy, 1994, p. 1). For some this includes the pure pleasure of knowing and understanding, as support for the University of the Third Age has shown. The encouragement of learning for personal reasons and for the enlargement of the human spirit without disclosure of motive remains one of the obligations of a civilized society.

One of the most promising developments in this field is the 'Educating Cities' movement. Dedicated to the ideals of lifelong learning in support of the complete spectrum of corporate and private learning, the movement sees the city as the unit in which coalitions of learning providers, both public and private, offer better coordinated, more readily available opportunities. The movement does not discriminate as to the purpose of learning or by age, gender, race or other factor; it embraces lifelong learning for all. It encourages learning whether formalized, structured or otherwise. The movement attracted 900 delegates from 130 cities in 43 countries to its second congress in Gothenburg in November 1992, and seems to offer real opportunity to bring integration to fragmented provision and purpose (OECD, 1993).

Other projects work in rural areas. They may lack the resources of the city and the strength of an international organization to support it, but the people show much the same enthusiasm for learning and independence of spirit in its pursuit.

Interlocking Fields of Action

Without commitment to become a learning society, Britain's economic decline will continue. But other action is required too. A group of Japanese industrialists were visiting a British factory recently. At the end of their tour the managing director asked them if they had noticed anything that should receive the firm's attention. After demurring politely several times the head of the delegation brought out a piece of paper and said, 'Well if you really would like to hear our observations we did note these fifty-three things.' Numerous studies at home and abroad show some agreement on the action needed to move Britain not just forward but into the first division of developing nations. The list (in no order of priority since many of the fields of action interlock) include:

- The need for a clearly defined and vigorously pursued national strategy. (This is a theme developed by Tony Cann in his chapter on structural matters.)

- Little changes without investment. It is needed in premises, equipment, the introduction of information technology into manufacture, management and servicing, research and development, learning and much else. But the list is significant because so many of the items depend in some way on learning. To be effective, research and development need intelligent focus, advanced learning kept up to date, effective management and the use of information technology. The source of investment raises other issues. For example, Sir John Banham has recently pointed out that Britain invests less than its competitors because Britons spend more as consumers than they do. This and other factors explain in part why our machines are older (therefore less competitive) and we invest less in learning than we could (Banham, 1994). The other investment issue is the practice of our financial institutions to concentrate upon financial returns over the short term rather than long-term growth potential as the criterion for bank lending or foreclosure. It is a limitation on growth.

- The application of research to the economy requires a sharper focus with a close match with existing and potential sectors of competitive advantage and determined diffusion of research findings into commercial activity.

- High standards of managerial competence and qualification. Once again the lessons from other countries is that the quality of management relates closely to qualifications, continuous updating of skill and internal appraisal (Northcott *et al.*, 1991). The implications for learning are again key.

- A well-motivated, loyal, dedicated and actively cooperative workforce is a feature of every successful economy. We have made substantial improvements in this field in the last decade and a half by legislative control, better management and through increased perception of economic forces. Understanding economics and accepting them as personally relevant is a form of learning and there may be scope for more structured provision in, for example, the joint study of company economics by managers and trades union officials.

- Every major study highlights learning as fundamental. 'There is little doubt from our research that education and training are decisive in national competitive advantage,' writes Michael Porter summarizing the conclusion of one of the most thorough analyses (Porter, 1990). 'The quality of the available labour force is probably the most important competitive variable between countries,' says the Director General of the CBI (Davies, 1993). It is vital in itself and it contributes significantly to most other fields of action. (For this book, Christopher Ball examines the evidence of the connection between learning and national and personal prosperity in his chapter 'Learning Does Pay'.)

Action on many fronts is needed to move Britain forward and one book cannot (as Christopher Ball reminds us at the end of his chapter) explore all the issues. Learning serves many purposes both for the common good and as matters of private choice. There are unresolved tensions between individual freedom and the obligations which society can place upon them which can only be settled in the maturing of the learning society.

The interrelated issues of the sub-title 'The learning revolution, the economy and the individual' are recurring themes in the book. They are not used to delineate parts, though most chapters have a particular emphasis. In the end though, all of them point to the need for Britain to pursue the goal of becoming a learning society as a matter of urgency.

References

BALL, C. (1990) *More Means Different*, London, The RSA.
BALL, C. (1991) *Learning Pays*, London, The RSA.
BANHAM, J. (1994) *The Anatomy of Change: Blueprint for a New Era*, London, Weidenfeld and Nicolson; extracts and summary published in the *Sunday Times* 27 March and 3 April 1994.
BERRYMAN, S.E. and BAILEY, T.R. (1992) *The Double Helix of Education and the Economy*, New York, Institute on Education and the Economy, Columbia University Teachers College Box 174 Columbia University New York 10027.
BRADSHAW, D. (1994) 'How Rover cars is becoming a learning organisation', *Synapse*, London, The RSA.
BURGOYNE, J. (1992) 'Creating a learning organisation', *The RSA Journal*.
DAVIES, H. (1993) 'A credit to your career', address to a CBI Conference, 22 June 1993.

FAURE, E. (1972) Letter to the Director General of UNESCO presenting the report *Learning To Be*, Paris, UNESCO.

GIRLING, R. (1994) 'The smart way to work', *The Times Magazine*, 12 March.

HAHN, C. (1993) 'The importance of manufacturing in a robust economy', *RSA Journal* June.

HANDY, C. (1989) *The Age of Unreason*, London, Hutchinson.

HANDY, C. (1994) *The Empty Raincoat: Making Sense of the Future*, London, Hutchinson.

HEYCK, T.W. (1984) *The Transformation of Intellectual Life in Victorian England*, London, Croom Helm.

THE NATIONAL COMMISSION ON EDUCATION (1993) *Learning to Succeed*, London, Lawrence and Wishart.

NORTHCOTT, J. and A POLICY STUDIES INSTITUTE RESEARCH TEAM (1991) *Britain in 2010*, London, PSI Publishing.

OECD (Organization for Economic Cooperation and Development) (1993) *City Strategies for Lifelong Learning* and *Lifelong Learning in Educating Cities*, Gothenburg, Gothenburg City Education Committee.

PORTER, M.E. (1990) *The Competitive Advantage of Nations*, London, Macmillan.

REICH, R.B. (1991) *The Work of Nations: Preparing Ourselves for Twenty-First Century Capitalism*, London, Simon and Schuster.

SIMON, B. (1991) *Education and the Social Order*, London, Lawrence and Wishart.

SPENCER, H. (1861) *Education, Intellectual, Moral and Physical*, London, Williams and Moorgate.

WILLE, E. (1990) *People Development and Improved Business Performance*, Berkhampstead, Ashridge Management Research Group.

Chapter 2

Learning Does Pay[*]

Christopher Ball

Introduction

Learning pays. Or does it? It is striking that such an apparently simple claim can be so controversial. On the one hand, Peter Usher (1994) — writing from the point of view of an industrial employer — deplores 'an excess of academic discussion' which may 'cast doubt on what should (be) taken as axiomatic'. And a recent CBI report, *Thinking Ahead* (1994), which calls for further expansion of higher education, argues that: 'Higher education is a prime source of highly skilled people, a key contributor to a dynamic economy and central to the future competitiveness of UK business'. On the other, James Murphy (1993 and 1994) has recently argued that the belief 'which sees the expansion of higher education as benefiting the country economically . . . is no longer defensible'. And a report from the London School of Economics (Bennett, Glennerster and Nevison, 1993) argues, that 'the financial returns to post-compulsory education and training are mixed. . . . In some cases the return to training and education may even be negative.' What are we to make of this?[*]

The Nature of the Assertion

The claim that 'learning pays' embraces nations, organizations and individuals. It is commonplace and repeated world wide: 'The age of technology, information and communications rewards those nations whose people learn new skills to stay ahead . . . in a world that rewards learning' (America 2000, 1991); 'The survival of firms today depends on the day-to-day mobilization of every ounce of intelligence' (Matsushita, 1985); 'The costs of dropping out of secondary school are discernible and significant: Canadian society will lose more than \$4 billion over the working lifetimes of the nearly 137,000 youths who dropped out instead of graduating with the

---

[*] This chapter develops the themes first set out in *More Means Different* (RSA, 1990), *Learning Pays* (RSA, 1991), *Profitable Learning* (RSA, 1992) and 'Profitable Learning: a Note on Murphy's reply to Johnes' (*Oxford Review of Education*, forthcoming 1994).

class of 1989' (Lafleur, 1992); 'There is little doubt from our research that education and training are decisive in national competitive advantage' (Porter, 1990). In the UK, the idea that learning is profitable underlies the National Training and Education Targets, the 'Investors in People' movement, and aphorisms like 'the more you learn, the more you earn'.

In my own discussions of these themes I have tried to make explicit three important hidden qualifications of the claim that learning pays. The first lies in the word 'learning', which is not intended to be synonymous with conventional education and training. It is far from that. The title of my RSA report *More Means Different*, (Ball, 1990), was intended to signal as clearly as possible that the expansion of higher education which I then looked for (and which has now occurred) should not result merely in 'more of the same'. Learning includes the products of both education and training, the processes of both formal and informal learning, and the various types of learning: skills, knowledge, understanding, experience, attitude, values. . . . Most importantly, it shifts the emphasis from the activities of the teacher or trainer towards the development of the student. The statement that 'learning pays' reveals a serious claim about the value of human development.

The second qualification affects the word 'pays'. Learning 'pays off' or adds value in many ways — personally, socially and economically. The claim that learning pays is obviously an economic statement, but it is not only (or merely) economic. Nonetheless, the value of personal and social benefits can also be expressed in economic terms. Moreover, the old-fashioned contrast between the values of employment and of private life make less and less sense today. The fourth of the National Training and Education Targets for Foundation Learning calls for 'education and training provision to develop self-reliance, flexibility and breadth'. But such qualities also lie at the very heart of traditional liberal education.

The third qualification can best be expressed by an analogy. When my doctor tells me that 'exercise is healthy', I know that he will not be moved by me reminding him that some forms of exercise can cause injury, or even death. He means to convey that **appropriate** exercise is beneficial. Similarly, the slogan 'learning pays' implies — not that all learning will prove valuable — but that appropriate learning provides benefits of various kinds, especially economic ones. You must learn the right things, at the right time, in the right way. Properly understood, the claim provides a yardstick for measuring the effectiveness of our learning. If it fails to provide benefits, then its relevance and/or quality must be questioned. Learning should pay, as the London School of Economics (LSE) report implies.

Who benefits? It is important to recognize that the assertion covers three very different kinds of beneficiary: individuals, organizations and nations. Different arguments and different kinds of evidence will be needed to demonstrate the value of learning for each of them. For example, the first is given some support by figures showing that educational 'drop-out' correlates with lower life chances and indeed reduced life expectancy. It is the completely unqualified who find the most difficulty in securing work of any kind. Moreover, 'once unemployed, those with the least qualifications have been the ones with the most difficulty in getting back to work' (Northcott *et al.*, 1991). Recent statistics issued by the Department of Employment for the last quarter of 1993 showed that, while 10 per cent of the whole UK workforce was unemployed, only 8.8 per cent of those with A-level (or equivalent) qualifications, and just 5.1 per cent of graduates, were out of work. The so-called 'poaching problem', whereby employers are discouraged from training their staff because they then find that they are attracted to better jobs with their competitors, is a strong indicator of the added value of learning for the individual, although it is often adduced as evidence that learning does not pay organizations!

As for organizations and companies, the growing movement to develop Learning Organizations is founded on the assumption that learning pays, not just individuals, but also the companies and organizations to which they belong. For example, the Arup Partnership (Ove Arup) has grown from 400 to 4,000 employees over twenty years, using training and development as the basis of its approach to recruitment, retention and motivation, with all employees involved in Continuing Education and Training, a budget of over £3 million a year and at least 10 per cent of everyone's time committed to learning. The Chairman, Sir Jack Zunz, argues: 'We believe that learning pays for us, and will continue to do so'. As more and more organizations become accredited 'Investors in People' they are discovering the validity of this assertion for themselves.

It is, of course, most difficult of all to prove the claim that learning pays nations. There are inevitably a number of factors involved in developing the competitive strength of a nation. A 'world-class workforce' may well not be a sufficient condition for international success, but it is almost certainly a necessary condition. The so-called 'Confucian societies' of the east, which have achieved such remarkable economic growth and prosperity in recent years, clearly believe that their success is rooted in education and training. Today, the countries of the Pacific Rim have three fundamental qualities in common with some earlier remarkable societies (like Scotland in the later eighteenth and nineteenth centuries, or Jewish societies): family loyalty, hard work, and the learning habit. I doubt whether national competitive success will be possible in the next century for countries which have not effectively fostered all three of these characteristics.

Testing the Assertion

How can it be proved whether learning pays? There are a number of difficulties, well exemplified in the arguments presented in the previous paragraphs. First, it is important to distinguish correlation from causation. If there is a significant correlation between graduates and employment, this might be explained in any of three ways. Possibly, success in gaining a job and a degree are both the result of some third factor such as the status of parents, schooling or personal qualities. Alternatively, it might be the case that employment is the cause of graduation — if, for example, employers systematically encouraged their staff to work for part-time degrees. Each of these possibilities must be excluded, and neither can be wholly excluded, before it is safe to assert that the correlation of graduate and employment status indicates that the former necessarily and regularly causes the latter.

Secondly, we are dealing with phenomena which by their nature are likely to have multiple causes. If, for example, the success of a small business depends on the *quality, availability* and *price* of the product (or service), then the contribution of the learning of the workforce to these critical factors will be both diverse and indirect. It is rarely possible to isolate the effects of learning or carry out controlled experiments.

Thirdly, the advantages of learning tend to develop over the longer term; short-term benefits are difficult to demonstrate. The dramatic expansion of UK higher education which has occurred during the last five years has not yet produced clear and obvious benefits for the British economy, although what may be the start of a correlation can be perceived. However, it is important to recognize that the demonstration of the link between learning and (national) prosperity depends on being able to show that the nation is more prosperous *than it would have been if the learning* (in this case, the expansion of higher education) *had not taken place*, not that the nation has in fact prospered, either absolutely or relative to other countries, over the period in which the 'increase of learning' took place.

What criteria might be judged adequate for settling the question of whether learning really does pay? The problem is rather like setting out to prove that the sun rises in the east. Most people can't be bothered with the challenge of proving something that is obviously true. But the pedants insist that the sun does not rise at all: the apparent effect is the result of the Earth spinning on its own axis. Both groups are correct — from their own point of view. As far as the assertion that 'learning pays' is concerned, we might apply the tests of intuition, experience, research — and the serious implausibility of the converse.

Common sense tells us that learning pays. It is intuitively true — whether for the infant seeking to decode the mother-tongue, the child learning to read or mastering simple arithmetic, the young person learning to drive, cook, lay bricks, sew, dance or draw, or the adult seeking to read music, a map or a balance sheet, or acquire the seven cardinal virtues. Our intuition informs us that such learning pays off — adds value — and our experience confirms it.

Indeed, research repeatedly demonstrates that learning pays — in two different ways. First, and obviously enough, the enormous achievement of modern scientific research in increasing human understanding of natural phenomena has yielded countless advantages (and a few disadvantages) to mankind. The benefits of science and technology have economic value for the individual (e.g., availability of spectacles or the contraceptive pill), for the company (e.g., plastics or the microchip), and for the nation (e.g., telecommunications or radar).

Secondly, there is a growing body of research which demonstrates that learning has paid in specific cases. Some of the most important contributions are: Joan Payne (1990) *Adult off-the-job Skills Training: An Evaluation Study*, (especially chapter 8); The Training Agency Funding Study (1989) *Training in Britain: A Study of Funding, Activity and Attitudes*, (especially pp. 29–34); the work of Professor Sig Prais, especially discussion paper 191 on *Vocational Education and Productivity in the Netherlands and Britain*, NIESR, November 1990; and the work of Professor Mike Campbell, Director of the Policy Research Unit at Leeds Metropolitan University, especially (1994) *Education, Training and Economic Performance*. The last of these presents evidence which demonstrates that, both at an international level and at a regional level in the UK, 'there is evidence of a clear association between education/training and economic development and performance'.

Equally significant is the recent initiative of the Economic and Social Research Council to invite applications under a new research programme entitled *The Learning Society: Knowledge and Skills for Employment*. Some £2 million are to be invested over four years 'to provide better answers than are currently available' to the following strategic questions:

- What are the main characteristics of a learning society?
- What are the links between learning and economic success, between training and competitiveness, and between education, innovation and wealth creation?
- What economic, political and cultural factors are preventing or facilitating the progress of the UK towards becoming a learning society and how can the impact of the former be minimised and the impact of the latter be maximized?
- What are the theoretical gaps in the understanding of the processes of learning and the complex interrelationships between employment, training and education?
- What is to be learned from the advances being made in this area by our partners in the European Union and by other leading industrial countries in America and the Far East?
- What changes should be introduced to the current systems of post-compulsory education, training and continuing education to respond to the challenges represented by a learning society?

- What national policies need to be adopted to speed the transition to a learning society?'

Of course, the outcomes of this research programme will not be available for some time, but the second question raises all the issues discussed here. It would not have been asked in this way if the likely answer was: 'there are no links'.

Finally, it seems worth addressing the argument derived from the implausibility of the converse. What would it mean if learning did not pay? It would imply that systems of education — schools, colleges and universities — had no positive economic effect. Or that there was no relationship between the general educational and technological skills of the workforce and the level of productivity. Or that those disabled from learning in various ways suffered no economic disadvantage thereby. But such conclusions seem absurd.

The Modified Claim

It will be clear from the foregoing arguments that the assertion 'learning does pay' is in fact a rather crude simplification of a more subtle, modified claim, namely that 'good learning provides a variety of benefits, including economic profit'. Is this circular? If the benefits of learning define its virtue, it may be argued that the modified claim is merely a self-fulfilling statement. But I don't think that it is so.

Once again, the analogy of physical exercise is helpful. Some forms of exercise (like bare-knuckle boxing) are harmful; others (like hill-walking) are beneficial. Appropriate exercise is good for you. And the same is true of learning. The correlation between some forms of learning and benefits — some of which can be expressed in economic terms — is both significant and best explained on the assumption that the former causes the latter.

The modified claim, as has been suggested above, offers a measure of the value or effectiveness of our learning. Where learning does not pay (or add value), it is by definition not good. We learn laziness and greed; we learn to lie and cheat. But, quite apart from moral turpitude, the ordinary processes of education and training can be evaluated by the modified claim, and where there is no evidence of benefit they must be found wanting. The modified claim counters the 'education for its own sake' or 'training at all costs' approaches. Whatever the difficulty in practice, it implies that in principle it should be possible to observe the benefits derived from (good) learning. Where academic and useful learning are set in opposition to one another (as in the UK), and the former is valued above the latter, it is hardly surprising that the outcome is unsatisfactory: 'Every month that passes more evidence is presented to strengthen the case that the "academic mould" is the single most important reason for the under-performance of the UK economy in the twentieth century' (Morgan, 1990).

Unfortunately, educational research has seemed less interested in addressing these questions than their importance might have led us to expect. It is a problem both of attitude and method. There are three particular difficulties: the gap (or is it gulf?) that exists today between the worlds of educational research and educational policy; the relative value of speculative and empirical theory; and the problem of applying to an uncertain (but different) future the findings of research into the past.

Having at least a toe-hold in each of the worlds of educational research and educational policy (e.g., as a member of the editorial board of *The Oxford Review of Education*, and of the CBI's Education and Training Affairs Committee) I am acutely conscious of the distance between them. As an example of the lack of communication, I note that the *Review* has not as yet reviewed *Towards a Skills Revolution* (CBI, 1989), possibly the most influential report on UK education since the Robbins Report; while the CBI report, despite a range of references, never once refers to a paper in the *Review*. While one example is hardly decisive, I believe that too often today those who formulate and implement policy and those who undertake research in education are not in touch. At worst, the two sides reveal a relationship of mutual contempt.

Within the world of educational research there is a somewhat similar division between those who adopt a speculative approach and the empiricists. *More Means Different* (Ball, 1990) like almost all my work in education followed the former tradition; its critics (e.g., Murphy and the LSE report) belong to the latter. Both are desirable and necessary. Yet I have the impression that, while empirical research seems to be more rigorous and 'scientific', speculative research is more useful. The manipulation of data sometimes appears to be an alternative (or an impediment) to thought.

But the most serious problem is the one which permeates most of the disciplines of social studies. It is the analogical application of a methodology borrowed from the natural sciences — where it is normally possible to limit the variables before starting research, repeat experiments, and derive general propositions which remain true over time and space — to a field of enquiry (human affairs) where none of these three features of the scientific process obtain. These difficulties are well-known, but are nonetheless disabling for that. In particular, the gradual transition from relatively stable societies to ones which change at an increasingly remarkable rate must call into question a methodology which measures the patterns of the past in order to 'improve practice' in the future. The working assumption that we are thereby comparing like with like is false too often for comfort.

Some Examples of Beneficial Learning

(i) Pre-School Learning

My recent report, *Start Right, The Importance of Early Learning* (Ball, 1994), makes the case for believing that 'pre-school education pays'. It argues that 'good pre-school education leads to immediate and lasting social and educational benefits for all children — especially those from disadvantaged backgrounds. Investment in high quality and effective early education provides a worthwhile social and economic return to society. The latest finding is that "over the lifetime of the participants, the pre-school programme returns to the public an estimated $7.16 for every dollar invested".'

The research evidence for these conclusions is set out in the second chapter of the report, and supported by two authoritative appendices, the first by Professor Kathy Sylva on *The Impact of Early Learning on Children's Later Development* (appendix C), the second *A Summary of Significant Benefits: The High/Scope Perry Pre-School Study Through Age 27* (appendix D) by Lawrence J Schweinhart and David P Weikart. The latter shows that high quality pre-school education correlates with (and is responsible for) better High School grades, fewer arrests for criminal acts, higher monthly earnings, less reliance on social services, and more house ownership than was the case for the matched control group which received no pre-school programme. The authors conclude: 'The lifetime economic benefits to the pre-school program participants, their families, and the community far outweigh the economic cost of their high-quality, active learning pre-school program. If the program had not been offered, the direct costs to society in lost labour-force participation, increased criminal behaviour, and additional welfare support would have far exceeded the program's costs.' Professor Sylva's study reveals that these findings are consistent with, and supported by, a range of other research work undertaken in several countries and at different times.

(ii) Primary Education

Article 28 of the United Nations *Convention on the Rights of the Child* recognizes the right to education: ratifying nations should 'make primary education compulsory and available free to all'. Its aim is the 'elimination of ignorance and illiteracy throughout the world'. Literacy is the key to personal, social and national development. The Save the Children Fund has shown how the achievement of literacy by children (and parents) is the first step towards economic development. The chain of cause and effect works like this. Those who can read, learn to observe elementary rules of health care. This in turn enables parents to gain confidence in the survival of children into adult life. Without this confidence, parents are unlikely to limit the size of their families and so the control of populations becomes impossible. Development is defeated by uncontrolled growth of populations. UNICEF seeks $25 billion a year to control the major childhood diseases, halve child malnutrition, reduce child deaths by four million a year, bring safe water and sanitation to all communities, make family planning universally available, and provide a basic education for all children. The attainment of the last of these objectives (basic education) by itself will enable poor communities to make substantial progress towards the remaining goals. Investment in effective primary education provides significant social and economic returns for both developing and developed nations. Indeed, the World Bank policy study of *Education in Sub-Saharan Africa* (1988) claims that:

> Without education, development will not occur. Only an educated people can command the skills necessary for sustainable economic growth and for a better quality of life . . .

> Greater investment in education can, at this time in Africa's history, be expected to yield broad economic benefits. These benefits include higher income and lower fertility. The research evidence to this effect is compelling . . .

> Increased investment in the quality and quantity of education can be expected to reduce fertility. In general, there is a strong negative relationship between how much education a woman receives and the number of children she bears during her lifetime. Men and women with more education, in addition to having fewer children, tend to live healthier and longer lives. And numerous studies have shown that parents' education affects children's survival and enhances their physical and cognitive development.

(iii) Secondary Education

In this section I consider the relative value of learning a second language in different linguistic situations. The contrast I wish to draw is one between communities and countries where English is not the first language, and those where it is. There can be little doubt of the value of learning English as a second language in the developed nations (and most developing nations) where English is not the first language. This is because English has more or less become a universal second language, like Latin in medieval Europe. People are partly cut off from much advanced thought, many forms of cultural expression and large numbers of their fellow human beings, if they cannot speak and understand English. Even (monoglot) speakers of well-established languages like French, Russian or Chinese are becoming partially isolated without a command of English. Both the educational programmes and the success of learners in such countries demonstrates the real and perceived value of learning English as a second language. English is the 'world language', and it pays to learn it.

But this remarkable (and obvious) fact presents a problem for nations where English is the normal first language. What is the value of learning a second language (other than English) in such countries as the UK, the USA or Australia? What educational policies make sense in such linguistic situations? What motivation is there to encourage children (or adults) to master another language? For most (English-speaking) people the opportunity costs of learning a second language are too high for it to be worth the time and effort. And the main reason for this is that for most people no single (non-English) second language is sufficiently important to be worth the investment. We need half a dozen; and since that is not a practical proposition, we learn none (well).

The point of this analysis is not to applaud or deplore the position, but to observe that it shows that *different* second languages have *different* values for *different* groups of people. Learning languages does pay (or can pay), but it does so differentially.

(iv) Technical Further Education

In the past one of the most obvious kinds of 'profitable learning' has been found in technical further education. Apprenticeships, trade skills, the mastery of a craft have all had an obvious economic value. The plumber, bricklayer, dress-maker, chef, hairdresser, motor mechanic, short-hand typist, pilot, dentist, midwife — all know (and prove) that learning pays. The point is too patent to elaborate. But an important underlying principle is worth emphasizing: the return on any skill or piece of knowledge depends on the market for it. And markets change in various ways.

Technological change introduces new forms of skill (word-processing, for example) and makes others redundant, such as short-hand skills. Plumbers must be able to work with plastic as well as metal piping. Chefs must learn how to use microwave ovens. The work of pilots and dentists is transformed by new technology. Because of the speed (and acceleration) of technological change these forms of technical learning often become obsolescent and lose their value quite quickly. Technical learning pays, but not for long. Nonetheless, it is generally true that the experience of learning one set of skills makes it easier to learn a second set.

Of more enduring value are the personal skills (like teamwork, adaptability, communication or leadership) which are *transferable* to new situations and different sectors of employment. At a higher level still are the conceptual skills (like problem solving, imagination, creativity or metaphoric power); such skills have a very high value. One of the most interesting challenges — for the individual, organization or nation — is to find an appropriate balance (and mix) between technical, personal and conceptual learning. In the past we have tended to overemphasize the first at the expense of the other two. Today it is becoming clear that personal and conceptual learning are both more challenging and more rewarding than technical learning. While it is easy to prove that technical learning pays, and more difficult to show the direct economic value of personal and conceptual learning, my firm belief (derived from observation and experience) is that these forms of learning are the most valuable.

(v) Higher Education

The evidence and arguments for the view that higher education pays were set out in my RSA report, *More Means Different* (1990). They need not be repeated here. I believe that the arguments used in that report have stood up to scrutiny. More recently the CBI has developed the argument still further in *Thinking Ahead* (1994). Citing the intensity of global competition and the consequent need for people prepared for working lives of innovation and responsiveness to change as among the most important reasons for seeking to increase government targets for participation in higher education, it concludes 'Higher education is the prime source for many of the qualities that make up such people: creativity, analytical skills and problem-solving abilities.'

However, although the evidence of differential unemployment suggests that graduates are more likely to secure jobs than non-graduates — and that (in consequence) higher education pays the individual — there is an interesting problem in trying to separate the 'positional benefits' from the 'inherent value' of graduation. Do graduates outperform non-graduates in the employment market because of what they have learned? Or merely because they have been 'sorted' into a higher-labelled category? What difference would it make if everyone (or if no-one) were a graduate?

The idea that learning pays implies that in three different ways a wholly graduate workforce would be more fully employed than a wholly non-graduate workforce in the same situation. The first is the argument that the problem of 'skill shortages' would disappear — or at least be reduced. The second is the fact that higher levels of education correlate with increased mobility. A wholly graduate workforce would be relatively mobile and readily available to fill jobs wherever they were created — in the UK, EU or beyond. The third is the probability that graduates would be more apt to create work for themselves — by means of self-employment or starting new small businesses — than non-graduates. Will this happen as a result of the current expansion of higher education? Only if the implications of the warning that 'more means different' are heeded.

(vi) Continuing Education and Training

The idea of the learning organization is now almost a commonplace. But it lacks precision. The current 'working' definition states that: 'a learning organization is one which facilitates the learning of all its members and continuously transforms itself' (Jones and Hendry, 1992). Learning organizations recognize that learning pays, that we live in a world which rewards learning, that the more people learn the more they earn. Though each of these claims needs careful analysis and some qualification, the motivation to create and develop learning organizations derives from the idea of the profitability of learning. One of many companies that has begun to develop the idea of the learning organization is Unilever.

In April 1993 the Heads of Unilever's UK businesses agreed a learning policy at their National Conference and set annual targets for 1993–95. Unilever's learning policy is as follows:

Unilever believes that a policy of continuous learning and improvement — throughout the whole of the workforce — is an increasingly vital component of business success. Amongst other things, this will involve Unilever companies in:

- increasingly widespread commitment to continuous improvement and total quality;
- continuously raising the skill-levels of all employees;
- encouraging all employees to develop themselves;
- moving towards an organizational learning culture.

Such learning is most likely to be effective when it can be linked to business performance measures through which it can be monitored and evaluated.

The four learning targets for 1993 were:

(i)   progress towards (or achievement of) *Investors in People* status;
(ii)   introduction of regular audits of the skill-levels of the workforce and comparison with operational skill-needs, to form a basis for planning and monitoring training;
(iii)   establishment of individual learning targets for all managers;
(iv)   extension of the implementation of National Vocational Qualifications, with clear achievement targets for the end of 1994.

As a whole, the Unilever companies have made impressive progress with these targets. Like other companies, they are finding three particular challenges: the selection of the appropriate 'currency of learning' (e.g.,

National Vocational Qualifications); the difficulty of developing a true learning culture in the workplace; and the problem of 'proving the pay-back' on investment in training and development. None of these has easy solutions, but in the third case the arguments presented in this chapter for 'the modified claim' provide a measure for the value of a company's investment in the continuing learning of its workforce.

Conclusions

This paper has explored a serious claim about the value of human development. Properly understood, the assertion that 'learning pays' offers a measure of the value and effectiveness of individual learning. Neither traditional ideas of 'learning for its own sake' nor enthusiastic campaigns for 'training at all costs' help learners (or those who provide for them) to distinguish between more and less effective and valuable learning. The idea that *learning should pay* does just that.

As has been repeatedly noted, the idea that learning pays is a truism — 'a self-evident truth, a trite or commonplace statement'. Why then do so many people find it controversial or difficult? The reasons are cultural, rather than rational. Typically, objections to the assertions seem to be either shallow or cynical (or both) — revealing that the objectors do not *want* (rather than do not *believe*) the statement to be true.

For example, it is often objected that public figures like Richard Branson, with limited formal education, demonstrate that learning is not necessary for financial success. For two reasons this is an inadequate objection. First, such people inevitably turn out on closer study to be brilliant informal learners, although their formal education may not have been especially successful. For most of us, it is the case that our informal learning is far more important and influential than our formal education and training. Secondly, while holding fast to the claim that learning pays, I have not argued that this is the whole story. 'Confucian societies' (and 'Confucian companies') apparently draw their success from three fundamental qualities: family loyalty, hard work, and the learning habit. All three are needed.

The poaching problem, discussed in the second section of this paper, is an example of a different kind of objection. As in the case of powerful multi-national companies, where effective organizational learning may not necessarily benefit the nations in which they operate, the poaching problem reveals a conflict of interest, not a contradiction of the claim that learning pays. While learning undoubtedly can pay individuals, companies and nations, it is not always the case that what is good learning from the point of view of one of these beneficiaries will necessarily be valuable and effective from the other points of view. But the problem (though real) is often overstated, and can usually be resolved by good management practice.

Graduate unemployment is also often quoted as evidence that learning does not pay. This is a particularly interesting objection since it does justice neither to the facts nor to the argument. The facts are that higher qualifications lead to lower unemployment and higher earnings (Campbell, 1994). This is true over a wide range of countries. In the UK it has recently been the case that the gap between graduation and first employment has been widening, probably as a result of the recession combined with the expansion of higher education. This phenomenon is reflected in the 'first destination statistics' collected some six months after graduation. We lack any systematic picture of the position one, two or three years after graduation. But nonetheless, as noted earlier, the unemployment rate for the graduate portion of the workforce was 5.1 per cent in late 1993, compared with an overall rate of 10 per cent. Even if it were the case that graduate unemployment was equal to, or higher than, general unemployment (which it isn't), this would not disprove the thesis that learning pays: it would merely demonstrate that something was seriously amiss with university education.

What are the implications of accepting the claim that 'learning does pay'? There seem to me to be three. First, each of the potential beneficiaries (individuals, companies, nations) need to be much more rigorous in ascertaining, evaluating, and enhancing the effectiveness and value of learning. Too often this is either taken for granted or rejected as improper. That the evaluation of learning is undoubtedly difficult is no excuse for not attempting to do it.

Secondly, and in consequence, there is a major challenge to research to find ways of testing (and, it is hoped and expected, of demonstrating) the links between learning and economic success. The ESRC's new research programme is a most welcome response to this challenge.

And thirdly, and finally, there is the question of culture. The UK stands apart from most other nations — certainly most other developed countries — in finding problems with the idea that learning pays. Our culture reveals distinctive (and, I think, bizarre) attitudes to both the idea of learning and the aim of economic success. These attitudes (discussed briefly in *More Means Different*, 1994, pp. 22–32) need to be further challenged and confronted. But that would require another book, or at least a further chapter . . .

References

AMERICA 2000 (1991) An Education Strategy, Washington, US Department of Education.

BALL, C. (1990) *More Means Different*, London, RSA.

BALL, C. (1991) *Learning Pays*, London, RSA.

BALL, C. (1992) *Profitable Learning*, London, RSA.

Christopher Ball

BALL, C. (1994) *Start Right: The Importance of Early Learning*, London, RSA.

BALL, C. (1994) 'Profitable learning: A note on Murphy's reply to Johnes', *Oxford Review of Education*, (forthcoming).

BENNETT, R., GLENNERSTER, H. and NEVISON, D., (1993) *Learning Should Pay*, London, LSE and BP.

CAMPBELL, M. (1994) *Education, Training and Economic Performance*, LMU.

CBI (1989), *Towards a Skills Revolution*, The Report of the Vocational Education and Training Task Force, London, CBI.

CBI (1994) *Thinking Ahead: Ensuring the Expansion of Higher Education into the 21st Century*, London, CBI.

Education in Sub-Saharan Africa (1988) A World Bank Policy Study.

JOHNES, G. (1993) 'A degree of waste: A dissenting view', *Oxford Review of Education*, **19**, pp. 459–64.

JONES, A.M. and HENDRY, C. (1992) *The Learning Organisation: A Review of Literature and Practice*, HRD Partnership.

LAFLEUR, B. (1992) *Dropping Out: The Cost to Canada*, Conference Board of Canada.

MATSUSHITA, K. (1985) *Why the West Will Lose*, Privately printed pamphlet.

MORGAN, P. (1990) *Breaking the Academic Mould*, BTEC Council Strategic Seminar.

MURPHY, J. (1993) 'A degree of waste: The economic benefits of educational expansion', *Oxford Review of Education*, **19**, pp. 9–31.

MURPHY, J. (1994) 'A degree of waste: Reply to Johnes', *Oxford Review of Education, 20*, pp. 81–92.

NORTHCOTT, J. *et al.* (1991) *Britain in 2010*, London, PSI.

PAYNE, J. (1990) *Adult off-the job Skills Training: An Evaluation Study*, Sheffield, The Training Agency.

PORTER, M. (1990) *The Competitive Advantage of Nations*, London, Macmillan.

PRAIS, S. (1990) *Vocational Education and Productivity in the Netherlands and Britain*, NIESR discussion paper 191.

THE LEARNING SOCIETY (1994) *Knowledge and Skills for Employment*, ESRC.

UNILEVER (1994) *Towards a Learning Organisation*, Progress of Unilever UK Companies in 1993, Unilever.

TRAINING IN BRITAIN (1989) *A Study of Funding, Activity and Attitudes*, The Training Agency Funding Study.

USHER, P. (1994) 'Learning does pay', *RSA Journal*, **CXLII, 5447**, p. 28.

Chapter 3

Education and Training: An Historical Perspective

Jon Ainger and Roy Harrison

Introduction

The performance of the British education and training system over the last century has had a fundamental effect on our economy. We are currently having to strive hard to compete at a world-class level and, as the two previous chapters have shown, there is an economic imperative to the drive to improve the quality of national learning. The 'World Competitiveness Report' (IMD, World Economic Forum, 1994) bases its findings on a combination of hard data and perceptions of top executives. It considers information on unemployment, the availability of skilled labour and levels of in-company training. In 1994, the report ranked the UK seventeenth out of the twenty-two OECD countries in terms of its human resources. Figures produced by the National Institute of Economic and Social Research in 1993 give cause for concern over the number of 16-year-olds reaching the equivalent of GCSE grades A to C in Maths, the national language, and one science (Green and Steedman, 1993). The figures for other countries in these areas are: Germany 62 per cent; France 66 per cent; and Japan 50 per cent; with the UK bottom of the league at 27 per cent. The percentage of the German workforce with vocational qualifications at the craft level is 56 per cent, compared with our 20 per cent. At the crucial supervisor level, only 45 per cent of our supervisors have any formal qualifications, compared with 93 per cent in Germany (Davies, 1993).

So, Britain remains a long way behind its major competitors even after recent efforts to improve. But we are improving, not only in what we achieve through education and training, but also in our ability to learn from the past.

The story of Britain's attempts to define and pursue effective policies for learning during the last 150 years has been told many times. This chapter, however, is concerned with the search for radical solutions during the past thirty years and the opportunities for progress offered by our achievements to date.

Jon Ainger and Roy Harrison

The Industry Training Boards

In the early 1960s, entry to skilled work was still largely through apprenticeships. They were based on occupations rather than industries and used the serving of time, rather than the meeting of a defined level of skill, as their mark of success. In fact, much employment lay outside the scope of the system, as many occupations had no apprentice scheme at all. Many employers gave no encouragement (and no time off) to attend further education and technical colleges, so although these establishments had expanded there was a very substantial potential population outside their scope. The Industrial Training Act of 1964 was an attempt to tackle these issues. It set up the Industry Training Boards (ITBs) on a tripartite basis consisting of representatives from government, employers and unions. The Act gave the Boards real powers to define policy, lay down standards and test against them and send young people to college. The Boards were also able to impose a training levy on employers within their scope.

In 1964 the introduction of the training levy had general support because there was increasing concern among government and employers about the phenomenon of poaching. The root cause of this problem was that, at a time of economic growth, there were simply not enough qualified applicants to fill the vacancies that existed. Some firms, therefore, had to spend money on training if they wished to remain in business. This opened up the possibility of other firms free-riding on this training expenditure by 'poaching' the recently qualified trainees and paying them a marginally higher wage.

Pressure was therefore building up for expenditure on training to be spread more evenly among employers. The levy/grant system attempted to do this by requiring all firms whose expenditure on training did not reach the statutory minimum laid down by the ITBs, or whose training did not meet the necessary criteria, to pay a levy to a sectorally based fund. This money would then be distributed in the form of a grant amongst those employers whose training matched the Board's requirements.

The Industrial Training Act provided the framework for training in the UK until 1974. ITBs raised £200 million a year through the levy, over 90 per cent of which was paid back to employers in grants towards approved training. Originally it was anticipated that more than 100 ITBs would be created, but by 1972 there were just 27, covering over 15 million workers between them. In most cases the Boards had a number of industries within their scope brought together because of their apparent affinities. The fewer than expected numbers of ITBs created problems of size and flexibility which were to prove important later. One of the main reasons for the eventual phasing out of the structure set up by the Industrial Training Act was the fact that the ITBs were too broadly based and did not represent accurately the training needs of all the companies in their sector.

Most of the eventual criticism of the Industrial Training Act was centred around the bureaucratic administration of the levy/grant system. It was inevitably cumbersome and most of the problems it created were at the margin, rather than with large firms or clearly defined sectors. Thus firms which were peripheral to the sector, small or specialized firms and firms which required a less skilled workforce, were all disadvantaged. It was found to be almost impossible for a central body like an ITB to develop criteria for the awarding of grants which matched each individual firm's training needs. Small firms especially felt that the criteria were not appropriate, were inflexible and out of touch. Indeed some firms followed a policy of maximizing their grant returns, thus distorting the training they had previously undertaken for business needs.

The philosophy of 'cost redistribution' that underpinned the Act was based on the idea that, through their company-based training, workers were receiving transferable skills that would enable them to perform any job in their sector. In practice, much of the training that firms undertook was job specific and the benefits were largely lost when individuals changed jobs. This meant in fact that the levy/grant system could reinforce inequities that already existed.

By the early 1970s, the process of 'disengagement' from the levy/grant system by firms who showed an adequate level of training was under way. Increased levels of exemption for many small firms also were beginning to show that the system was not fulfilling its early promise. In response, the Department of Employment (DE) published the White Paper *Training for the Future* (DE, 1972), which called for the training levy to be phased out. The ITBs were asked to concentrate on their other roles which, it was felt, they had been performing well. These included identifying their industry's particular requirements, providing advisory services, setting sound standards of training, developing good training programmes and encouraging the establishment of group training schemes. Where a clear consensus for continuation of the training levy system existed at industry level and the Secretary of State agreed, it was possible for the system to continue — as is still the case with the construction industry through the Construction, and the Engineering, Construction Industry Training Boards[*].

Any judgment about the performance of the Industry Training Boards has to be qualified because the scale of their activities varied considerably. This makes it difficult to generalize about their work. It was the first attempt to coordinate training activity and create a coherent policy at national level, and there were some positive results. The introduction of

---

[*] The construction industry has its own special circumstances, including the necessity for genuine mobility of labour, a relatively low skilled workforce, and a contracting system producing different employers, different tasks and different sites with each new job. All these factors make training difficult to plan and deliver.

ITBs undoubtedly raised the absolute numbers of people undergoing training in Britain. There was a rise of 15 per cent from 1964 to 1969 with a falling off thereafter, reflecting the slower rate of economic growth and a lessening of the impact of ITBs' grant schemes. ITBs also helped to improve the quality and efficiency of training in each sector. This was largely due to careful and detailed analysis within each industry of what was needed and how to deliver it.

The Industrial Training Act achieved much but was weighed down, fatally in the end, by bureaucracy and inflexibility.

The Manpower Services Commission and Beyond

Training for the Future highlighted the failure of the Industrial Training Act. Following up the report, in November 1972, the government announced that a nationally-based Manpower Services Commission (MSC) would replace much of the sectorally-based structure that the Industrial Training Act had set up. The MSC was brought into being by the Employment and Training Act of 1973, and assumed formal responsibilities on 1st January 1974.

The Manpower Services Commission was obliged by law to consist of three members nominated by the CBI, three from the Trade Unions, two from local authorities and an educator. It ran both employment and training services. Only education and training should concern us in this chapter, though there were times when training policy was used to help in the handling of unemployment issues.

Although introduced under the Heath Government, the MSC became a funding priority for the Wilson and Callaghan Governments from 1974. By 1979 the work of the MSC had become embedded, and it had become accepted as a surrogate branch of government. The Conservative Government under Margaret Thatcher was not a natural ally of the MSC but, while high levels of unemployment persisted, the Cabinet considered that it could not afford to reduce its powers. Training schemes for the unemployed were impossible to delegate elsewhere while there was no infrastructure to take responsibility.

The MSC was a powerful organization. It was the only national body concerned with training from 1974 until the announcement of the introduction of the Training and Enterprise Council (TEC) network in December 1988. The period of the MSC's hegemony was, however, characterized by rising levels of unemployment and two prolonged recessions. This meant that its role in providing an overall strategy for the education and training market was somewhat diluted by continual pressure to perform as a 'stopgap to unemployment'.

Training for the Future set up the Training Opportunities Scheme (TOPS), and this provided the main work of the MSC when it was launched. Training for adults through TOPS was carried out in Skill Centres and in further education colleges. In 1976 the MSC document *Towards a Comprehensive Manpower Planning Policy* (1976) was launched, followed in April 1978 by the Youth Opportunities Scheme (YOPS). YOPS combined training with a strong element of work experience for young people, and was the forerunner of the Youth Training Scheme (YTS).

The MSC initially survived the change in Government in 1979 and continued in its role to oversee training. The New Training Initiative (NTI) was launched in 1981 and marked a new period of development for the MSC. The programme comprised a number of elements including a commitment to develop a Youth Training Scheme (YTS). This was highly innovative in training terms. YTS applied the latest thinking on training practice to a government scheme and introduced it into participating companies. Training programmes were developed which set out objectives and outcomes. Records of achievement and core skills training were incorporated and training schedules included release to attend related further education college courses. The effect within companies was frequently to encourage managers to review their own training programmes and employees to seek company training which adopted YTS best practice.

In 1983 the Technical and Vocational Educational Initiative (TVEI) was launched. The transition between education and employment was seen as a particularly crucial area needing urgent attention, and the TVEI was designed to tackle this. It was an attempt to link education and training and give a more 'industry-friendly' feel to the transfer between school and work. It invested new money in improving work experience for students and developing the school curriculum to include greater coverage of the world of work. It is seen by some commentators as one of the most successful education and training programmes of the 1980s. Though funding for the initiative is now coming to an end, the work it began has become increasingly embedded in routine school practice.

In fact the MSC's activities began to involve it increasingly with the education sector and this began to blur the distinction between education and vocational training, which had traditionally been treated as separate policy areas. The MSC was valuable to the Department of Employment because it could deliver policy initiatives rapidly while the Department of Education and Science (DES) was obliged to depend on the Local Education Authorities (LEAs) for the implementation of initiatives.

The announcement in 1988 of the introduction of the Training and Enterprise Council (TEC) network marked the beginning of the end for the MSC. The YTS was restructured and renamed Youth Training (YT), and delegated to the TECs. The MSC was a surviving example of the tripartite, corporatist top-down approach that had dominated British politics since the Second World War. Its remit had never explicitly included education, although its initiatives in the education field had highlighted the symbiotic link that exists between the two learning routes, and as a result had highlighted the need to view learning as a whole.

1988 also saw the passing of the Education Reform Act which launched the National Curriculum and increased the autonomy of schools and further education colleges through local management. The Education Reform Act also opened up the possibility of schools opting out of local authority control altogether. Many of the reforms it provided for are still having a major impact on fundamental school practice.

New Approaches

New thinking on learning has blossomed since the mid 1980s and there has been something close to a consensus on the future objectives of education and training in this country. The twin themes of individual empowerment and lifelong learning have now been adopted by a wide range of different key interests.

Thinking on education and training has generally been well ahead of practice. In 1976, the Prime Minister, Jim Callaghan, in a now famous speech to mark the laying of the foundation stone for an extension to Ruskin College, Oxford (Callaghan, 1976), started what became known as 'the great debate' on education. This was almost the first time that the link between the education system and employment became an arena for debate.

The speech highlighted the central theme that the education system must be more directly geared to producing the skills that individuals and employers need. He pointed out that industry was not satisfied with the products of the education system and that the best educated showed very little desire to join industry. This was partly a by-product of the fact that there was 'insufficient coordination between schools and industry'. The theme of lifelong learning was also given a public airing as he set out individuals' need for an 'appetite for knowledge that will last a lifetime'. His speech covered many areas that are now seen as valid but that were controversial at the time. He said that the education system should provide individuals with 'essential tools' (or core skills in today's terminology) and that schools should teach to a core curriculum. A great debate on education was crucial because 'there are simply fewer jobs for those without skills'. The education of children and young people was crucial because 'the future of our country' depended on it.

Since 1976 there have been several contributions to this debate which are now seen as especially significant. In 1979 the Further Education Unit (FEU) published the report *A Basis for Choice* which placed emphasis on some of the areas that Callaghan had highlighted as ripe for change. *A Basis for Choice* was produced by a study group which concerned itself with post-16 pre-employment learning.

They set out three principles for the development of post-16 pre-employment courses. The first was that the system of provision should encourage the development of a realistic vocational focus as the course progressed. The second was that equality of status should be achieved between vocational and academic routes. The third principle called for recognition of the importance of participating in 'learning experiences' away from the teaching of basic skills.

The report recommended that a 'common core' curriculum should be developed which would reflect the consensus view about the kind of general education to which everyone should have a right. The importance of widespread learning was highlighted by the 'Training in Britain' survey (DE, 1989), carried out eight years later in 1987, which still found that 42 per cent of the workforce could not imagine undertaking training of any sort. Those with no qualifications showed the least propensity of any group to undertake training, drawing attention to the key role played by the availability of qualifications.

Competence and Competition (NEDO, 1984) was commissioned jointly by the National Economic Development Office (NEDO) and the MSC. The report highlighted the fact that Germany, the USA and Japan all saw a clear link between investment in education and training and competitive success:

> The efforts which each makes are on an impressive scale and collectively they set a standard against which our own must be measured if British industry is to compete and thrive against international competition and if managers and workers in Britain are to realise their full potential.

It stated that

> To remain competitive, British companies need to develop among their employees the ability to learn and the habit of learning. . . .

It also observed that

> The time has come for individuals to see that their desire for learning is relevant to their employment roles.

A Challenge to Complacency (Coopers and Lybrand, 1985), a follow up to *Competence and Competition*, outlined ways in which British firms could be 'encouraged to recognize and shoulder their responsibilities collectively and individually, and ensure that their ability to compete is not further eroded'. The report found that few employers thought training sufficiently central to their business for it to be a main component in their corporate strategy. It also found that: 'a surprisingly high proportion of the senior executives . . . had only a limited knowledge of the scale of resources devoted to training within their own company'; and that 'few companies said they saw a direct link from training activities to profitability; in fact the link was often explicitly stated as being the other way round — buoyant profits led to increased training expenditure'.

The report's recommendations were based on three themes. Theme 1 was 'exhorting and encouraging companies to invest in training'. Theme 2 was 'harnessing the interests of individuals as a means of bringing pressure to bear on employers'. The third theme was 'improving the operation of the training market to make it easier for companies to define, and obtain from external providers, the training they require'. One final development which the report felt was necessary was the development of a clear structure of qualifications based on the achievement of set standards or competences.

The shortfalls of the system of vocational qualifications that existed were identified by the DeVille Working Group, commissioned by the MSC and the Department of Education and Science (MSC, DES, 1986). It identified five main points for action. These were:

creating a larger and better qualified workforce;

reducing the confusion of the present qualifications system;

bridging the unhelpful divide between so-called academic and vocational qualifications;

devising vocational qualifications that related more directly and clearly to competence required (and acquired) in work;

and building on what was good in current practice.

The response of the Government was to introduce the National Vocational Qualification (NVQ) system, announced in the July 1986 White Paper *Working Together — Education and Training* (HMSO, 1986).

Britain's management performance was another area that came under scrutiny. Two reports published in April 1987, *The Making of Managers* (NEDO, 1987) and *The Making of British Managers* (Constable and McCormick, 1987) respectively compared management education in five countries, and identified the areas which needed improvement in Britain. Both reports noted figures which highlighted the gap between Britain and its competitors. For example, 85 per cent of top managers in both the USA and Japan had degrees, compared with 24 per cent in Britain. In 1987, 90,000 people entered management roles, while just 12,300 obtained a management qualification of any description. In *The Making of Managers*, Professor Charles Handy identified a way forward by suggesting the setting of professional standards for managers which were expected from practitioners in other walks of life. His ideas proved to be the forerunner of the Management Charter Initiative (MCI), which has become the management 'lead body' and successfully set professional management standards.

These different strands have been drawn together by, among others, the Confederation of British Industry (CBI). The final and, in many ways, most crucial piece of the jigsaw that still had to be put in place was the placing of education and training in an area called 'learning' and the tackling of the subject as a whole. The CBI did this with its report *Towards a Skills Revolution* (CBI, 1989).

The CBI report set out the employer agenda for starting and sustaining the skills revolution. Its two main themes were for individuals to be put first in the education and training system and for the need to engender a culture of lifelong learning. The report argued that individuals are the only source of sustainable competitive advantage, and that efforts must, therefore, be concentrated on mobilizing their commitment and encouraging self-development and lifetime learning.

The report put forward in all forty main recommendations to sustain the skills revolution and three were of particular importance.

First, the report recommended that National Targets be set up to focus attention on the need to increase attainment of qualifications, and to highlight the differences in achievement between Britain and the rest of the world.

Secondly the report recommended that a learning system for the 16–19 age group called 'Careership' should be introduced. The four main elements of Careership were:

a coherent qualifications system that allowed transfer between academic and vocational routes and provided all young people with the opportunity to acquire core skills;

high quality and impartial careers guidance that enabled young people to make the right choice for the development of their career;

personal profiles for young people embodying both a National Record of Achievement and an action plan to achieve individual targets;

and a cash credit empowering all 16-year-olds to choose their future learning path.

Thirdly, the report set out a ten point action programme for organizations to become 'Investors in Training' and provide a systematic system for the development of employees based on the experience of world-class systems. This was the inspiration for what has now become the 'Investors in People' standard, helping companies achieve the change in culture that will allow them to become 'learning organizations' that make the fullest use of their people's abilities.

The successive publication of these and other reports has had a cumulative effect. Britain's system of education and training has indeed begun to respond to the challenges that face it.

The Current Position

The introduction to this chapter highlighted the need for Britain to improve its education and training performance. This improvement can be achieved through the creation of a learning society, via a learning market. Over the past six years a number of elements have contributed to the development of a nascent social education and training market system in this country. There is still some way to go before it is fully achieved.

The primary requirement for the effective working of any market is that it has a transferable, recognised 'currency'. In Britain, the currency for learning is the National Vocational Qualification (NVQ). NVQs are primarily intended for use in the workplace for those already employed. NVQs are assessed in terms of 'competence' to fulfil a specific occupational role. This approach allows *all* prior learning (be it formal or experiential) to contribute towards the achievement of a qualification, opening up the possibility of a qualification to many who have previously felt excluded from learning of any kind. NVQs will begin to provide a coherent overall framework for vocational learning as more and more occupational areas have awards accredited by National Council for Vocational Qualifications (NCVQ). As yet its impact has not been fully realized — the framework does not yet cover all occupational sectors and still has to make real inroads at the professional level. As the NVQ network becomes more embedded its value as a currency for learning will become more apparent (CBI, 1994a).

The second main element for the creation of a learning market is more flexible and wide-ranging choice for the individual and the employer — i.e., improved supply.

The 1988 Education Reform Act provided schools with increased control over their own budgets. Local management of schools became a statutory requirement — the LEA is now obliged to devolve to each school 90 per cent of its budget, retaining the last 10 per cent for services such as transport and special needs. In addition to this change, it became possible for schools to opt out of LEA control altogether and become 'grant-maintained' — funded directly from the centre by the Funding Agency for Schools (FAS). Schools which have chosen to opt out have 100 per cent control over their own budgets. With increased responsibility for their own budgets, schools are now better managers, but the change in their funding regime is essentially a means to an end — to allow them to respond to local needs more effectively. League tables and parental choice are helping to focus schools on the need to do this.

The Further Education Funding Council (FEFC) uses elements of output-related funding for Further Education (FE) colleges. This has improved efficiency both in terms of the use of resources and the completion of courses. Output related funding is a positive step towards rewarding good outcomes.

Schools and colleges, however, remain a delivery mechanism for learning. Just as important for achieving an improvement in the supply of learning is the 'product' they provide. There are now several new opportunities for learning available.

For pre-16 students, the National Curriculum now includes a compulsory technology element, providing a broadly based technical education for every pupil. The introduction of the General Certificate of Secondary Education (GCSE) in 1988 has meant that more students have been able to demonstrate their ability in a more competence-related way than under the previous knowledge based 'O'-level system. Achievement rates have, as a result, risen steadily.

The introduction of General National Vocational Qualifications (GNVQs) for teaching in schools and colleges offers an alternative to traditional examinations so that more young people can learn in a manner appropriate to them. The initial takeup of GNVQs has been very encouraging, and demonstrates that there has been a pool of latent demand for more broadly based high quality vocational qualifications. Despite their newness, GNVQs have already had their own impact on post-16 staying-on rates. GNVQs are designed to be compatible with and a preparation for both entry into higher education and into employment, and the achievement of NVQs. The expansion of the GNVQ and the NVQ system over the next two years will mean further opportunities for learning for those who have not yet been given the chance to demonstrate their talents.

In higher education, old and new universities alike are providing courses which more closely match the needs of young people. As the traditional graduate market undergoes a period of change, students require broader and more work-related learning to improve their chances of getting a job. As the old polytechnics have become the new universities, creating a more level playing field, the competition to recruit high achieving 18-year-olds has grown.

On the training side, Modern Apprenticeships and Accelerated Modern Apprenticeships will provide new work-based vocational routes for high achievers. The two initiatives (which cover 16–19-year-olds) from the Employment Department may well begin to help bridge the perceived gap between the academic and the vocational route. They will rely on the collective efforts of employers, training providers, FE colleges, TECs and Industry Training Organizations (ITOs). Parents and students realize that in the future low-skill jobs will be lost and new higher skilled jobs will be created. The elusive concept of 'parity of esteem' between academic and vocational learning will only be achieved when individuals see that there are routes through vocational learning which offer as genuine a route to high skill-level employment as the more traditional path through higher education. The third crucial element in a learning market is demand. Only if demand is high enough for these new opportunities will Britain reap the full benefits of the recent changes.

There is substantial evidence to suggest that employers and individuals are realizing the central importance of improved learning. There has been a rapid increase in the number of 16-year-olds staying on in full-time education. The overall proportion of 16-year-olds in full-time or part-time education has risen in the last five years from 69.9 per cent to 80.0 per cent (DE, 1994). The demand for higher education has risen even more dramatically. In 1980–81, the proportion of 18–19-year-olds entering higher education was 13 per cent. By 1993–94, the rate had risen to 31 per cent. The number of mature students in the first year of courses in British institutions increased by 77 per cent from 134,000 to 237,000 between 1980 and 1990 (CBI, 1994b). Employers have also begun to realize the value of investing in training. Contrary to the experience of previous recessions, the CBI's Industrial Trends Survey indicates that spending on training and retraining by companies held up impressively from 1990 onwards (CBI, 1990–4).

Several initiatives are playing a crucial role in increasing the demand for learning. The employer-led Training and Enterprise Councils (TECs) (Local Enterprise Companies, LECs, in Scotland) have responsibility for the implementation of government training schemes. TECs are regionally based, with a remit which also covers the development of enterprise in their areas. TECs are a crucial vehicle through which businesses have more opportunity to influence the creation and the direction of local, regulated, learning markets.

Investors in People (IiP) is another major initiative, helping companies to develop human resource policies encouraging individuals to improve their learning. The development of companies into 'learning organizations' is a vital component part of any efficient learning system. IiP is a quality standard with which companies can be accredited if they meet stringent criteria for becoming effective 'learning organizations'. The standard requires companies' managing directors to declare publicly their commitment to develop all of their employees all of their working lives and to introduce the organizational systems to ensure that this happens in practice. This must be done in such a way as to ensure that individual development and the achievement of business objectives go hand in hand. This process of 'culture change', that many British companies are now undergoing, is seen as a necessary one if they are to survive and compete effectively into the twenty-first century. IiP can provide a route by which improved breadth and depth of learning undertaken by people in British companies allows those organizations to regain the elusive competitive edge.

Piloting of the Youth Credit pilots by the TECs has been largely successful and they will be available nationwide for 16- and 17-year-olds leaving full-time education in 1995. Financial credits empowering individuals to purchase the learning of their choice are an important route to achieving a greater emphasis on outcomes, and for increasing the demand for learning from individuals. Credits for learning make clear what an individual's entitlements are and encourage the search for good advice and guidance on how to spend their money. Improved careers guidance for 13-, 15- and 17-year-olds, as announced in the Competitiveness White Paper (HMSO, 1994), will help young people choose the courses that are right for them. If consumers of learning are to be given credits, it is essential that they are well informed. Greater levels of information will allow a more efficient working of the learning market.

Education Business Partnerships which provide better links between schools and industry are another important way of helping to create better informed consumers. The presence of these consumers also encourages providers to tailor the courses they offer to the individual's needs. One consequence of increased flexibility of provision and improved guidance in schools should be reduced drop-out rates — identified by the Audit Commission in *Unfinished Business* (Audit Commission, 1993) as a major source of Britain's failure to compete effectively in terms of its people's skills.

The reform that will perhaps do the most for Britain's ability to deal with education and training as a single whole — i.e., as 'learning' — is the introduction of a learning credit. This proposal was made originally in the CBI Report *Towards a Skills Revolution* (1989). The Competitiveness White Paper has promised, among other things, that the Government will consult widely on the possibility of introducing learning credits for all 16-year-olds. Individuals would be able to purchase learning along any path, including 'A'-levels in a sixth form, GNVQs in a school or FE college, or NVQs in work or on government training schemes. The learning credit would remove the distinction in young people's perceptions of the different routes of learning. This credit for young people is an early indication of the type of market choice that we can expect to see in the future for learners of all ages.

Britain still requires a quantum leap in skills if we are to compete at the highest level. Achievement levels are rapidly improving, but have fallen short of what is necessary. The National Education and Training Targets (NETTs), agreed by all the key players as a result of the CBI's recommendation in *Towards a Skills Revolution*, are proving valuable in highlighting the task ahead. The new thinking has begun to have a real influence on policy, but it is vital that the changes are fully embedded before we are able to observe their real impact. It is not overstating the case to say that learning is the key to Britain's future.

References

AUDIT COMMISSION, OFSTED (1993) *Unfinished Business*, HMSO, London.

CALLAGHAN, J. (18 OCTOBER 1976) 'Speech by the Prime Minister the Rt. Hon. James Callaghan, MP, at Ruskin College, Oxford', 10 Downing Street, London.

CONFEDERATION OF BRITISH INDUSTRY (1989) *Towards a Skills Revolution*, CBI, London.

CONFEDERATION OF BRITISH INDUSTRY (1990–4) *Quarterly Industrial Trends Survey*, CBI, London.

CONFEDERATION OF BRITISH INDUSTRY (1994a) *Quality Assessed: The CBI Review of NVQs and SVQs*, CBI, London.

CONFEDERATION OF BRITISH INDUSTRY (1994b) *Thinking Ahead*, CBI, London.

CONSTABLE, J. and MCCORMICK, R. (1987) *The Making of British Managers*, BIM/CBI, London.

COOPERS & LYBRAND (1985) *A Challenge to Complacency: Changing Attitudes to Training*, MSC/NEDC, London.

DAVIES, H. (1993) *A Social Market for Training*, Social Market Foundation, London.

DEPARTMENT FOR EDUCATION (1994) *Statistical Bulletin 10/94*, HMSO, London.

DEPARTMENT OF EMPLOYMENT (1972) *Training for the Future*, HMSO, London.

DEPARTMENT OF EMPLOYMENT (1989) *Training in Britain — A Survey of Funding, Activity, and Attitudes*, HMSO, London.

FURTHER EDUCATION UNIT (1979) *A Basis for Choice*, FEU, London.

GREEN, A. and STEEDMAN, H. (1993) *Educational Provision, Educational Attainment and the Needs of Industry: A Review of Research for Germany, France, Japan, the USA and Britain*, NIESR, London.

HM GOVERNMENT (1986) *White Paper — Working Together: Education and Training*, HMSO, London.

HM GOVERNMENT (1994) *White Paper — Competitiveness — Helping Business to Win*, HMSO, London.

IMD, WORLD ECONOMIC FORUM (1993) *World Competitiveness Report 1994*, 14th ed., Switzerland.

MANPOWER SERVICES COMMISSION (1976) *Towards A Comprehensive Manpower Policy*, MSC, Sheffield.

MANPOWER SERVICES COMMISSION, DEPARTMENT OF EDUCATION AND SCIENCE (1986) *The Deville Report — Review of Vocational Qualifications in England and Wales*, HMSO, London.

NEDO (1984) *Competence and Competition*, MSC/NEDC, London.

NEDO (1987) *The Making of Managers*, MSC/NEDC/BIM, London.

Chapter 4

Lifelong Learning: A Brave and Proper Vision

Naomi Sargant

Lifelong and lifetime learning are two current versions of attempts to find a suitable name for post-compulsory learning. Both have the advantage, from the adult learner's perspective, that they can include both education and training. 'Lifetime' derives particular support through its acceptance and inclusion by the Confederation of British Industry (CBI) and Employment Department (ED) in their agreed Lifetime Learning Targets for Education and Training. 'Lifelong' is preferred within European organizations and is broader in its inclusiveness.

For most people, the term education has been so closely associated with 'schooling' and the classroom, as immediately to invoke negative memories and attitudes. School was compulsory, and was for many people a place to leave as soon as possible. The idea that it is desirable, let alone necessary, to go on learning and being judged as competent or not throughout life is quite threatening. To learn for pleasure or for leisure is one thing, but to be required continually to update oneself or retrain for another career is quite another. Learning is a necessary entry-point to the information society and it must be made available to older people as well as to the young.

The Open University: A Monument?

The fact that there is much latent demand for learning among adults is shown by the impact and undoubted success of the Open University (OU) which celebrated the 25th anniversary of its foundation in 1994. Set up primarily to provide 'second chance' opportunities for adults, it did not set out to rewrite the curriculum of higher education, but to demystify it and make it more widely available through the use of the media (McIntosh *et al.*, 1976). The evocative challenge of its first Chancellor, Baron Crowther, on the occasion of his installation to be 'open as to people . . . open as to places . . . open as to methods . . . and open, finally as to ideas' (Crowther, 1969) provides a continuing inspiration for its own community and a continuing challenge to conventional institutions.

Its birth was attended by much cynicism, and indeed the *Times Edu-cational Supplement* (TES) commented on the 1966 plan:

> But what would happen in a university of the air? The numbers
> attracted to it would certainly be out of all proportion to the
> numbers that stayed the course. Can we really afford the fantastic
> cost that this would entail. The Government gives no estimate. It
> is just as well . . . This is one of those grandiose schemes that does
> not bear inspection while so much else that is already begun is half
> done. We shall need to be very sure that it is necessary before we
> commit ourself to the expense. (TES, 1966)

Twenty-five years on it has produced 130,000 graduates and gained world-wide recognition as well as many institutional imitators. Its post-natal history has been documented elsewhere, most recently in *Learn & Live* (OU, 1994).

Most important to this chapter is its commitment to adult learners: learners under 21-years-old were positively to be excluded. More than 200,000 people study with the OU each year, 75 per cent of students are in full-time employment and contributing to the national economy while they study. One third of its graduates had less than the minimum entry requirements for a traditional university. The remit for higher education was significant; but the OU displays some of the qualities of a monument: an achievement to be celebrated, but one gazed at in admiration while nothing around or beneath changes.

While Jennie Lee, then Minister for the Arts, worked on plans for the OU, the more orthodox planners in the Department of Education and Science under their Secretary of State, Anthony Crosland, had just pub-lished the White Paper *A Plan for Polytechnics and Other Colleges* (DES, 1965). They were to provide full-time and sandwich courses for students 'of university quality' but in more vocational and applied areas of study and courses in the same areas 'but of a somewhat less rigorous stand-ard . . .'. Adults studying part-time were implicitly to be part of their mission. Most important was their third role; to provide for 'tens of thou-sands of part-time students who need advanced courses either to supple-ment qualifications, or because for one reason or another, they missed out on the full-time route' (Crosland, 1965). In the event, while polytechnics (now universities) shed much of their lower-level work over the years, they have maintained a major commitment to part-time study and hence to adult opportunities.

'Access' was not, in the early 1970s, a matter of concern for most institutions of higher education, nor indeed for the new Government. The bulge in the birth-rate had only reached primary schools, and the qualifi-cation and participation rates remained low. Neither did the new polytech-nics, with a few exceptions, develop or expand their part-time provision.

Indeed, as late as 1978, the DES in a discussion paper, 'Higher Education into the 1990s' (DES, 1978) expressed the complacent view, 'that there was no evidence of any unsatisfied demand for part-time degrees'. This was despite the fact that the OU was having to turn away several thousand applicants for part-time degree-level study each year, many of whom, such as non-graduate teachers, had strong vocational and work-related motives for study.

The answer to this contradiction lay in the nature of the provision made by conventional universities and its inaccessibility to working adults. The OU was attracting a large number of students, not because it was cheap or easy, but because it gave the learner the choice about how, when and, in particular, where to learn (McIntosh and Woodley, 1978). Additionally its credit structure was more flexible, a characteristic which was to become more valuable to learners as equivalence and transferability of credit arrangements with some individual universities, and more significantly between the OU and the Council for National Academic Awards (CNAA) were agreed.

Creating a Wider Vision: The Advisory Council for Adult and Continuing Education

A practical step forward was taken in 1977, in England and Wales at least, with the setting up of the Advisory Council for Adult and Continuing Education (ACACE). Part of its remit was 'to promote the development of future policies and priorities; with full regard to the concept of education as a process continuing throughout life' (DES, 1977). This was excitingly new and the Notes of Amplification provided by the DES still stand as a brave and proper vision:

> Increasingly we have come to realize that education and training cannot adequately be provided by school and post-school ('front-end') provision; for a variety of personal, social and vocational reasons, adults need to be able to return to education and training throughout life, to explore new avenues or pursue existing interests further . . . Post-school education and training is increasingly seen as a continuum permitting many different combinations of modes of attendance, subject areas and levels of study intended to meet the almost infinite variety of students' needs and motivation. Adult education and all the other administratively convenient bundles of provision do not therefore have rigid boundaries. Continuing education requires us to think in a student-centred rather than an institution-centred way. (Jones, 1977)

Though ACACE was limited by the fact that its role was advisory, its membership, while not representative as such, covered a very wide spread of involvement from the CBI to the TUC, from the MSC to broadcasting and libraries as well as more conventional providers. This breadth of membership gave it real strength and its Chairman, Richard Hoggart, in urging it not to be afraid to be radical, ensured that its 'reach' should exceed its 'grasp'.

Its paper *Towards Continuing Education* (ACACE, 1979) was designed to provoke discussion, rather than assume agreed solutions, and argued strongly that a shift from the 'front-end' model of education, in which adults are equipped with all the educational baggage they need for their whole lives at the beginning of it, to a model in which opportunities continue to be available throughout life was vital. It proposed the distinction between initial and post-initial education rather than between compulsory and post-compulsory. More important, it preferred not to differentiate between education and training, and criticized the term non-vocational education. It argued from the point of view of the learning adult, not from the point of view of existing provider institutions, funders or embedded vested interests.

There were however structural obstacles and Peter Newsam pointed out that most educational administrators had a background in schools and not in adult work, and would not necessarily be sympathetic to continuing education. He also warned of the 'fallacy that falling rolls would release more and more resources from a fixed total to be redeployed to adult education'. This, he said, was just not the way the Treasury operated and reminded his audience that 'thought is free; it's action that runs up the bills'. He also noted 'the diseconomies of decline' (Newsam, 1979).

In its six-year life ACACE did much valuable work, made evident through its thirty-four publications, but it did not succeed in its most important task. In its final publication (ACACE, 1983) it criticized itself for failing adequately to raise the level of excitement about the education of adults and for failing to persuade the Government to extend its life and make it an official development body rather than merely an advisory one. No decision as to the future of its work had been made at the point the Council was closed down, and the Government response, when it came, was a 'mouse': they offered the National Institute of Adult Continuing Education (NIACE) £50,000 to set up a 'development unit' later called the Unit for the Development of Adult Continuing Education (UDACE) under the wing of NIACE, and added a similarly small amount for a unit (to be called Replan) to develop education for the unemployed, another of ACACE's pieces of unfinished business. When this sum was offered to NIACE, a number of people who had bridged both organizations considered it derisory and thought it should not be accepted. It is, however, easy to understand why NIACE was interested in accepting it; but it became another clear example of one educational grouping being played off against another: a government strategy which has continued in this area.

ACACE's major report *Continuing Education: From Policies to Practice*

(1982a) argued that all adults should be entitled to continued opportunities for education throughout their lives. It did not propose to set up a new 'sector' of such education or develop a new curriculum but to make the 'best' more widely available and give the education of adults an increased priority in the allocation of resources. Issues focused on were:

- the removal of barriers to access;
- the provision of information, advisory and counselling services;
- ways in and through the system, including flexible and modular structures and what would now be termed progression routes;
- the accessibility of institutions, including the need for a network of local centres near people;
- new patterns of learning including open and distance learning and broadcasting;
- issues of financing of provision;
- and financial support for learners, including entitlements.

These issues are all still on the agenda. That report proposed and ACACE's final report ended '. . . by restating the proposition that the time has come for this country to give the same serious attention to the education of its adults as it gives to the education of its children' (ACACE, 1983).

Richard Hoggart and his colleagues on the Council were genuine in their self-criticism, but they were equally critical of attitudes in the country as a whole. In their final paper, they noted 'the complete absence of any references to continuing education in public speeches about the future of our society . . . during the election campaign of 1983'. Two of their major reports *Continuing Education: From Policies to Practice* and *Education for Unemployed Adults* (ACACE, 1982a; 1982b) had been sitting on the then Secretary of State's desk for 18 months and a year respectively. Keith Joseph had, 18 months earlier speaking to the NIACE Annual Conference on the Continuing Education Report's publication, described it as 'insidiously seductive' (he was later to explain that from him this was a compliment) but that people had to understand that this was an area for private funding for which people should pay themselves. This proved to be a foretaste of future stronger policies.

The Vocational Takeover

With the demise of ACACE, and the limited funding offered for continuing work to NIACE, the initiative in the development of opportunities for adults passed from education to training, and from the Department of Education and Science (DES) to the Manpower Services Commission (MSC). The MSC had been created by the Employment and Training Act, 1973 and lasted until its transformation into the Training Commission in

1988. It was one of the small number of quangos which survived the attacks of that time, finding a role which was also acceptable to the incoming Conservative Government. Ainley and Corney (1990) describe the MSC as having set itself three tasks:

> In the widest context . . . it aimed to abolish completely the dichotomy between education and training that had emerged during the nineteenth century. Within the policy-making context, the MSC's goal was to elevate the importance of education and training and redefine its contribution to productivity and national development. At the institutional level, the MSC attempted the complete overhaul of Britain's education and training system.

It is not surprising that the MSC became seen as a rival to the DES and there was real tension between them. The MSC soon adopted the term 'Vocational Education and Training' (VET) in an attempt to show their interrelationship. An example of a positive, but limited, riposte from the DES in the 'adult' area was their Discussion Paper on *Continuing Education: Post-experience Vocational Provision for Those in Employment.* (DES, 1980) This complicated formulation (soon referred to as PEVE) focused on the importance of mid-career courses of vocational education for those at work. It noted: 'This does not deny either initial education, which indeed is likely always to take a large share of education resources; retraining of the unemployed; or general continuing education for adults.' In a footnote, it commented:

> By vocational is meant anything which is broadly relevant to the individual in his development in working life, whether or not it is directly or immediately relevant to his present job. Education should be construed broadly, as embracing activities which might be regarded as training.

ACACE, still working on its long-term plans, was somewhat concerned about this more instrumental direction. The paper, however, made it clear that any such shorter term practical solutions 'need not prejudice any long-term and more general developments across the whole field of continuing education which might be pursued in the light of advice from ACACE'. The use of *continuing* in the narrower and 'post-experience' sense has however tended to become the accepted sense of its use in higher education since that time.

Separately, Jim Prior, as Secretary of State for Employment, had been interested in setting up an analogue to the OU to meet adult training and retraining needs at technician and related levels. The resultant Open Tech Programme was not to be a new institution, but a planned and coordinated range of commissioned projects with two key tasks: to open or widen access to existing training provision and to make new education and training provision which from the beginning can best be met through open learning. Providers were pump-primed to produce open learning materials which would then be widely available, but 'on the assumption that adults retraining through the Open Tech Programme would have to pay for their own self-improvement' (Ainley and Corney, 1990).

It is not possible to review this period in detail. However, the departure of John Cassels for the Cabinet Office in 1981 and his replacement as Director of the MSC by Geoffrey Holland, and the replacement of Richard O'Brien, as Chairman, by David (later Lord) Young, who had been advising Keith Joseph at the Department of Trade and Industry were particularly significant. This is an area where it is not possible to disengage attitudinal issues from the individuals engaged in policy development. According to Ainley and Corney (1990):

> Young's appointment indicated that the future development of the MSC would be in strict accordance with the overall direction of government policy. The MSC might be used to deal with political crises, as and when they arose. Otherwise, its main function was to keep the anti-inflationary strategy on course. Training would be left to the market and would aim to encourage industry to develop and apply the new technologies.

There was as yet no obvious connection with investment in human capital and with the need for an adaptable and flexible trained workforce. The most urgent task for the MSC was to help to deal with mass unemployment, especially mass youth unemployment, which the government was increasingly funding through the Youth Opportunities Programme.

The MSC Picks Up the Adult Baton — But Drops It

John Cassels had prepared a consultative paper *A New Training Initiative* (NTI) (MSC, 1981a) which aimed to replace the various temporary employment schemes with a permanent, national and comprehensive training programme for all young people. Behind it were all the now well-known arguments about adaptability and flexibility, the unpredictability of the labour market and no single job for life. Arguing that training and re-training for the entire workforce was not only important for the survival of individual firms and for employment prospects but that both were also a cure for unemployment, the NTI argued for the development and improvement of apprenticeships, the chance for all young people under 18 to continue either in full-time education or training and for the *opening up of widespread opportunities for adults* (emphasis added). The last of these was expressed in generous terms: 'We must open up wide opportunities for adults, whether in employment, unemployed or returning to work, to acquire, increase or up-date their skills and knowledge during the course of their working lives' (MSC, 1981b).

This far-seeing statement of adult needs was not to be matched by the allocation of financial resources: youth training remained the priority of the Government. The MSC published their follow-up *A New Training Initiative: An Agenda for Action* (MSC, 1981) and, on the same day, the Secretary of State for Employment, Norman Tebbit, published *A New Training Initiative: A Programme for Action* (The Department for Employment, 1981) proposing a £1 billion scheme of vocational preparation for people between the ages of 16 and 18. After this age, it said 'the cost of training is basically a matter for the individual employer'. The Youth Training Scheme was to start in 1983, and the valuable Training Opportunities Scheme (TOPS) scheme was to be closed down to help pay for it. Adults, and particularly women returners, would therefore be worse off, as the joint TUC–Labour Party statement *A Plan for Training* pointed out (TUC and the Labour Party, 1984).

Geoffrey Holland, Director of the MSC, found what he described as '. . . the Government's obsession with the young' unhelpful and was concerned at the major shift away from support for adults. Since the budget that was retained for work with adults was now too small to enable any significant provision of training, he determined that the most fruitful strategy would be to concentrate on changing public and private attitudes towards the desirability of adult training, particularly among employers.

The result was the publication of the MSC's discussing paper *Towards an Adult Training Strategy* (MSC, 1983a) and its subsequent *MSC Proposals for Action* (MSC, 1983b). The Foreword of the Discussion Paper, signed by David Young, then Chairman, was encouraging:

> . . . In the view of the MSC, adult training and retraining will be every bit as important in the 1980s as Youth Training. . . .
> At the moment adult training and re-training are poor relations. They do not have sufficient priority or attention and they need to find a place on the agenda of employers, unions, the education service and all who are concerned with our training and vocational education system. (MSC, 1983a)

The paper argued the economic case for an adult training strategy, suggesting:

> more effort should be put into training and re-training those already in employment or about to start a new job, rather than into speculative training or training for stock. Providing the skills base for an economy which is not only viable but flourishing will be the most practical way to open up more opportunities for unemployed individuals.

It identified as particular priorities the management of change, the building of a more flexible and responsive training system to provide access to training for individuals. The language was already one of modules and standards of competence, of continuity and progression. The importance of information and expert advice assisted by the potential of information technology with increased accessibility through open learning systems such as the Open Tech and the OU were discussed. Their follow-up proposals for action included now familiar paragraphs: A National Awareness Campaign, Action at National Level, Achieving and Measuring Competence, Local Level Collaboration and Working with the Market. The Commission saw its role as acting as a focus for the national debate, working with others on achieving adult training objectives, using its resources to form opinion, provide information and act as a broker. It needed also to set an example with its own programmes and resources. The proposals included a number of useful detailed proposals with cross-references to the Open Tech programme and to the work of ACACE. An earlier proposal that an adult entitlement for training should be considered had not found favour in internal discussions in the MSC. What did emerge was the first reference to a national loans scheme.

In order to raise awareness of and the need for adult training, the MSC commissioned the first significant research into the quality, nature and cost of adult training, management attitudes to training and the relationship between adult training and business performance (IFF Research Ltd, 1985). This indicated that while employers considered that adult training was an essential investment, what they actually invested amounted to only 0.38 per cent of pay roll. High-performing businesses were twice as likely to train, and train twice as many employees, as low-performing businesses. High-performing businesses had increased their training by 25 per cent over the last five years while low-performing businesses had reduced their training by 20 per cent.

It was clear to people reading the fine print that the MSC was from then on to take over and actively pursue many of ACACE's policies but was, not surprisingly, to relate them to only training rather than the broader field of continuing education. While some adult educators were cynical about the MSC's motives, others, more pragmatic, welcomed them as setting precedents which could be built upon in better times. Since then many of the policy developments in this area have indeed come from the Manpower Services Commission and its successor bodies, under the guidance of Geoffrey Holland and his colleagues rather than from the DES.

Education Returns to the Ring

The fact that many policy developments on continuing education came from the MSC does not mean that there was no movement on the 'education' side, though this tended to be within the institutional group-ings rather than through the DES. The University Grants Committee (UGC) established a working party on continuing education in December 1982. The Business and Technician Education Council produced a policy statement titled *Continuing Education for Business and Industry* in April 1983 (BTEC, 1983) and in the same month the National Advisory Body for Local Authority Higher Education (NAB) established a group with wide-ranging membership to consider and advise on the appropriate role and extent of continuing education provision and how it might be fostered. Its first key recommendation was that 'the provision of continuing education should be accepted as a major objective of higher education' (NAB, 1984a). Later in the same year, the NAB and the UGC agreed a joint statement with the recommendation that 'the provision of continuing education in order to facilitate adjustment to technological, economic and social change and to meet individual needs for personal development' be adopted as an explicit national aim for higher education and be added to the 'four pur-poses of higher education' enshrined in the Robbins report of 1963 (NAB, 1984b).

The mid 1980s saw some hardening of attitudes. Some points stand out. Employers were expected to pay for the costs of training their em-ployees and the divide between providing education and training for the employed and the unemployed widened. For example Lord Young, then Secretary of State for Employment, refused to allow the emergent Open College to serve the unemployed as well as those in work, though the air-time offered by Channel 4 (lunch-time on weekdays) had been offered on that basis. The College's Chairman, Michael Green, said vehemently: 'I did not agree to be the chairman of a college for the jobless . . .'.

The DES Lags Behind

The DES continued to be mainly pre-occupied with the education of the young and with initial rather than post-initial education. The main thrust of the 1987 Education Reform Bill was at school level. However, at the same time as responsibility for higher education was to be removed from local education authorities, their duty to secure the provision of adequate further education to meet the needs of their areas was clarified. Unfortun-ately the Bill now differentiated between the straightforward provision of full- and part-time education and training for persons over compulsory school age (other than higher education) and the quaintly-worded second category of 'organized leisure-time occupation provided in connection with the provision of such education and training'. This it spelled out as mean-ing, 'in such organized cultural training and recreative activities as are suited to their requirements . . .'.

This distinction and the way that it is misused has been damaging.

Reappearing in the White Paper *Education and Training for the 21st Century* (DES, 1991), it paved the way for the separation of general adult educa-tion from supposedly more worthwhile areas of study. The give-away is, of course, the misuse of 'leisure' as an adjective to describe such courses. The connection with leisure is the simple one that the vast majority of adults who study use their own leisure-time in which to study. Many people who are engaged in work-related study are also using their own time for it, sometimes because their employers will not provide it. And of course, what may appear as a leisure interest now, may become rel-evant for future employment. Often motivation is known only to the learner and cannot be determined by categorizing courses or identifying sources of provision. This is an increasingly sterile argument as working patterns change with people undertaking a larger number of different jobs, living longer and having more leisure throughout life.

The limitation of this distinction is seen most clearly by the success of the employer development schemes being run in an increasing number of companies. The original Ford scheme, the Employee Development and Assistance Programme (EDAP) arose from the 1987 collective agreement between Ford and their Trade Unions. It provided for a company contri-bution of £40 per head for all 49,000 employees into a jointly managed fund, from which any employee could then draw up to £200 per annum for education, training or health and lifestyle pursuits. The key points are that the choice of what to do is left entirely to the individual, it is not expected to be work-related, neither is the study or activity carried out in work-time, though tuition will usually be offered on work premises. Response to the scheme, and to others like it, has been far higher than anticipated, and many people, once their confidence and interest has been secured have been encouraged to move on to more demanding areas and often vocationally relevant areas of study.

More of a problem arises for smaller companies in implementing such a scheme, but there are projects developing in some TEC areas to provide a framework for a number of local small- and medium-sized enterprises working together, and also where large companies, such as Rover, are opening their study facilities to their suppliers. These schemes provide an imaginative bottom-up complement to Investors in People (IiP). It is possible to see these strands of activity contributing to the idea of a learn-ing organization.

The emergence, in the 1980s, of the CBI as a major force in shaping policy for education and training lifted the debate nationally. Its report *Towards a Skill Revolution* (CBI, 1989) placed much emphasis on the indi-vidual. Working with others, the CBI also helped to establish the National Training and Education Targets (NETTS) (quoted in full on page 143) required to meet the strategic priorities for action laid down in *A Strategy for Skills* (ED, 1991). The target dates are close. Those for foundation learning seem likely to be met. Achievement of the adult targets seems less certain though IiP UK Ltd, who have the job of getting IiP adopted, report a gathering momentum in their area. Moreover some of the value of these targets is that they focus attention on, and legitimate work towards, the achievement of these goals.

Of the strategic priorities of *A Strategy for Skills* (*op. cit.*), the third is particularly relevant for this discussion: 'individuals must be persuaded that training pays and that they should take more responsibility for their own development'. It is the setting of this strategic priority which has led to the creation of a new department in the Training Enterprise and Education Directorate (TEED) under the banner of 'individual commitment'. It brings with it echoes of Keith Joseph and David Young, the implication being that while it is clearly a priority, and professional endeavour can be expended on this area of work, the task is to focus on 'hearts and minds' and not on anything that costs money and which would directly support individuals. The positive result of this is active encouragement within the Employment Department and the TECs of the development of coherent individual commitment strategies locally, and the commissioning of much new research which is providing valuable new information for providers.

In addition the TEC National Council set up a Working Group 'to address the web of complex issues that influence the commitment of individuals to lifetime learning in particular, and to the learning market in general'. This Working Group has recently reported to a joint DE/CBI conference on Learning and Individuals with a number of proposals including:

- a major and sustained PR campaign to increase motivation and awareness by individuals and employers of the benefits of lifetime learning;
- incentives for individuals to fund their own learning;
- rapid expansion of information, advice and guidance services at all ages to increase the efficiency of the learning market;
- improved responsiveness of learning suppliers to customer needs. (TEC National Council, 1994)

While not new, these are all laudable and the issue of financial incentives breaks some new ground. But essentially the policy returns to exhortation and rhetoric, but little action.

The other major influence on public attitude has been the Royal Society for the encouragement of Arts Manufactures and Commerce (RSA). The reports of Sir Christopher Ball, now the RSA's Director of Learning, are referred to elsewhere in this book, notably in Chapters 1 and 2. Here we note that *More Means Different* (Ball, 1990); *Learning Pays* (Ball, 1991); *Profitable Learning* (Ball, 1992); *Start Right* (Ball, 1994); and the commitment of the RSA to the development of a learning society have been valuable in changing perceptions and attitudes.

Adult Learning: Who Should Pay?

While many, though not enough, employers have been prepared to train their own employees in work-related skills, they have done this in the knowledge that their workforce has been expected to be basically stable. The decline of manufacturing industry and the increase in part-time low-skilled jobs, often taken by women (as is discussed in Chapter 1), has changed this. Few employers have funded non-work-related training, and by reverse, some employees have paid for their own work-related studies either if their employer would not, or, as often, when they wished to change employer.

A sequence of research studies funded by the ED's Individual Commitment Branch provide valuable new information on underlying attitudes both of employers and learners. The research shows first that the pattern of employer expectation is mirrored by the expectation of adult learners more than half of whom 'agree that employers or government should pay for learning that is to do with jobs or careers' (IFF Research, 1994). Secondly, the study of Individuals' Attitudes notes that:

> Non-learners were more likely than learners to feel that they themselves should *not* be expected to pay for job-related learning (43 per cent and 36 per cent respectively). This group was also more likely to feel that employers or government should fund vocational learning. (SCPR/ED, 1994)

Similarly a recent study of general adult learning carried out for Adult Learners' Week, 1994, shows that while adults consider that individuals themselves should pay two-thirds of the costs of courses which do not lead to qualifications, they reverse the proportions for courses leading to qualifications and consider that two-thirds of these costs should be borne by employers or tax-payers (NIACE, 1994).

Another serious issue is that training is not provided equitably across the workforce. A matching study on Employer's Attitudes (PSI/ED, 1994) records that 95 per cent of employers provided training for some or all of their employees, but as other research has shown, provision was greater for higher occupational groups and amongst larger organizations.

Neither are opportunities for training spread equally between men and women, or between ethnic groups. More training is recorded among the already better trained, and the 1992 Summer Labour Force Survey showed that in every industrial sector except energy and water, women received proportionately less training than men. Since the main growth in the workforce is among women working part-time, the situation is less than encouraging. Research among adult learners show fewer women engaged in current or recent learning in the work place, 12 per cent of women compared with 18 per cent of men (Sargant, 1991). A companion study among the main ethnic minority groups shows only 8 per cent overall learning at work compared with the 15 per cent overall in the national survey (Sargant, 1993). This is not due to their lack of interest in learning, since they show higher rates of learning both formally and informally than the population of Great Britain as a whole.

Entitlements Make Good Sense

The expectation that all post-compulsory training and work-related education can be left to employers has always been mistaken. Proponents of Paid Educational Leave made the same assumption at a time when very many women were not in the workforce and were not therefore eligible for it. That is one reason why ACACE argued for a broader form of entitlement, which was including rather than excluding since people in paid employment are now a minority of the population (ACACE, 1982a). ACACE argued for two forms of entitlement. The first was designed to give to those adults who had left school early the equivalent educational and financial opportunities that are already available to those who take the elite escalator through 'A'-levels to a degree. Along these lines, Sir Christopher Ball had usefully suggested that we learn to recognize 'deferred progression into further and higher education as normal and sensible' (Ball, 1989). The second would be a 'topping-up' continuing educational entitlement which people could choose to use regularly or save up for whatever they most required throughout their adult lives.

Over the past decade there has been continued but fitful discussion of such strategies as entitlements, paid educational leave and sabbaticals. One idea was entitlement for the over-fifties picked up by the Labour Party in a policy review. There are, of course, already a number of schemes which are effectively forms of entitlement: mandatory grants for higher education and training credits, for example. It is clear from such precedents that it is possible to plan an entitlement policy which is not open-ended and can be allocated within agreed priorities.

Turned on its head, the agreement that adults following the Employment Training programme are supported to the tune of their dole money plus expenses is, in fact, a form of entitlement. It is, of course, limited to those who have been unemployed for over six months and the Learning for Work entitlement is even more limited. The 21 hour rule, the concession to unemployed claimants of benefit which allows them to study part time whilst looking for work as long as the course does not exceed 21 hours per week, frustrates people because it comes near an imaginative entitlement but fails to achieve it.

The Training Agency and its successor TEED have been serious experimenters with versions of entitlements, the most significant being the piloting of a number of youth training credit schemes through TECs which the Government is now committed to offering to all young school-leavers by 1995 (President of the Board of Trade *et al.*, Cm 2563, 1994). Entitlements for guidance for adults are now built into Skills Choice, experiments with credits for Open Learning are proving very successful and adult training credits are also being tested out. In parallel with these initiatives is the expansion of Career Development Loans and recently the announcement of Small Firm Training Loans. While none of these projects form the basis of an overall policy, there is no question that the existence of these schemes has had a significant effect in changing attitudes.

Little changes without new ideas. Sir Geoffrey Holland recently suggested a framework against which the Labour Party's idea of a sattelite University for Industry might develop. It includes many of the planks of recent and current innovation: assessment of prior learning, paid educational leave, modular structures with Credit Accumulation and Transfer Schemes (CATS), complete choice of where and how to study, and the use of new technologies. He also suggested that the unique ingredient which could help drive the project could be individual training accounts rather than entitlements. The idea is that both the employer and the worker could make contributions into such an account which would be tax-relievable and could be called on 'as and when' for people's education and training needs. It is encouraging that the *Competitiveness* White Paper suggests that the 'Government will consult TECs, financial institutions and other bodies on how to take such arrangements forward . . .' (President of the Board of Trade *et al.*, 1994). However, as usual such ideas raise issues of universality and equity: not everyone has an employer and small employers are less able to engage in such funding. Moreover the structural changes in the labour market outlined in Chapter 1 mean that as far fewer people expect to have tidy careers, working with a single employer or in one career throughout their lives, training accounts will therefore need to be portable.

It is extremely difficult to deal with the lack of opportunities and inequities without any government or taxpayer intervention. And, as the research shows, individual commitment and motivation are extremely difficult to encourage when there are no visible job opportunities. Government policy is to move responsibility for funding education and training from the state to the employer and to the individual. In line with this, the *competitiveness* White Paper emphasizes the need for young people

> to learn how to take responsibility for their own decisions and to appreciate the crucial importance of investing in skills. At the same time the providers of education and training should be responsive to their customers. The Government therefore sees attractions in providing all 16–19 year-olds with **learning credits** with a real cash value. (*op. cit.*)

It emphasizes that such a far-reaching change in funding would need careful preparation and proposes wide and open consultation. It would certainly impact on 6th forms, on independent schools and on further and higher education. But combined with the notion of individual training accounts, it is possible to see the beginning of an overall entitlement strategy. What we have at the moment are a number of accidental planks of support. The most privileged learners, as Jeff Rooker (1993) in his discussion paper 'Opportunity and achievement' made clear, are the conventional entrants to full-time higher education, even though loans and grant cuts are putting pressure on them. The only other schemes that pay for subsistence/living costs are Employment and Youth Training and the benefits under the 21-hour rule.

Jeff Rooker suggests, as did ACACE, a life-time entitlement to higher education, an educational account to be drawn on after school. He emphasizes five guiding principles: equity, quality, continuity, access and accountability. He focuses on the fact that part-timers get no financial assistance, neither do OU students, and that discretionary grants are being cut with the pressure on local authorities caused by rate-capping. Subsidized loans are made available to full-time degree-level students while tax relief is available only for the costs of study of NVQs. The system is neither rational or equitable.

Policy for those in employment and the unemployed is determined by the Employment Department, working with the TECs. Policy for those not in employment is, effectively, determined by the Treasury operating with the other side of its brain. The failure is to see that these are two sides of the same brain, that patterns of work, non-work and leisure are changing and that the costs and benefits to society of a well-trained and educated population are social as well as economic and long-term as well as short-term. Of course resourcing training in a flexible and changing labour market is more difficult but it is vital that we do not plan for a divided workforce and a divided society. Economic necessity and the reality of the arrival of the information society may persuade the government to change its policy and priorities. Otherwise we shall continue paying only lip-service to what really is a 'possible vision' and condemn many to living in an information-poor society.

References

ACACE (1979) *Towards Continuing Education*, Leicester, ACACE.
ACACE (1982a) *Continuing Education: From Policies to Practice*, ACACE.
ACACE (1982b) *Education for Unemployed Adults*, Leicester, ACACE.
ACACE (1983) *In the Corners of our Time*, Leicester, ACACE.
AINLEY, P. and CORNEY, M. (1990) *Training for the Future*, London, Cassell.
BALL, C. (1989) *Aim Higher*, London, RSA.

BALL, C. (1990) *More Means Different*, London, RSA.

BALL, C. (1991) *Learning Pays*, London, RSA.

BALL, C. (1992) *Profitable Learning*, London, RSA.

BALL, C. (1994) *Start Right*, London, RSA.

BTEC (1983) *Continuing Education for Business and Industry*, London, BTEC.

CBI (1989) *Towards a Skills Revolution*, London, CBI.

CROSLAND, A. (1965) Speech at Woolwich Polytechnic, 27 April.

CROWTHER, G. (1969) Chancellor's inaugural speech at the Open University, 23 July.

DE (1981) *A New Training Initiative: A programme for action* (Cmnd 8455), London, HMSO.

DES (1965) *A Plan for Polytechnics and Other Colleges*, London, HMSO.

DES (1977) 'Terms of reference and functions for The Advisory Council for Adult and Continuing Education', London, HMSO.

DES (1978) 'Higher Education into the 1990s: A Discussion Document', London, HMSO.

DES (1980) *Continuing Education: Post-experience Vocational Provision for Those in Employment*, London, HMSO.

DES (1991) *Education and Training for the 21st Century* (Cm 1536), London, HMSO.

ED (1991) *A Strategy for Skills* (Cm 1810), London, HMSO.

IFF Research Ltd (1985) *Adult Training in Britain*, London, IFF Research Ltd.

IFF Research Ltd (1985) *Employer Expectations of Lifelong Learning*, London, IFF Research Ltd.

JONES, D.E.L. (1977) 'Notes of amplification to ACACE', *The Oxford Review of Education* (1979) **5**.

MCINTOSH, N.E. *et al.* (1976) *A Degree of Difference*, London, The Society for Research into Higher Education.

MCINTOSH, N.E. and WOODLEY, A. (1978) 'Combining education and working life', *CORE*, Vol 3, no 1.

MORI (1994) *What Price the Learning Society*, Leicester, NIACE.

MSC (1981a) *A New Training Initiative: A Consultative Document*, London, MSC.

MSC (1981b) *A New Training Initiative: An Agenda for Action*, London, MSC.

MSC (1983a) *Towards an Adult Training Strategy*, Sheffield, MSC.

MSC (1983b) *A New Training Initiative: MSC Proposals for Action*, Sheffield, MSC.

MSC (1983c) *A New Training Initiative: Adult Training*, Sheffield, MSC.

NAB (1984a) *Report of the Continuing Education Group*, London, NAB.

NAB (1984b) *A Strategy for Higher Education in the Late 1980s and Beyond*, London, NAB.

NEWSAM, P. (1979) 'Providing for a system of adult education', Keynote address to the NIAE Annual Study Conference, University of Nottingham, April.

NIACE (1994) *The Will to Learn*, Leicester, NIACE.

OPEN UNIVERSITY (1994) *Learn and Live*, Milton Keynes, The Open University.

POLICY STUDIES INSTITUTE (for ED) (1994) *Employers Attitudes to Lifelong Learning*, London, HMSO.

PRESIDENT OF THE BOARD OF TRADE, *et al.* (1994) *Competitiveness: Helping Business to Win* (Cm 2563), London, HMSO.

ROOKER, J. (1993) 'Opportunity and achievement', *The Times Higher Educational Supplement*.

SARGANT, N. (1991) *Learning and 'Leisure'*, Leicester, NIACE.

Naomi Sargant

Sargant, N. (1993) *Learning for a Purpose*, Leicester, NIACE.
Social and Community Planning Research (for ED) (1994) *Individuals Attitudes to Lifelong Learning*, London, HMSO.
TEC National Council (1994) *Individual Commitment to Lifetime Learning*, London, The TEC National Council.
TUC and the Labour Party (1984) *A Plan for Training*, London, TUC.
Times Educational Supplement (1966) Leading Article, March 4.
UDACE (1992) *Working with UDACE*, Leicester, UDACE.

Chapter 5

Human Learning Potential

Ken Richardson

Introduction

Some concept of human potential (and thus of learning and development) underlies every educational (and probably every social) system. Too often (at least since Plato's *Republic*) this has consisted of a pessimism about people's potentials. And this pessimism is widespread today:

> We have underestimated the human potential to learn. . . . As a consequence both the motivation to learn and the provision of learning opportunities have been unsatisfactory. (Ball, 1992, p. 4)

Indeed, the very concept of potential usually implies a foregone conclusion — something with a pre-determined limit. This connotation has been expressed in the many devices (e.g., IQ tests and scholastic exams) for quantifying people's potentials, predicting their future performance, and thus determining access to different levels on the educational and employment ladder. This institutionalization of the concept of potential has, in turn, had a powerful effect on people's self-conceptions of their own potential, and reduced their motivation to learn. Thus Ball (1992, p. 5) can point to '. . . a pernicious "conspiracy" in our society between ideas of human potential, assumptions about unemployment need, provision for education and training, and the motivation of young and mature people to learn'.

The argument of this chapter is that breaking this conspiracy will entail a Copernican revolution in our view of the nature of human learning potential. The ingredients of a new vision are, however, available in recent psychological research and theorizing about human potential. The purpose of this chapter, therefore, is to look at some traditional views about human potential and then show how these have been modified by recent psychological research. The gist of these studies is that, instead of being lumbered with built-in potentials, humans are uniquely able to create their own potentials. I shall attempt to pull out some of the pedagogical and social conditions enabling and disabling this creativity. Then I shall attempt to spell out the implications of the view for understanding knowledge, and education and training.

Potential as Inherent Limitation

The dominant conception of human learning ability for at least the last century and a half has been that of inherent, essentially unchangeable, mental 'strength' or power, varying across individuals according to their genes (Richardson, 1991b). Against the backcloth of Darwin's theory of natural selection this conception has been given a remarkable degree of credence by people generally. The Darwinian notion of inherited variation of potential and of a natural 'sorting out' of the strong from the weak, chimed in wonderfully with a class-structured and imperialistic social system. In the 20th century, it has had a powerful hold on the minds of psychologists and educators as well.

This view, in fact, still furnishes our most common metaphors and models for learning ability. Thus learning in the school is seen as a kind of natural selection process in which the 'strong' learners are sorted out from the 'weak' learners by a neutral curriculum. Tests of many sorts are taken to be indicative of children's and young people's potentials, rather than merely current states of interest and motivation. Concepts such as 'bright' and 'dull' children pervade the national curriculum and discussions around it. The Darwinian metaphor lurks within every ministerial remark about the curriculum 'bringing out' or allowing children to develop their individual potential. And it pervades further and higher education, and job selection and promotion, where current or recent performance is seen as indicative of a fixed potential limiting future performance.

The Failure of the Metaphor

The consequences of a Darwinian metaphor of potential are devastating for most individuals, education and society in general. They are damaging for many, if not a majority, of individuals by means of a vicious psychological circle. Very soon after entering school, at five years, children become scrutinized for 'signs' of their congenital potential for learning, and become labelled accordingly (Rogers, 1991). Usually this potential is actually assessed on the basis of a number of social, linguistic and personality characteristics, rather than learning ability as such. Even facial appearance and other aspects of physical self-presentation have been shown to play an important part (Langlois, 1986). Negative labelling leads to poor self-expectations, low self-esteem, low sense of control over own destiny, and thus poor motivation (Rogers, 1991). Teachers see their natural selection function as a highly important and indeed 'professional' task, although vast swathes of human creativity are lost in the process. Yet the whole gearing of the school and education system to a hierarchical job market makes it difficult for teachers to conceive of their role in any other way.

So entrenched is the metaphor of inherent potential, that most people seem unable to entertain the possibility of it not being a valid one. Yet it has always been difficult to confirm, objectively, that the sorting out is really taking place on the basis of learning potential. What are taken to be signs of potential are, at best, only very weak predictors of future performance at almost all levels of the education/training system, and in working life afterwards. Thus, Fulton and Elwood (1989), researching for The Training Agency, pointed out that the usual criterion for access to higher education — 'A'-level results — has very low predictive power. In one large-scale study (Sear, 1983; *c.f.* Leitch, 1990) it was found that 'A'-level scores accounted for less than 10 per cent of the variance in university performance. A recent meta-analysis of over twenty studies confirms this general picture (Peers and Johnston, 1994).

It is perhaps not surprising, in view of this, that many studies have shown that there is little relationship between academic performance and performance in the workplace at any level even, ironically enough, for future academics. For example, a meta-analysis by Cook (1988) reported correlations of around 0.1 between academic achievement and subsequent job performance. And there is little if any association between so-called 'measures of potential' like IQ, and actual job-performance (Ceci, 1991). Recent reviews in the USA (where a similar metaphor of potential prevails) report 'little or no relationship between academic and practical tasks' in a wide variety of unskilled, professional and managerial domains (Wagner, 1994, p. 146). Thus, we seriously need to ask why we cling to a concept of potential which, in terms of sheer utility, grossly underperforms.

One reason for the persistence of the concept may be its crucial role as a social ideology. Like ideologies generally, adherence to the Darwinian notion of potential involves people in an elaborate pretence. One prominent aspect of this pretence in schools is that in order to be 'authentic', and a fair sorter of potential, knowledge must come in specially packaged forms. This usually means 'knowledge' detached from the local environmental and socio-economic fabric in which children actually live — greater awareness of which might actually promote responsible cirizenship. The process of packaging knowledge as a means of sorting out potential, is illustrated by Perret-Clermont and Bell (1988, pp. 276–7) on the subject of sets in school mathematics:

Set theory as elaborated by mathematicians becomes in the hands of curriculum experts (who are influenced by politicians and other subject experts) the notion of 'sets' as an object of the school curriculum. . . . This version of 'sets' then becomes the object of a lesson or exercise as it is transformed by teachers in the class-room. This transformed [deformed?] object finally reaches the child who in turn re-contextualizes the notion of 'sets' as an object to be learned. Thus, at the end of this process the [naive] psychologist discovers that there is little in common between the notion of 'set' as initially elaborated by the mathematician and the notion of 'set' as learnt by pupils.

Further research has drawn attention to how this pretence is maintained in schools and colleges. In schools, as Edwards and Mercer (1985) observed, most of the subject knowledge acquired consists of 'ritual knowledge', and what children are *really* learning are various 'discursive devices' through which they try to keep the teacher happy. And at higher levels it has frequently been shown how 'A'-level and university students steeped in objectified curriculum knowledge are totally incapable of translating it to, and thus understanding, real-life practical situations in corresponding domains. Howard Gardner (1993, pp. 3–4) describes the results of a large number of studies on both sides of the Atlantic, as follows:

Perhaps most stunning is the case of physics. . . . (S)tudents who receive honours grades in college level physics are frequently unable to solve basic problems and questions encountered in a form slightly different from that on which they have been formally instructed and tested. . . . Indeed, in dozens of studies of this sort, young adults trained in science continue to exhibit the very same misconceptions and misunderstandings that one encounters in primary school children . . . essentially the same situation has been encountered in every scholastic domain in which inquiries have been conducted.

Of course, it is dangerous to generalize too much: many parents and teachers know that children, students and trainees are successfully learning something useful and interesting. The question is whether the success can be attributed to some persistent potential inherent to individuals, rather than more transient motivational or personality attributes, and whether it has any long-term import. Far too many teachers appear to adopt a fatalistic attitude to this question. Thus research has suggested that teachers rarely use a consistent theory of positive pedagogy in the classroom. The dominant education principle seems to be the more passive one of 'let individual potential do its work', and pupils are seen overwhelmingly as learners *by* results (i.e., by their potential) rather than any clear learning process (Parsons, Graham and Honess, 1983).

Finally, the metaphor has struck and perpetuated a damaging élitism that has divided education and training, the social consequences of which have been very serious. On the one hand, the teaching of knowledge detached from social roots has produced the 'emptiness' so often attributed to academic knowledge — the example of physics undergraduates who can 'parrot' theories but fail to apply them to ordinary practical problems is only one reflection of this. On the other hand, it has fostered the shallow view of 'units' of labour to be trained in practical skills divorced from conceptual awareness of the social context of their application. This paternalism has fostered, in turn, a self-abnegation of potential:

> It is not uncommon to find massive training programmes which routinely schedule people at all levels of the organization from top management through semi-skilled ranks, for participation in courses prescribed by someone in line or staff management. The fault with such a system lies not so much in the content of the course as with the sources of initiative it represents. In essence, it undermines self responsibility by conditioning people to be outer directed, to wait for directives and cues from authority figures. It leads to dependency relationships and complacency based on the feeling that the 'management' knows what is best for them and will see to it that that they are trained and utilized effectively. (Myers, 1989, p. 163)

In sum, admissions and promotion policies in education and occupational selection seem more designed to perpetuate an ideology of inherent ability than a scientific pedagogy. The metaphor of potential as a kind of genetically-determined mental strength, naturally selected in the education system, is itself a great failure for individuals and for society. I have tried to show in this section that the metaphor has little empirical foundation. I will argue in the next section that is has little biological, psychological or even just logical foundation, either.

From Genes to Learning

The idea of genes somehow setting our learning potential whilst our 'environmental' experience determines how much of it is actually reached is a model of development that dominates educational folk psychology. But it has been increasingly rejected in recent years in scientific studies. Humans are learning organisms *par excellence*. We now have a better understanding of how this came about, and, by virtue of that, understand the nature of learning potential more clearly.

What is remarkable about the general acceptance of the Darwinian metaphor of learning potential is that, whereas genes produce potentials as random variations that are blindly selected by current environments, learning is precisely the opposite of this. Learning evolved as a means of creating new potentials in individuals, in an organized, targeted, non-random manner, on a recurring, lifelong, basis. Instead of 'fitting' individuals to environments by chance, learning is a system for anticipating, developmentally adapting to, and actively changing, environments (Richardson, 1995).

There are many biological (even Darwinian) arguments to support this notion (Plotkin and Odling-Smee, 1979). Survival by genetic potential is fine for relatively stable or only slowly changing aspects of environments. But when organisms have to contend with changeable environments, when tomorrow's world requires different potentials from today's, this system proves inadequate. Instead of coding for pre-determined potentials, the genes selected in such conditions were those which supported self-organizing systems of developmental and behavioural regulation. These new 'cognitive' systems utilize information other than that in the genes, and thus, in an important sense, supersede the genes as new sources of potential.

The great advantage of such 'self-organizing' systems, then, is that they can continually create entirely original potentials that are unforeseen in either genes or environments. As Goodwin (1988, p. 54) observes, in such systems the organism has its own organizational principles, and traditional descriptions 'tend greatly to exaggerate the role of the environment on the one hand, and the role of the genes on the other' (Goodwin, 1985, p. 56). It should also be noted that the genes underlying such adaptable systems — as with any advantageous characteristics — can quite quickly become organized as a cooperative group and 'fixed' as a species-specific characteristic, common to all members of the species (Mayr, 1970). Indeed humans are remarkably alike genetically, sharing at least 99 per cent of genetic material (and we appear to have 98 per cent of genes in common with chimpanzees) whilst varying enormously, mentally.

Already we can see that it may be quite wrong to think of potential as something 'inside us' and varying in parallel with variant genes. Cognitive systems, generally, appear to have evolved for the continuous creation of *de novo* potentials. But humans have evolved another system of coping with an uncertain world — a social one — of even greater efficiency and potency. Cooperative action started to evolve as a unique *modus vivendi* of survival in humans at least two million years ago. Archeological analyses have shown how it coincided with new experience of extremely harsh and unpredictable conditions, but also how the advantages gained by early social cooperation triggered a rare virtuous cycle of evolution. The demands on the brain of operating jointly with other individuals are far more complex than those presented by the physical world alone. If you have any doubts about this consider moving a wardrobe downstairs with two other people — you need to integrate a multitude of stimuli, changing over fractions of seconds; continually re-adjust personal actions correspondingly; control personal feelings; and communicate rapidly and efficiently. These demands produced bigger brains, a capability for yet more complex social cooperation, still bigger brains, and so on, until we ended up with a brain three times that of our nearest biological relation — a learning brain.

The 'Efflorescence' of Potential

Humans are unique in the creativity of their potentials. But there is still much debate about how this learning brain actually 'works' in achieving that. Many have argued that it operates through the development of internal models or representations of the outside social and physical world. As Goodwin (1985, p. 59) describes them, such models '. . . make organisms independent of the environment by virtue of possessing internal copies of external patterns of variation'. A claim now frequently made of such characteristics is that rather than their form and their potentials being determined by genes or particular experiences, they are 'self-organizing'. Indeed, the poor predictability of 'performance indicators' across stages of education and real life itself probably reflects the fact that humans, rather than being simple 'input-output' systems, are being reactive to situations as self-organizing beings.

A currently popular view, in this vein — and one which brings us right back to the issues of this book — is derived from the work of the psychologist L.S. Vygotsky. As well as reminding us of the social context of human potential, this work brings into clearer focus the currently widespread problems of poor motivation and of social constraints on potential.

The learning system proposed by Vygotsky (e.g., 1988) works like this. Adaptive human behaviour invariably occurs as patterns of cooperative social activity which become internalized in the cognitive systems of the individuals involved. Among these patterns Vygotsky included all cooperatively organized activities: organized industrial production; various inventions for 'thought sharing' (e.g., number systems, language and writing systems); schemes for cooperative action (such as shared plans); a myriad social rules and principles (such as motoring rules); as well as 'hardware' tools and all human technological devices. In addition to developing organic 'tools' of survival, like the eye and the hand, therefore, humans acquire 'cultural tools' that are far more adaptable.

Human potential, in this view, is realized at least as much from the outside in as from the inside out. But it is crucial to appreciate the dynamic way in which new human potentials can be constantly created out of the interaction between individual and group. As Vygotsky argued, cultural change, new practices and new ideas arise because the relationship between individual and group is a dynamic, interactional one, not simply a handing over of a tradition. The individual mind is not a computer passively waiting to be programmed, it already contains abstract representations of countless other experiences. These will often conflict with, and react to, patterns currently being internalized (Vygotsky used the word 'clash'), producing novel resolutions. In this way, the relationship between individual and group allows the 'original ideas and creative contributions of individual minds' whilst explaining 'the achievement of social history' (Markova, 1990, p. 191).

The unconstrained, interactive human mind, in other words, may be a ferment of newly created potentials. Newell (1990, p. 114) called this phenomenon an efflorescence of adaptations:

> Humans appear to go around simply creating opportunities of all kinds to build different response functions. [In other species] (e)ach is to be understood by exploring the behaviour and physiological mechanisms that support it. Not so with humans. There is no enumerating their adaptations — they will invent new adaptations faster than they can be recorded.

Or as Donald (1991) put it:

> Our genes may be largely identical to those of a chimp or gorilla, but our cognitive architecture is not. . . . humans are utterly different. Our minds function on several new representational planes, none of which are available to animals. We act in cognitive collectivities, in symbiosis with external memory systems. As we develop . . . we reconfigure our own mental architecture in nontrivial ways. (Donald, 1991, p. 382)

All this 'ferment of potential' or 'efflorescence of adaptations' seems a world apart from the laborious and often fruitless process of learning as seen in contemporary institutions. Human economic performance constrained by a lack of learning potential seems a gross paradox. So how do we overcome this paradox?

Learning in Context

The solution, as I hope to show, will involve bringing learning back into context. Recent psychological research around this issue has brought us to face two great ironies. The first irony is that most knowledge acquisition in humans occurs in everyday social contexts, is often of great complexity, and occurs with great ease. It has often been pointed out that the language we all learn by the age of four years is the most complex intellectual feat any of us will achieve. But it doesn't occur by any kind of detached training. A large number of psychological studies have now shown how acquiring knowledge-in-context involves a remarkable process of negotiation between experts (adults, peers) and novices in which the former don't actually 'teach' so much as provide signposts and props for the 'guided rediscovery' of that knowledge by the novice (for reviews see contributions in Light and Butterworth, 1993).

Many observations of learning in context appear to have confirmed Vygotsky's view about the meeting between the mature forms of knowledge encountered socially and the more primitive forms in the novice. But it is crucial to be reminded again how this is usually a creative, rather than merely a replicative, process. In the course of this meeting, new versions may appear 'which', as Vygotsky put it, 'does not simply involve a stereotyped reproduction of chains formed in advance'. So that there is frequent reconstruction in individuals, leading to the vast creative diversity we find in human knowledge representations, new human conceptualizations and productive potentials frequently arise in the interaction between teacher and taught (for further discussion see Cole, 1985). This, then, is the natural form of learning in humans. It is unique to, and ubiquitous among, humans; it often involves knowledge of great complexity; and is brilliantly effective. The ease of its execution contrasts starkly with the pains of learning in schools and other educational institutions. As Bruner (1985, p. 29) puts it:

> The fact that we learn the culture as readily and effectively as we do must give us pause — considering how poorly we do at certain artificial, 'madeup' subjects that we teach in schools and whose use is not imbedded in any established cultural practice.

The second irony is that although educational institutions rightly stress the development of abstract knowledge and reasoning skills, this has typically been attempted in schools and universities, by detaching people from real-life contexts. Yet psychological research in the last decade or so has shown how abstract cognition only really flourishes when it is grounded in actual social and practical concerns. Some of this evidence comes from work which demonstrates substantially enhanced reasoning performance with tasks that are socially contextualized and thus make 'human sense' (Donaldson, 1978; Richardson, 1991a). Some of it comes from descriptions of the previously unsuspected complexity of reasoning (such as everyday mathematics) in everyday practical situations (Carraher, Carraher and Schliemann, 1991; George and Glasgow, 1988). But the psychological evidence is now such, that, as Butterworth (1993) notes, '. . . theorists are beginning to stress an *inextricable* link between contextual constraints and the acquisition of knowledge. . . . The contemporary view tends to be that cognition is *typically* situated in social and physical context and is only rarely decontextualized' (emphases in original). Donaldson (1978) has called the separation of disembedded intellectual forms from practical contexts a kind of apartheid: 'The paradoxical fact is that disembedded thinking, although by definition it calls for the ability to stand back from life, yields its greatest riches when it is conjoined with doing' (p. 83).

These two ironies — the ease and the abstractness of learning in context — cast into clearer perspective the crisis of human potential now facing most developed societies. The very technologizing of society and the rapidity of technological change are now, themselves, rendering the Darwinian metaphor obsolete. This is because we now need fewer and fewer people 'educated' with detached knowledge, or, conversely, blindly trained for automatized tasks in entrenched roles. Rather we increasingly need people, everywhere, with generic intellectual skills of critical analysis and insightful awareness, and *adaptable* practical learning. The really exciting prospect is that as the Darwinian metaphor erodes out of sheer social necessity, radically new institutional arrangements for education and training will come to be conceived. The final section hints at some possibilities.

Conclusion

Real improvement in the British education/training system will require a transformation in the culture of potential. Every educational debate over the last few decades has pre-supposed the Darwinian metaphor of potential as a starting point. This explains why little has really changed. The Darwinian metaphor has reduced learning ability to a genetically-determined potential (with many ideological spin-offs); encouraged a view of knowledge as something encapsulated and packaged; and separated abstract thought from practical contexts, to the detriment of both scholarship and training. In this conclusion I simply want to pull out some of the implications of the psychological arguments outlined above for the current (and perennial) education crisis.

The dilemma we now face can be simply expressed as follows:

(i) Society wants creative, potent people, both intellectually and practically;
(ii) Society also wants knowledge and intellectual skills that are abstract, generic and practical.
(iii) Yet people best develop abstract knowledge and create new potentials in (social) contexts in which they feel they have conscious participation wider than that of ritualistic learners or paternalized trainees.

If we want an efflorescence of learning, then, the following would appear to be the psychological pre-conditions:

We must reduce the division of labour between the 'thinking' part of an enterprise and its mechanical execution by hired labour. Divorcing people from a cognitive vision of the wider purposes of their learning will invariably result in learning of a most superficial and laborious kind. 'Cognitive enfranchising' of people can no longer be written off as the pipe dreams of educational theorists or collectivist ideologists: need for it is now being recognized at all levels of commerce and production.

The gulf between cognitive 'ownership' of the processes of organizations or institutions, on the one hand, and people as labour units on the other, is the most serious impediment to human creativity and productivity. 'We ought instead to think of "membership" . . . membership gives meaning, and responsibility, to those who work in the business. They cease to be instruments or employees and become enfranchised' (Handy, 1994).

This has all kinds of implications for education/training programmes. The situation currently developing in which employers send employees on increasing numbers of training courses as a kind of act of faith, and in which universities are falling over themselves to get into the training market (and thus risking their commitment to scholarship), needs to be carefully rationalized. First, vocational training courses need to be organized by people 'on the ground'. Indeed the logical (and psychological) place for occupational training is the workplace, with its social and economic context. The 'educational place' then becomes the locus of critical reflection on practices and policies in workplaces and the creation, at various levels of abstraction, of new theories of practical relevance. This will entail the development and use of the skills of traditional scholarship applied more closely to socially meaningful goals. Of course, many academics strive admirably, in the construction and presentation of courses, to use illustrations from 'real life' contexts (usually in the guise of case studies) for raising scholarly issues. But this is not the same has having students bring *their own* experiences of the practical situation into a more detached light and having them analysed and theorized at the abstract level. Yet this is much more likely to result in durable learning with practical consequences.

The corollary of such moves is that the work of scholars must become more overtly connected with social affairs and material contexts. While this will simply make explicit the connections between ideas and social contexts that are (and always have been) implicit, the benefits will be far wider than those already mentioned. Academic history, from the academies of ancient Greece (Robinson, 1981), through the rise of science (Rose and Rose, 1969) to 20th-century debates, shows that the most acute scholarship has always arisen around intense social concerns. But this also suggests that teachers and scholars will need to have periodic experience of the material and social conditions to which the knowledge they cultivate and manage appertains. This could apply as much to arts and 'cultural' disciplines as to the sciences and technology. Thus the traditional segregation between scholarship, practical skills and institutional decision making might need to be much reduced by the kind of periodic exchanges indicated very generally in Figure 5.1.

Figure 5.1: Domains of education and training requiring greater interchange of knowledge and thought

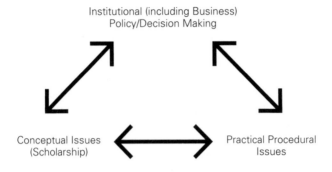

Institutional (including Business)
Policy/Decision Making

Conceptual Issues
(Scholarship)

Practical Procedural
Issues

What this implies is a closer collaboration between, and at least partial rotation amongst, traditionally segregated roles which will inevitably be reflected in education and training. Scholarship may thus become more productive because theories, variables and parameters are grounded in material and social concerns. By a similar process, practical problem-solving skills can become less encapsulated and less alienating. And decision making may become more enlightened and more realistic. Most important of all, new human potentials can arise in the many social and intellectual interactions that are opened up. Of course, all this also implies fundamental changes in practical arrangements for learning and teaching, and probably, indeed, in some of our other institutions as well — but that is another article, if not another book!

References

BALL, C. (1992) *Profitable Learning*, London, RSA.

BRUNER, J.S., (1985) 'Vygotsky: A historical and conceptual perspective', in J.V. WERTSCH (ed.) *Culture, Communication and Cognition: Vygotskian Perspectives*, Cambridge, Cambridge University Press.

CARRAHER, T.N., CARRAHER, D.W. and SCHLIEMANN, A.D. (1991) 'Mathematics in the streets and in schools', in P. LIGHT, S. SHELDON and M. WOODHEAD (1991) (eds) *Learning to Think*, London, Routledge in association with the Open University.

CECI, S.J. (1990) *On Intelligence . . . More or Less*, Englewood Cliffs, New Jersey, Prentice Hall.

COLE, M. (1985) 'The zone of proximal development: Where culture and cognition meet', in J.V. WERTSCH (ed.) *Culture, Communication and Cognition: Vygotskian Perspectives*, Cambridge, Cambridge University Press.

COOK, M. (1988) *Personnel Selection and Productivity*, Chichester, Wiley.

DONALD, M. (1991) *Origins of the Modern Mind*, Cambridge, Mass., Harvard University Press.

DONALDSON, M. (1978) *Children's Minds*, London, Fontana.

EDWARDS, D. and MERCER, N.M. (1987) *Common Knowledge*, London, Methuen.

FULTON, O. and ELWOOD, S. (1989) *Admissions to Higher Education, Policy and Practice*, Sheffield: The Training Agency.

GARDNER, H. (1993) *The Unschooled Mind*, London, Fontana.

GEORGE, J. and GLASGOW, J. (1988) 'Street science and conventional science in the West Indies', *Studies in Science Education*, **15**, pp. 109–18.

GOODWIN, B. (1985) 'Constructional biology', in G. BUTTERWORTH, J. RUTKOWSKA and M. SCAIFE (eds) *Evolution and Developmental Theory*, Brighton, Harvester.

GOODWIN, B. (1988) 'Morphogenesis and heredity', in M-W. HO, and S.W FOX, (eds) *Evolutionary Processes and Metaphors*, Chichester, Wiley.

HANDY, C.B. (1994) *The Empty Raincoat: Making Sense of the Future*, London, Hutchinson.

LANGLOIS, J.H. (1986) 'From the eye of the beholder to behavioral reality: Development of social behaviors and social relations as a function of physical attractiveness', in C.P. HERMAN, M. ZANNA and E.T. HIGGINS (eds) *Physical Appearances, Stigma and Social Behaviour*, Hillsdale, N.J., Lawrence Erlbaum.

LEITCH, A. (1990) *'Factors associated with academic failure: their role in identifying students at risk of failure'*, unpublished MSc Dissertation, The Open University.

LIGHT, P. and BUTTERWORTH, G. (1993) *Cognition in Context*, Hemel Hempstead, Harvester Wheatsheaf.

LIGHT, P., SHELDON, S. and WOODHEAD, M. (1991) *Learning to Think*, London, Routledge in association with The Open University.

MARKOVA, I. (1990) 'Causes and reasons in social development', in G. BUTTERWORTH, and P. BRYANT, (eds) *Causes of Development*, Brighton, Harvester.

MAYR, E. (1970) *Population, Species and Evolution*, Cambridge, M.A., Belknap Press.

MYERS, M.S. (1989) *Every Employee a Manager*, London, McGraw-Hill.

NEWELL, A. (1990) *Unified Theories of Cognition*, Cambridge, Mass., Harvard University Press.

PARSONS, J.M., GRAHAM, N. and HONESS, T. (1983) 'A teacher's implicit model of how children learn', *British Education Research Journal*, **9**, pp. 91–101.

PEERS, I. and JOHNSTON, M. (1994) 'Influence of learning context on the relationship between A-level attainment and final degree performance: A meta-analytic review', *British Journal of Educational Psychology*, **64**, pp. 1–18.

PERRET-CLERMONT and BELL, N. (1988) 'Learning processes in social and instructional interactions', in K. RICHARDSON, and S. SHELDON, (eds) *Cognitive Development to Adolescence*, Hove, Lawrence Erlbaum.

PLOTKIN, H.C. and ODLING-SMEE, F.J. (1979) 'Learning, change, and evolution: An inquiry into the teleonomy of learning', *Advances in the Study of Behavior*, **10**, pp. 1–42.

RICHARDSON, K. (1991a) 'Reasoning with Raven — in and out of context', *British Journal of Educational Psychology*, **61**, pp. 129–38.

RICHARDSON, K. (1991b) *Understanding Intelligence*, Buckingham, Open University Press.

RICHARDSON, K. (1995) 'The evolution of development', in J. OATES (ed.) *Foundations of Development*, Oxford, Blackwell in association with The Open University.

ROBINSON, D.N. (1981) *An Intellectual History of Psychology*, New York, Macmillan.

Ken Richardson

ROGERS, C. (1991) 'Early admission: Early labelling', in M. WOODHEAD, P. LIGHT, and R. CARR, (eds) *Growing up in a Changing Society*, London, Routledge in association with The Open University.

ROSE, S. and ROSE, H. (1969) *Science and Society*, Harmondsworth, Penguin.

SEAR, K. (1983) 'The correlation between A-level grades and degree results in England and Wales', *Higher Education*, **12**, pp. 609–19.

VYGOTSKY, L.S. (1978) *Mind in Society*, (edited by M. COLE, V. JOHN-STEINER, S. SCRIBNER and E. SOUBERMAN), Cambridge, Mass., Harvard University Press.

VYGOTSKY, L.S. (1988) 'The genesis of higher mental functions', in K. RICHARDSON, and SHELDON, S. (eds) *Cognitive Development to Adolescence*, Hove, Lawrence Erlbaum.

WAGNER, R.K. (1994) 'Context counts: The case of cogntive ability testing for job selection', In R.J. STERNBERG and R.K. WAGNER (eds) *Mind in Context: Interactionist Perspectives on Human Intelligence*, Cambridge, Cambridge University Press.

Chapter 6

Learning Theory: Harnessing the Strength of a Neglected Resource

David Bradshaw

Introduction

For a group of children in a school in Worcestershire, German lessons begin with an invitation to relax, close eyes, allow the mind to wander and to breathe deeply. The purpose is to set up a state of 'relaxed readiness'. This done, pupils listen to a play in German while following the text from a script, then they listen again while baroque music plays in the background and then for a third time with rather louder music and a quieter narration. Subsequent lessons reinforce the understanding of grammar through games, puzzles and 'activations' and develop the material used in the play.

Pioneered by Colin Rose, the 'Accelerated Learning' (AL) method is based on the theory that we learn foreign languages more effectively at secondary school age by using both sides of the brain — the step-by-step processes of the logical left side and the holistic understanding of the creative and aesthetic right — while the music helps to keep the right side engaged and gets the electric impulses of the brain working at a lower rate than that used for problem solving.

The method is a very long way from established practice. So are its results. One school compared the progress of a pilot group taught by a mix of AL and conventional teaching with other groups taught only by conventional methods. The pilot group's progress was markedly better (Watters, 1994). Other evaluations reported speeding up the learning of grammar by a factor of eight and another the learning of vocabulary by a factor of ten. Re-tests some months later proved that the learning was permanent.

The theory behind this remarkable advance is equally far from the ideas which have dominated our view of learning for most of this century. It combines new insights into how the brain works and of the nature of human ability, and although the research behind them go back several decades, it is only recently that they have achieved recognition as the central organizing principles for understanding learning. Even so, the

David Bradshaw

emerging consensus may be revised or superseded within the next few years if neurology continues to advance the boundaries of knowledge.

We have known that the activities of the mind take place in the brain for centuries and have attempted to describe and explain them for a hundred years or more. Almost all of this, however, was inferred from experiments on how people behaved in specific circumstances. Only in the last twenty years have we been able to start understanding the complex structures of the brain and how they work.

Among the first of these discoveries was that the two hemispheres of the cerebral cortex — the 'crinkled' matter on the top of the brain — have somewhat specialized functions. Although brain function is highly complex and it is easy to oversimplify its working, it is true to say that the left hemisphere tends to function in a linear and sequential way, processes language and is dominant in computing and manipulating numbers. It works things out step-by-step with one thought leading to another, develops and tests logical arguments and relates activities to time. The right hemisphere tends to be aware of things without using words and synthesizes experience into wholes, sometimes connecting information which appears disparate to the logical left hemisphere into new relationships. It sometimes fills in the gaps of available evidence making the leaps of insight we call 'intuition'. These can occur, as we say, 'in a flash' and no wonder; the right hemisphere is reported to work 1,600 times faster than the left. It is here, too, in the right hemisphere that aesthetic experiences, such as in music or the visual arts, are mainly processed.

Joined by the corpus callosum, the two hemispheres work so closely together that we are usually aware only of a single outcome. But there are occasional glimpses of the mind at work and of one hemisphere leading the other. Quentin Blake, the book illustrator, describes how after he has read a book to find its 'shape' and the sequence of the story he does his first drawings very quickly and spontaneously, often simply drawing whatever 'just came into his head'. Then he places the drawing over a light box with another piece of paper on top and draws thoughtfully using the first picture as his source of ideas on which to exercise his skills (Blake, 1991).

Other examples come from music where its aesthetic qualities are experienced on the right side while its form and other characteristics may be understood on the left. Certainly the pattern of a song is mainly a right brain function while the words are processed in the left. And as Accelerated Learning developed, Colin Rose points out, most people learn the words of dozens even hundreds of popular songs with little or no conscious effort.

In most cases it seems that one of the two sides of the cortex is in the lead. People with a speech impediment may stammer when *talking* about music during which the left side (where the impediment is located) is in the lead, but *sing* without difficulty since musical intelligence located on the right is then overriding the problem on the left. Another, day-to-day example would be in communication between two individuals where the verbal content of their interaction is controlled by the left side while the facial expressions are controlled by the right. As the two kinds of message are usually consistent, we seldom think about it, but we do notice when there is a contradiction between the two. In the example of language teaching, cited at the beginning of the chapter, the strengths of two hemispheres of the brain are brought into use simultaneously. Overall we have tended to neglect the special functions controlled in the right hemisphere, concentrating in the formal processes of education upon those on the left, and it is becoming clear that we can, and should, develop the right side to great advantage.

The New View of Human Abilities

Totally consistent with these findings about the cortex is the new view of human abilities, with the emerging preference for understanding them in terms of several abilities of equal importance rather than one predominating intelligence which can either operate on its own or organize subsidiary abilities like musical or spatial talent. Howard Gardner, the Harvard professor who has led the way in this field, identifies seven such abilities, calls them all intelligences to make the point that this is a clear break with past descriptions and gives them equal status in the process of learning (Gardner, 1985). Colin Rose and Louise Goll (1992) describe the intelligences like this:

Linguistic Intelligence — or talent with language is seen in the ability to write or talk well. Some people just seem to have the 'gift of the gab' or a fluent pen.

Mathematical/Logical Intelligence — or talent with maths, logic and systems is seen in the ability to deal well with numbers and to think logically. In everyday life we know people . . . who are razor sharp in adding up the odds on a bet, or at marking a score at darts!

Visual/Spatial Intelligence — or visual talent is the ability to visualize how things will eventually look or to imagine things in your mind's eye. Designers architects and artists would be an example, but this is the intelligence we all use when we use our sense of direction, navigate, draw a diagram or visualize how furniture in a showroom will fit into a room at home.

Musical Intelligence or talent with music is the ability to create and interpret music and to keep rhythm. Most of us have a good basic musical intelligence seen in our ability to learn a jingle or whistle a tune.

Bodily/Physical Intelligence is used when we run, dance, build or construct something. All arts and crafts use this intelligence [and]

> . . . people who are . . . 'good with their hands' . . . are showing a
> high form of [it].
> *Interpersonal Intelligence* is the ability to get on with others. Many
> people have an ability to make people feel at ease, to read others
> reactions and to be sympathetic to the feelings of others.
> *Intrapersonal Intelligence* or inner control is an ability for quiet ob-
> jective self-analysis. This leads to being able to understand your
> own behaviour and feelings.

The intelligences work together. Good communication between people
draws on both interpersonal and linguistic intelligences. A child making
a Lego model may use their visual and spatial intelligence in referring to
a diagram and their bodily and physical intelligence in the construction. It
is rare for someone to be equally gifted in all of the intelligences and each
one of us has his or her own pattern of development in which some of
them are more pronounced than others. Not surprisingly we tend to prefer to use those which are best developed, and this forms part of our
individual learning style: we prefer to use one or other of the senses in
receiving and handling information. Our thinking reflects our preferred
senses, too, some people think in visual images, some in sounds and
others through physical action.

The 'Single Chance Theory of Education'

One of the negative effects of previous views is that it has not only concentrated on the linguistic and mathematical/logical intelligences but has
neglected or even derided other forms of intelligence. Rose (1991), adapting Gardner, refers to this as the 'single chance theory of education': if
your preferred learning style happens to match that of the dominant teaching style (which is linear and heavily oriented to linguistic and mathemati-
cal/logical intelligences) you do well in the school system. After all, that's
what IQ tests measure. If you have a different learning style your chances
of success are less because there is a mis-match between your learning
style and the dominant teaching style. As a result non-verbal thinkers have
been made 'to feel inferior, and so begins a process of failure that will last
them all their lives' (Houston, 1991).

The aim must be for 'multiple chance learning' where teachers reach
the full range of intelligences and give children of all learning styles equal
chances. It has been done. Howard Gardner brings together an impressive
series of case studies of the theory in action in *Multiple Intelligences: The
Theory in Practice* (Gardner, 1993) and Gordon Dryden and Jeannette Vos
outline other successes:

- In Needham Massachusetts, John Elliot School has soared to the top
  of the state testing programme by using accelerated, integrative

learning techniques and teaching social competency skills and thinking skills.

- In New Zealand, primary school pupils up to five years behind in their reading age have caught up in as little as eight weeks, using a 'tape assisted' reading programme that matches their reading age to their interest level.
- In California, Texas and Pennsylvania ten-year-olds who were previously up to three years behind are now doing advanced high school mathematics. They are learning from a system where the teachers hardly ever provide answers but are specially trained to ask questions.
- A primary school in Greensboro North Carolina, has doubled its pupils test scores in mathematics and reading after introducing a system to check each student's learning style and catering to it. (Dryden and Vos, 1994)

It is one of the theories used in Rover Cars' success in becoming a learning organization, and it is the central theory in an experimental system of teacher training now being developed in Brunei.

A second aspect of learning style is our preference for one kind of activity over another. Some of us prefer concrete experience to thinking about it. For others the preference is the other way round. Others again have a marked taste for experimentation. Some like to build up knowledge step by step until a whole is finally built, while others need a conceptual framework first to make sense of the detail which is filled in later. This difference was identified by cognitive psychologists who called the two groups 'serialists' and 'holists' (Pask and Scott, 1975). The explanation is once again probably in a preference for forming understanding from the left side of the brain (the serial approach) or the right (the holistic approach).

The Process of Learning

A fuller explanation of learning style is in the process of learning identified and described by David Kolb. The key idea is that learning is the grasping of experience and turning it into knowledge; experience alone is not enough, it must be acted on in some way. Kolb's cycle has four stages: actual experience; reflecting on it; drawing conclusions; and testing them in practice (Kolb, 1984). Figure 6.1 sets the ideas out in visual form. This cycle is apparent very early in life:

> The infant immediately starts exploring the world looking, feeling, touching, smelling, as all higher animals do, from the moment of birth. Sensation alone is not enough; it must be combined with movement, with emotion, with action. . . . Subsequent

David Bradshaw

Figure 6.1:   Kolb's learning cycle

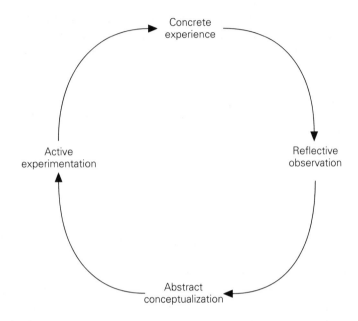

explorations — feeling the same object at different times, in different contexts — are never quite the same so that the initial learning is revised and re-revised again and again. (Sacks, 1990)

And the cycle can be observed in a child of three or four at play who will first experience by listening, touching or looking; then act on the experience, perhaps by questioning an adult; make sense of it by aligning it with previously acquired and 'processed' experiences; and use it as the basis for trying out variants of the same play.

Although everyone learns through this cycle, it is unusual to develop an equal facility in all four phases: rather we develop a preference for one kind of activity over another. At every stage the transformation of experience into knowledge has its own characteristics, with different forms of knowledge the result. This, in combination with our profile of intelligences and preferred senses, gives us our liking for one 'subject' over another and explains, in part, our work preferences too.

Kolb's cycle works at any age and for experience in any topic, subject or discipline. A teacher of English to students from ethnic minority groups recalls:

The RSA Diploma was action-based; our classroom experience informed the course throughout and was then illuminated by the theory. As it progressed I ploughed the understanding gained back into the classroom.

It works. But to adopt the Kolb sequence is unusual. The sequence of the phrase 'theory and practice' is more normal.

With an increase in work experience for school pupils, some schools have found the cycle particularly helpful in designing sequences of pupil activity so that the experience of being in the workplace is understood and learned in the sense of providing points of reference when considering possible careers (Miller, Watts and Jamieson, 1991).

Sandwich courses in higher education, in which periods of experience in employment aimed to bring reality to classwork, have seemed a good way of connecting theory and practice for several decades. But these courses have not always worked and the Kolb cycle helps to explain why. Firstly, the courses tended to begin with theory rather than concrete experience (though there would be enough previous experience of the topic for it to make sense). But, if the employment mentor did not relate the new employment experience to this theory, or the college tutor did not explicitly help to draw the connections between them then the two elements might not connect. Capable, self-motivated students who had already formed a conceptual framework out of grasped experience may have made the connections for themselves, but for many it did not happen. A similar lack of connection could occur in day release courses run by colleges of further education for apprentices or those on Youth Training schemes: but some tutors now use the Kolb cycle as the framework for planning the learning of their students.

Intelligences, Learning and Personality

Intelligences, learning style and learning preferences operate within a wider context and have a particular connection with personality type. Here the seminal work was done by Isabel Myers and Katherine Briggs who worked from the close observation of thousands of people interpreted by reference to the theories of Carl Jung. They show how behaviour comes from the interaction of our preferences in four dimensions:

1 Our normal range of extraverted (involvement in the outer world of people and things) and introverted (the inner world of ideas) behaviour.
2 Our reliance on concrete facts (sensing) and overall impression (intuition) in gathering information.
3 Our preference for applying logic to data (thinking) or principles (feeling) in coming to decisions.
4 Our tendency to reach decisions in a final way (judging) or to leave options open (perceiving) when dealing with the world around us.

In combination these characteristics give each one of us an individual personality type (Myers with Myers, 1980). And with an individual range of preference in all four dimensions, combined with the influence of our many abilities and our environmental heritage, every one of us is unique. Personality types are perceptible and definable, but not rigid; and they are helpful in our understanding of one another.

The Myers–Briggs typology has many applications. It aids our understanding of management style and can be used to help teams to work effectively in problem solving and decision making. The Myers–Briggs Type Indicator (MBTI) can help to indicate occupations in which people may be comfortable or ill-at-ease. It also helps to explain differences of teaching style and, because like types find it easier to understand one another than contrasting types, it sheds helpful light on the interactions between one learner and another and between learners and those who teach them.

The Myers–Briggs theory has also been applied in a number of school districts in America (especially in California) and is now being applied in Britain too. At Milton Keynes College, for example, the Principal and Chief Executive Ann Limb introduced the Myers–Briggs theory because she was impressed by its practical usefulness and its theoretical and ethical framework. Since 1988 a number of senior and middle managers have undertaken training in the Myers–Briggs theory and its applications, and some students have also been familiarized with the theory to raise their insight and awareness about themselves and others and help them to recognize and use their own strengths and take account of their least preferred functions — the 'shadow' side of the personality. Observations of tutors who have begun to apply the Myers–Briggs insights include:

- I'm an introvert; I didn't like to get up and move around the room;

- I now trust the process of unfolding, and as a teacher I'm not afraid of silence;

- It clarified the need for a variety of learning activities not necessarily to my taste;

- and one which catches the excitement of a common experience;

- This has given me permission to be myself. (Limb and Cook, 1994)

Information Processing

The conceptual starting point for each of the theories of learning outlined so far are very different from the theories of the behaviourists and cognitive psychologists who dominated the field for more than half a century. Both former approaches relied solely upon measurable phenomena for their data. The behaviourists accepted only the responses to stimuli observed in organisms. They saw behaviour as made up of public and testable acts, all of them the result of stimulus–response conditioning, but with the people who performed them as biological machines. They rejected phenomena such as thoughts, feelings or intentions as illusions, mainly because they were unreachable by their accepted methods of inquiry. Cognitive psychologists used experiments to isolate, define and measure such aspects of mental activity as perception, memory and learning. They worked with scrupulous care but there was always a methodological problem as they needed always to exclude from their experiments those variables which might distort the findings. Behaviourism and early cognitive psychology alike were also hampered by two things. Firstly, they could only infer from the results of experiments how the brain actually worked. Secondly (and more seriously), they were limited by their assumptions which excluded any phenomena which could not be reached by their research methods.

Behaviourism is now out of favour, and the new school of Cognitive Science has given the experimental tradition of the cognitive psychologists a broader context by incorporating some of the work described above. One of their current lines of research is based on the close similarity between some human mental activity and the information processing activity of computers. Concentrating (though not exclusively) on the analysis of tasks and the solving of problems, their theory of learning has been applied in the domains where cognitive psychology has always been most active — logical, sequential, mathematical and language-based activities. Here the applications have shown some success in improving classroom performance, for example, enabling children with a measured Intelligence Quotient (IQ) of 70 to read fluently (Bruer, 1993).

However, concentration on left brain activities may prove to be limiting, just as previous attempts to work from inference and analogy were. A further difficulty arises from the computer analogy: as Mihaly Csikszentmihalyi, Professor of Human Development and Education at the University of Chicago, points out it is:

> not that students cannot learn, it is that they do not wish to. Computers do not suffer from motivational problems, whereas human beings do. We have not found ways to program children so that they will learn the information we present to them as computers do. (Csikszentmihalyi, 1991)

Many of the developments cited here overlap but none of them either singly or in combination points to a complete theory of learning. Some incorporate other major theories. For example, Kolb absorbs the major

David Bradshaw

findings of Jean Piaget into his wider framework. These include the main developmental stages of intellectual growth from infancy to adulthood. (Some of Piaget's research methods and findings have been questioned in recent years but his concept of development has in general remained accepted and his work updated.) The overlap of the main approaches described in this chapter also interrelate. The experience at the beginning of the Kolb cycle is sensory. Early on a preferred sense is apparent in this stage and then the use of a preferred intelligence in the rest of the cycle. There is an overlap between Kolb's explanation of learning preferences and the Myers–Briggs typology of personality type. With sixteen possible combinations of the key factors, the Myers–Briggs typing is more sensitive than Kolb's. Kolb's analysis of mental processes however is more detailed. A complete synthesis is impossible, but the theories show no conflict and taken together they are compelling. And they work.

The Revelations of Neurology

Research continues in all of these fields and knowledge constantly expands. In particular, neurologists are now able to describe the minute structure of the billions of nerve fibres that make up the brain, and the electro-chemical impulses that run through them to sort, store (or discard), recall and combine the messages from our sense organs. So the connections between the brain at work and the attributes we know as the mind begin to emerge. Multiple intelligence, Kolb's learning cycle, preferred learning styles and personality types all help us to understand how we learn. They do not represent a comprehensive list of all helpful theories, but do represent those which appear to have been particularly helpful when it comes to application.

There are other factors at work too: motivation and confidence and the influence of social groups. The importance of motivation has long been recognized, though pinning down what motivates every individual is not always easy. But confidence is so frequently tied in with motivation that the two can only be taken together. Ken Richardson explores these issues further in his chapter on 'Human Learning Potential' (pp. 65–78). He also summarizes the relationship between social activity and learning observed by Vygotsky. The liberating effects of being trusted, of working harmoniously with others and of learning from experience that we can be successful learners, runs through all of the examples of learning described in Chapter 1 (pp. 3–11) and shown in the examples of the workers at Nissan's Sunderland factory, the team of cleaners at a Yorkshire college and the BBC engineer. They contrast strongly with some of the processes still used in some schools, colleges and universities.

In the case of language teaching described at the beginning of the chapter the frequency of the electrical impulses moving through the brain was seen to be one of the factors in the success of the learning. The theory behind this can be summarized as follows. Our brain operates on four main frequencies or waves measurable with an electro-encephalograph machine. When wide awake and alert and engaging in vigorous intellectual activity, like solving a difficult problem or making a speech, the brain transmits and receives at 13 to 25 cycles per second. This is often called the beta level. But this is not the best level for stimulating the long-term memory where brain-wave activity of 8 to 12 cycles per second is more effective. This is because this — the alpha level — links best with the subconscious mind where most of the information we learn will be stored. The other two levels are the theta, the phase between being fully awake and fully asleep where the brain waves change to between 4 and 7 cycles a second, and delta when we are fully asleep and the brain is operating at between 1 and 3 cycles a second (Dryden and Vos, 1993, pp. 162–5).

The many functions of the brain are normally integrated so that the mind works as a single entity. How this happens contributes to the process of learning and is itself a subject of major research. In the past its appearance of wholeness has been the cause of many misapprehensions particularly in the drawing of inferences from behaviour. We have so much still to learn from the functioning of the brain that most generalizations have to be framed with caution. But the information about the brain that is now emerging is indeed remarkable.

Perhaps the most intriguing conclusion to be drawn from what neurology has so far revealed is how different the actual processes of the brain are from those we have previously imagined. The brain is 'bitty' . . .

> outwardly coherent behaviour like talking and listening is subcontracted out all over the place. Nouns are stored here, adjectives there, syntax elsewhere. Verbs spelled by regular endings are learned using one sort of memory those spelt with irregular endings are learnt by another: for memory too has been atomised into so many pieces that psychologists cannot agree on their number. (*The Economist*, 1992–3)

It is here in the neurology of the brain, that the analogy with computers may perhaps prove most difficult to sustain. For example, learning is passed into the cerebral cortex via the hippocampus, an organ in the limbic system outside of the cerebral cortex. For a few weeks as it is recalled and used it is passed around the total system and then it is stored permanently. But if it is not recalled it is lost. Add this to the lack of grasped experience in the learning and we begin to see why last minute cramming can be so effective for exam performance and so insignificant in its long-term benefits.

Self-confidence — belief in one's ability to learn and to succeed — and motivation perhaps takes us to another part of the brain again. The limbic system, older in evolutionary terms than the cerebral cortex, is a group of structures concerned with learning as it relays information to other parts of the brain. It is also concerned with emotional states including fear, anger, flight and our feelings about territory and those emotions are closely associated with learning too. We remember emotional experiences like a first kiss or news of a bereavement with great clarity. We also remember classroom experiences with emotional content, the reward of praise for success or the effect of failure or humiliation. But there may be more to it than that. Does flight from confronting mental activity which has been stressful or a previous source of failure locate here? Or a sense of ownership that gives confidence? If so, the idea of the 'whole brain' takes on additional meaning. And if academic squabbles over 'ownership' of intellectual 'territory' originate in primitive feelings of territorial possession, then those who have witnessed some of the arcane debates in academic gatherings will have seen the left side of the brain being used in the service of feelings coming from the limbic system.

But this has taken us to the uncertain world of 'perhaps', 'maybe' and 'if'. It is tempting to draw conclusions beyond the state of current findings, but enough progress has been made to show why the inferential methods of the past failed to secure practical credibility and to support the use of neurology as offering more potential help. The methodology and techniques of neurology may be useful in cross-checking the findings of conventional psychological research. Howard Gardner's theory of seven intelligences for example is very attractive to learners; it seems to work where it matters. But it could be strengthened and refined by the processes of neurology. Closely connected is the work being done to relate the findings of neurology within the general theory of evolution and the science of genetics. In the field of evolutionary studies, for example, the phenomenon of consciousness, a puzzle to philosophers through the ages and dismissed by behaviourists as an illusion, is now thought to have evolutionary significance as a survival mechanism (Edelman, 1992; Humphrey, 1994). And as the influence of genetics in behaviour is more closely defined so the part played by environment becomes easier to pin down.

In Conclusion

The purpose of this book is practical. So as the research goes on, the issues for the learner and those who facilitate learning are those of application. Theories of learning tend to remain in circulation and use for some time after they have been updated or replaced at the research level. They are not discarded and replaced in the same way as are, for example, medical theories. This is partly because of the lack of a single unified theory, partly because of the dead-weight of theory still in circulation and a lack of a means of sifting it, and partly the scepticism with which teachers regard most theory. It has not been a secure guide in the past so it is understandable that new theory will be viewed with caution.

Emerging theory seems set to offer explanatory, predictive and practical power. Where it is applied it appears to be effective. We don't know everything but we know enough to start. Serving teachers need help to rid themselves of out-of-date, over-reliance on rule-of-thumb procedures and they need thorough acquaintance with the new approach to understanding and its applications. Teachers in training require a thorough grounding too. They do not need less theory; they need theory which works in practice. One step with great potential would be to establish a National Foundation for Learning to search out and screen emerging theory and stimulate its application. Recommended by Sir Christopher Ball in *Profitable Learning* (Ball, 1992) the RSA is now developing proposals to bring it about.

Over the past decade and half there has been much reform of structures, management and curriculum. Commenting on the failure of the American school system to produce adequate results for all and on the reforms now being introduced Bruer observes, '. . . proposed solutions include school-based management, market incentives, more testing and greater school accountability. . . . We run the risk of changing our schools without improving them' (Bruer, 1993, p. 7). His concerns fit the British scene very closely. Opting out, Local Management of Schools and competition for pupils stimulate efficient management of schools as institutions, but do nothing to improve the effectiveness of teaching within them. In post-compulsory education, the incorporation of colleges, the introduction of strong marketing in determining what courses will be offered and improvement in curriculum content can all help to make what is available more relevant. But the heart of the matter is the individual learner. We are able as never before to work with the grain of their motivations, abilities and learning style. The time has come to make use of learning theory as a dynamic and totally relevant resource. The failures of past theories to work in practice should not deter us from seeking those that will, and the evidence that such theories are now becoming available is abundant.

References

BALL, C. (1992) *Profitable Learning*, London, RSA.

BLAKE, Q. (1991) on 'Speaking volumes', BBC 2.

BRUER, J.T. (1993) *Schools for Thought: A Science of Learning in the Classroom*, Cambridge, Mass., The MIT Press.

CSIKSZENTMIHALYI, M. (1991) 'Thoughts about education', in D. DICKINSON, *Creating the Future: Perspectives on Educational Change*, Aston Clinton, Bucks, Accelerated Learning Systems.

David Bradshaw

DRYDEN, G. and VOS, J. (1993) *The Learning Revolution*, Aston Clinton, Bucks, Accelerated Learning Systems.

The Economist 26 December 1992/8 January, 1993.

EDELMAN, G. (1992) *Bright Air and Brilliant Fire: On the Matter of the Mind*, New York, Basic Books.

EDWARDS, B. (1979) *Drawing on the Right Side of the Brain*, Los Angeles, JP Tarcher.

EDWARDS, D. and MERCER, N. (1987) *Common Knowledge: The Development of Understanding in the Classroom*, London and New York, Routledge.

GARDNER, H. (1985) *Frames of Mind*, London, Paladin Books.

GARDNER, H. (1993) *Multiple Intelligences: The Theory in Practice*, New York, Basic Books.

HOUSTON, J. (1991) 'Educating the possible human' in D. DICKINSON (ed.) *Creating the Future: Perspectives on Educational Change*, Aylesbury, Accelerated Learning Systems.

HUMPHREY, N. (1994) 'The private world of consciousness', *New Scientist*, 8 January.

KOLB, D. (1984) *Experiential Learning*, Englewood Cliffs, New Jersey, Prentice Hall.

LEAKEY, R. and LEWIN, R. (1992) *Origins Reconsidered: In Search of What Makes Us Human*, London, Abacus Books.

LIMB, A.G. and COOK, M. (1994) 'Using Myers-Briggs type indicator in a College of Further Education', *Synapse*, 1994:2, London, RSA.

MILLER, A., WATTS, A.G. and JAMIESON, I. (1991) *Rethinking Work Experience*, London, Falmer Press.

MYERS, I.B. with MYERS, P.B. (1980) *Gifts Differing*, Palo Alto, California, The Consulting Psychologists Press.

ROSE, C. and GOLL, L. (1992) *Accelerate Your Learning*, Aston Clinton, Bucks, Accelerated Learning Systems.

SACKS, O. (1990) 'Neurology and the soul', *The New York Review*, 22 November.

SPRINGER, S.P. and DEUTSCH, G. (1989) *Left Brain, Right Brain*, New York, Freeman.

WATTERS, K. (1994) 'Accelerated learning — A new approach to language teaching', *Synapse*, London, RSA.

Chapter 7

Curriculum and Curriculum Process for a Changing World and an Uncertain Future

Anne Jones

'Plus ça change, plus c'est la même chose.' We sometimes speak and write as if we were the first generation to meet and tackle unprecedented change, or to debate endlessly the appropriate balance between knowledge skills and attributes. Not much remains of my degree in Modern Languages, long past its sell-by date, but what is seared on my brain is the simple truth of Montaigne's (1580 and 1953) sixteenth-century words: 'Je préfère une tête bien faite à une tête bien pleine'. Too often the quest for knowledge, even now, becomes the quest for facts, stuffed into the computer-like head, until the brain seizes up, loses its creativity and innovatory thoughts, and its sharp cutting edge. Too often the quest for certainty in an uncertain world, where the whole order of things is about to be transformed into something rich and strange, itself puts a block and a damper on the creative and imaginative acceptance of that emerging new order. Too often we have not learnt to ride the waves of change, and enjoy them, but rather we try to hold back the tide. In doing this, we also too often neglect the inner core of our own being, which is what will really give us the strength, not only to survive, but more importantly to thrive in the next phase of human existence. As Montaigne put it 'Connaîs-toi toi-même'. That is the only certainty from which we can venture into the unknown.

The last few years have brought seismic world change: collapse of cultures, economies, political and religious orthodoxies. Giants turned into pygmies, enemies into friends, world powers into third world powers, poor economies into world-class economies, ill-educated nations into knowledge-driven nations, top nations into third-rate nations. In the new 'borderless world' (Ohmae, 1990), businesses are run on a global scale in real time, with a workforce which could be anywhere in the world: for example, most of the paperwork and number crunching for British bankers is now done in northern India. Yet, simultaneously, as work becomes more global, local cultures become more important, and people cling more tightly to their ethnic roots. What we are experiencing is not cosmetic or superficial: it is a transformation just as great as the Renaissance, the

Industrial Revolution, or before that, the decline and fall of various world empires. And the process continues, as Thurow's (1993) survey of current trends and their consequences demonstrates with graphic realism. My view is that the world is once more in the chrysalis stage, and what will eventually emerge will be totally different from what preceded it. Whoever would have thought that butterflies could develop out of caterpillars?

Against this changing background, the debate about the curriculum seems out of proportion. Furthermore, the assumptions behind the debate are often based on outmoded concepts of what makes a good education. The concept of Britain as a learning society has not really caught on. The motto used to be 99 per cent perspiration, 1 per cent inspiration. In truth, what we need now in our workforce is more like 50:50. Yet current trends in education too often reflect the pint-pot, stuffed head, remember and regurgitate model of education, and the more the panic about 'standards' increases, the more education is pushed back into rote learning, counting and testing. Just as we need to release the creative energy, imagination and ideas of our people, if we are to survive economically, we appear to be reducing learning to league tables, standard scores and testing to destruction. And despite mutterings about lifelong learning and releasing the potential of all our people, most of the systems and structures still reinforce the idea that education is something you take in a great lump between the ages of 5 to 16, or if you are lucky, 5 to 21.

This is what I call the 'boa constrictor' model of education, swallowed in one gulp, not very well digested and fairly rapidly eliminated. Much more appropriate in today's climate would be a 'slow release' model, something like that which can now be produced in fertilizers, soap powders or cold cures; the kind of education which is provided at a time, stage, place and in a style which is appropriate to the learner's needs. Furthermore, in the new 'New World', the learner will be the driver of the learning, which may not necessarily be provided by the education system, but will come, as it always in fact has come, from a variety of sources. The real curriculum is the whole of life. The trick will be to help people to understand, to record that which they have learnt, and to get it verified if need be.

So, 'revenous à nos moutons', as Rabelais (1533 and 1955) said as he wandered from his original theme. The debate about the balance between knowledge, skills and attributes takes many forms: know that versus know how; content versus process; learning how versus deep learning; rote learning versus action learning. What I have observed over nearly forty years in education is that balance is rarely ever reached. The pendulum swings backwards and forwards, from one extreme to another. When I was a young School Counsellor, I recall the words of a very distinguished HMI (School Inspector), who said that he never took trends in Education very seriously: if you stayed where you were, the fashion would eventually swing back towards you. He was describing the kind of natural oscillation between the two poles of most human behaviour, and is reflected in individual as well as corporate behaviour. In my lifetime, the education system has constantly rearranged the deckchairs and tacked from side to side, but it has not fundamentally changed. As T S Eliot (1954) put it: 'Where is the life we have lost in living? Where is the wisdom we have lost in knowledge? Where is the knowledge we have lost in information?'

That is, until recently. In my youth, the emphasis was on *inputs*: filling people up with knowledge, teaching them well — 'Learn 'em', as Rat said in *Wind in the Willows*. Then in the 1960s and 1970s came the idea that the *process* was all important — 'it ain't what you do, but the way that you do it'. The predominant idea was that learning how to learn was the most important function of the education system. Now the emphasis is on *outputs* — what it is that the person knows, understands and can do as a result of the educational process. And even more recently comes the concept of *impact* — what is left after the process has finished and the outputs have been counted. Is there anything there at all, or has the boa constrictor fodder merely gone in one end and out the other? Has any real value been added to this person? Or are they merely just as intelligent or slow as they were at the beginning. Even more sophisticated is the concept of *intellectual* capital. Has the intellectual capacity of this person been extended, has their practical capability been increased, has their understanding been deepened and attitudes broadened? What are they doing with this capital: counting it, using it, making it grow, or keeping it 'under the bed'?

No-one really knows the answer to these questions. Although there is a lifelong quest here for educational researchers — more than enough work to keep them busy for ever — valid conclusions on a grand and enduring scale will never be reached since the ball-game, the context and the goal posts are swinging around endlessly. By the time megatrends have been measured, the object of the research will have disappeared or altered beyond recognition. This point was particularly brought home to me when I was responsible for education programmes within the Department of Employment. One of these, the Technical and Vocational Education Initiative (TVEI), was probably one of the most researched initiatives of all time. Thousands of pounds were spent on research which was, by the time it finally came out, looking at issues which were no longer of prime interest. More disturbingly, there was no conclusive evidence as to whether or not the initiative had been successful. Those of us who were closely connected with it were convinced that its net effect was even greater than the sum of its parts — but we would say that wouldn't we? The plain truth is that it is almost impossible to disentangle what causes what in this multi-faceted fast-moving world. It reminds me of those sparkling crystal cut balls which used to hang in the middle of dance halls, whirling endlessly and catching the light in a myriad of different ways. Measuring learning accurately is like trying to catch a falling star. But you still recognize it if you see it.

Swings and Roundabouts

The various curriculum movements over the last fifty years illustrate what I have been saying. What follows is a gross exaggeration, with notable exceptions, but the general trends were definitely there. The products of the 1944 Education Act were largely brought up on a knowledge driven curriculum, except that it was not knowledge driven so much as fact driven. In those days I was really good at remembering miscellaneous facts about Britain: Kings and Queens, major towns, big battles, rivers. But it was only when I learnt to drive that I realized how hopeless my actual sense of geography was. Poems and times-tables were chanted in class. In the air-raid shelters too, where there was hardly any vision, let alone visual aids, we chanted, recited, quizzed, repeated and sang our way through the day, trying hard to remember what we were told and repeat it when asked. And even though I could do mental arithmetic then at the speed of light, ever since I left school I cannot even remember those times-tables which I used to rehearse and manipulate with such confidence. Learning by rote didn't really work then and it works even less well now when there is too much to remember. We do not seem to have registered that knowledge now depreciates at the rate of 7 per cent a year, and therefore 'know how' becomes more important than 'know what'. I was, I think, saved by going to a rather unusual secondary school (Harrow Weald Grammar) which was way ahead of its time in getting facts into perspective, and in giving its pupils considerable responsibility for the management of their own learning. But that was not the norm.

So in the 1960s, 1970s and 1980s, came rebellion against the curriculum of the 1930s, 1940s and 1950s: what was the point of all these facts if people did not know how to use them, how to apply their knowledge, how to think for themselves? Emphasis began to switch to the *process* of learning — getting pupils to manage their own learning, use initiative, research and find out for themselves, work in teams, make presentations, interview each other and even 'real people'. Along with this set of ideas, which only took hold slowly and patchily, was the idea of pastoral care and the development of the *whole* person.

The rebellion was not only against what was too often a narrow, passive curriculum, but also against the suppression of the individual. The telling, controlling, testing culture of rote learning had encouraged passive dependency and conformity in pupils. For some pupils, those who found learning difficult, it had also induced a feeling of fear and failure, a reject label which did nothing to inspire and motivate them and a lot to switch them off education for the rest of their lives. So as an antidote to all this, and as the comprehensive school movement took hold, there developed a new emphasis in schools (which had always been present in the best of the previous schools) in building a 'caring community' in which the needs of each pupil were addressed. There sprang up systems of pastoral care, individual counselling and guidance, and extra support for those with learning difficulties. The Pastoral Care System began to rival and even dominate the academic systems (Jones, 1984). Many schools began to take on all the problems of society, and the role of teacher became blurred with that of social worker. Teaching methods changed with a growing emphasis on mixed ability, group work, investigative work and a cooperative rather than a competitive culture. Everyone was to be valued equally, at least in theory.

The thrust behind this movement (of which I was part) was admirable. Its aim was to counterbalance the over rigid and sometimes negative systems of the past, and to release the potential of all pupils. The Newsom report, *Half our Future* (Ministry of Education, 1963) stressed the 'waste of talent' for the nation if we did not nurture and develop all our pupils. The down side of this era was that it went too far. The swing to 'caring' began to detract from the quest for achievement. For some reason, we seemed as a nation to find it difficult to combine high academic standards and high standards of personal development. The swing from one extreme to another was too great.

But even this pastoral/academic split was not the whole problem. There was also the neglect of capability, that is the ability to translate theory into practice, to take an idea and implement it, to design, produce and to use the end product to good effect. What we really needed to develop was head, hands and heart, a kind of three-legged stool, in balance and stable, and able to withstand considerable pressure. Developing the intellect and the emotions is all very well, but practical ability counts too. So we still had a two-legged, rather than a three-legged stool, and the result was lopsided. In the early 1980s, the RSA's 'Education for Capability' movement did a great deal to put this right, and certainly brought the problem into public consciousness. My Cantor lecture at the RSA in 1985 (Jones, 1985) emphasized this point first-hand. Progress has been made with the result that today's curriculum outcomes are couched in terms of what the learner knows, understands and can do. This is an enormous breakthrough. I like to think that a paper I wrote with colleagues for the Secondary Heads Association in 1983 also helped to bring about this shift in emphasis. In a 'View from the Bridge' (Secondary Heads Association, 1983) we defined desirable areas of learning; added economic literacy, computer literacy and technological literacy; and advocated a modular structure; a role for schools in continuing education; lifelong learning; a negotiated curriculum; records of achievement and action planning; prevocational education (bridging the academic/vocational divide); and opportunities for people to manage their own learning and thereby become more mature.

During the 1970s and 1980s the emphasis on process to balance the previous emphasis on content was welcomed, but it put insufficient emphasis on outcomes and ultimately the process became an end in itself.

Process in this sense is quite different from 'process re-engineering' which is a way of using the process to improve the outcomes continuously. On the contrary, in schools and colleges of the 1970s and early 1980s, process too often appeared to take away from achievement, hence the panic now about standards.

International Competition

In the meantime, the Pacific Rim countries, with their high achievement rates in compulsory and post-compulsory education still put a great emphasis on knowledge, but it is not always sufficiently acknowledged that their students are also capable and good with people. In the UK we need to keep head, hands and heart in better balance. In most cases, this now means putting more emphasis on 'head'. Knowledge workers will be almost the only workers of the future. We need every ounce of brainpower we can develop if we are to remain 'world class' and competitive as a nation.

In 1990, I was privileged to visit the United States, Canada, Japan, Korea and Singapore on behalf of the Department of Employment and with the aim of investigating what effects the revolution of information and communication technologies was having on working practices. More importantly, I looked at the implications for the education system: what kind of education would be needed to equip people for this kind of global, instant, real-time economy? I came back convinced that we had got it wrong in the UK. We now had *too* little emphasis on knowledge, precision, attention to detail, rigorous methodology, delivery on time. My comments upon my return follow:

1   In terms of competitive advantage, the UK is way behind these other countries. We have not begun to grasp in reality the order of magnitude that these technological changes bring about. It is like going into a new dimension where everything is on a different plane. It is not a step change but a sea change into something new and strange. We are not prepared.
2   We know intellectually that we are going to need more highly skilled people and fewer unskilled people but will these highly skilled people be able to think in 3D rather than 2D? Will they be able to work in teams to solve impossible highly technological problems. Will they be able to be self-motivating and self-managing? How will they react to a paperless world, in which there are virtually no supervisors, no secretaries, no middle people? A world in which the technologically illiterate might as well be deaf and dumb? Yet this is what we saw in Pratt and Whitney, Nova Scotia, Canada.

3 We know intellectually that training is a 'good thing', yet in every country we visited our questions about training were regarded as 'odd'. Without exception, training was built into the workplace system, very often in cooperation with the local community college which delivered more effectively and cheaply than private providers. Most companies had their own learning 'businesses' with sophisticated learning systems, fully accredited by the local college, with virtually continuous training built into the job. In Seattle, USA, the Boeing Company has a motto on its wall: an engineer has to be retrained every two years.

4 We may think intellectually that Japan is merely a copycat nation, simply replicating other nations' high-tech inventions. We may think that the Japanese are uncreative thinkers, low on innovation and poor at people considerations. How wrong can we be! Major companies invested nearly all their profit in Research and Development (R&D) with hardly any going to the shareholders, and innovation is the most highly prized quality in an employee. Qualities looked for in the employees (lifelong employees with lifelong training) were: 'bright, positive, dynamic, optimistic, balanced and in harmony, able to make a positive contribution'. The competition is there but it is achieved through teamwork and cooperation:

> to achieve the success as a global cooperation we believe
> that mutually rewarding co-existence must be the guiding principle of all our actions. (Canon)

5 We may think intellectually that because few companies have fully integrated computer manufacturing systems, that there is not much to worry about: 'No, they are not fully integrated, they have a few islands of integration', we say reassuringly to ourselves. But the global companies in the East and the West are preparing *now* for a fully integrated system; preparing their staff, their markets, their products. Cutting down on staff? No way — the aim is increased productivity. A Sapporo Beer plant in Tokyo runs on thirty people but has quadrupled its productivity. Computers mean you can employ more people because you can produce more, and increase your share of the world market. Making people redundant is alien to the Japanese culture, though even they may not be able to keep this up for ever.

6 We may think intellectually that countries like Korea must be way behind — third world countries making spare parts for Japan? Not any more! Korea seems to have thrived on adversity, with war followed by oil crises, because it has invested massively in technology. Hyundai Electrics was only set up in 1983 and is

now the largest conglomerate in Korea. It naturally has its own state of the art resource/training facilities. All employees take courses in management, salesmanship, computers and foreign languages. In Korean primary schools, all pupils are taught basic skills using computer learning programmes. In secondary schools all pupils are computer literate, able to word process and use modern technology. Ninety-four per cent of the pupils now go to High School, which ends at 18.

7   We may think intellectually that Singapore is too small a country to be much of a threat internationally. Do not be mistaken! Here again, strategy and action were as one: a programme of computer assisted learning in primary schools; IT skills in secondary schools; 100 per cent IT training programme for the **Whole** workforce up to senior manager level — with a Government subsidy for employers; forward investment in people and in R & D to keep at the leading edge of technology; and getting other bigger countries with more space to do the big manufacturing jobs for them.

8   Surprisingly Japan did not appear to have a work-related curriculum, nor to teach computer skills in schools. No need to when the pupils are taught to work in teams for long hours, and deliver to targets from the age of six. Work habits learnt at school matched those needed in work. This includes looking after those with learning problems.

9   The good news is that TVEI still holds up as a bold national strategy with all the right components. Maybe we should be even bolder about stressing the importance of achieving high standards of success in exams, especially maths, science, technology, IT and languages. But we are absolutely right to stress as well as much as we do the 'person' and 'task management' skills. None of the other countries put as much stress as we do on these, nor on links with industry. So these additional factors *could* be our trump card. If we could pull off the trick of continuing to achieve an increased participation rate in post-16 (relevant and appropriate) education, and better exam results, we *could* still rule the world.

10 But this will not happen if working practices in industry do not change. TVEI pupils will want to go to work in places where their skills and capabilities are used, otherwise they will become disaffected and frustrated. We are preparing our future workforce but are we preparing our workplaces?

11 The 'future shock' is fundamental not cosmetic, in most cases a change of organizational culture, management styles, working practices, education and training provision, value systems and human relationships. Incremental changes will not be sufficient. Only those companies that take a strategic view which they

follow up with action will survive in the competitive global economy which is already with us. In other countries, companies are tackling these issues with a precision and determination. If they have not done so already, islands of integration will suddenly snap into fully integrated systems. What are we going to do, now, to overcome our apparent competitive disadvantage in the world market? Jones (1990a)

Looking back it seems to me that we had taught our pupils about the information technology revolution but we had not systematically taught them how to take part in it. That may be because we, the adults, were not then sufficiently confident at using these new technologies. Most of our young people have taught themselves and now surpass their elders in competence and capability. Nevertheless, the fact remains that our targets for school leavers still do not include explicit competence in Information and Communication Technologies (ICT). Contrast this with, the example of Singapore, admittedly a small country, but one where all school leavers are technically proficient in ICT, and where a programme of adult IT literacy ensures, at government expense, that all managers are ICT trained.

What was also disturbing to note from this visit was that there was a marked difference in approach to education and economic success between the West and the Pacific Rim countries. In the United States and the UK in particular there was, and still is, a great emphasis on education-business partnerships: a great deal of energy and time spent on getting the two 'sides' to talk to each other and understand each other better. In the Pacific Rim this was deemed to be unnecessary. The pervading culture included an agreed implicit assumption that economic survival depended on being competitive on a world scale. There was no need to muddle up and confuse the roles of education and industry; everybody accepted that economic success depended absolutely on each sector developing the potential of its people to the utmost. As Pascale and Athos, 1985 put it: 'the core of management is precisely this art of mobilizing and pulling together the intelligent resources of all employees of all the firm' (Pascale and Athos, 1985). And this task has been ruthlessly pursued with a great deal of apparent success. We might feel that 'all round' development has been neglected at the expense of high-tech performance, but we may be wrong even about that. If we do not take this competition seriously we are in danger of deluding ourselves. It used to be said that the USA fostered individual brilliance and collective mediocrity, whereas Japan fostered individual mediocrity and collective brilliance. Whatever the truth of this, in the UK we certainly need to target both individual and collective brilliance.

The fact remains that the Pacific Rim countries are pushing, and successfully, for ever higher standards of academic achievement, *albeit* on rather narrower indices than we have been pursuing in the West. This fact is reflected in the numbers now staying in education to 18 and/or completing

Higher Education. This would not in itself constitute such a threat to the UK economy if it were not combined with other factors. In the UK we have a rapidly ageing workforce, and in Europe in the year 2000 more people will retire than will join the labour market. We also have an expensive and relatively unskilled workforce. In the Pacific Rim countries, conversely, there is a growth in numbers of young people, who themselves are well educated and highly skilled. These countries therefore have a growing number of highly competent skilled workers, who are relatively cheap to employ. So, in thinking about the curriculum for a changing world and uncertain future, we have to take account of the international competition, and to do this on a number of dimensions. To maintain and re-secure our leading edge, we need to think and act very fast. And we certainly cannot afford to waste the talent locked up and under-developed in our existing workforce.

Organizational Changes

If this set of factors were not enough, we need also to examine the changing nature of organizations, the effects this is having on people and the kind of curriculum they will need if they are to survive in this uncertain future. Just as Britain does not yet truly have a learning culture, so some organizations are not yet truly learning organizations. Senge (1990) defines a learning organization as one where people continually expand their capacity to create the results they fully deserve. This requires a change of mindset even more complicated than organizational reshuffling, if the creativity of all members of the organization is to be released. As Einstein said: 'I never discovered anything with my rational mind'.

My observation is that a large number of organizations now know about and talk about the kind of dramatic changes that are taking place in organizations, but very few of them have actually worked out the implications of these changes, or what they should be doing now if they are to sustain their businesses. Comfortable lip-service is paid to flatter hierarchies, delayering the organization, even the concept of the learning organization, but little changes fundamentally, even when the flattening and delayering actually takes place. The shape of the organization might change, but the assumptions on which it works do not, so nothing really changes. If organizations are unable to manage this transition from caterpillars to butterflies (or whatever else emerges) for themselves, then they may have to break down completely in order for a new kind of organization to emerge, one which is more appropriate to this brave new world.

How will individual learner-workers fare in this anomic environment? I do not have the answers, though they may be more simple than we imagine: it is easy to become overwhelmed by complexity. In any case, people have to work out for themselves the answer which is appropriate in their circumstances. However, the trends are very clear, and are borne out by an in-depth series of interviews which we in the Brunel Management Programme (based at Brunel University) have recently undertaken. The organizational trends noted were hardly surprising, and only confirm the predictions of the organizational analysts such as Handy (1994). Universally reported were the following trends.

1   Smaller organisations — dramatically smaller, with a growing trend for setting up devolved autonomous units or cost centres, each of which had to be self-sufficient.
2   Flatter hierarchies — with several tiers of management stripped out.
3   Focus on customer care — for sustained growth.
4   Partnerships with suppliers.
5   Strategic alliances with other former rivals.
6   Great hope pinned on Business Process Re-engineering.
7   Continuous change on a global scale as a permanent backcloth.
8   Shift from management to facilitative leadership.
9   Focus on continuous learning and self-development.
10 Collaborate team working to retain competitive leading edge.

Devolvement to autonomous sub-units requires a whole new order of integrative mechanisms: who has the picture of the whole? Is this now irrelevant? The stripping out of layers of hierarchy may have gone too far: have the right people been moved out? Senior managers may no longer be used for implementing decisions rather than taking them: workers will need a lot of support to develop their 'management skills'. The 'core' business may now be too lean: is there sufficient experienced manpower around to carry the remaining core business? The question of how to build in appropriate continuous development in a changing context, and particularly without an organization to belong to, may be difficult. New role models and working practices will need to be developed. *Quis custodet?* How will individuals sustain their learning or get support for their learning? They will not be able to depend on their large organization to pay, and even if they regroup into small organizations, they may find themselves under too much pressure for survival to make time or resources available for formal learning.

The fact is that in the future lifelong learning will no longer (even if it ever did) come from lifelong employment. This is not necessarily a bad thing though it does raise enormous questions about who pays. Expensive management training courses will not be in the reach of most individuals. However, my own view is that lifelong learning will become more of a reality when people depend less on their employing organization and more on their own initiative to ensure their own continuous professional development. If learning pays, who will pay in the future? Certainly not the large organization of yesteryear: such organizations will rarely exist and, instead, we are likely to move to cooperative self-help learning organizations. Perhaps those people who work alone or in very small organizations will get their support and professional sustenance from professional bodies who should, along with careers guidance workers, assume much more importance.

The Handy (1989) 'clover-leaf' organization, with a third employed, a third subcontracted as needed and a third providing services to the core, has come upon us with a vengeance; in some cases the 'hard core' third may be hard pressed to cover all that is needed for basic survival — too lean and mean could mean extinction. But the corollary of all this is that organizations as we have known them are breaking down completely. It could be that at least two thirds of the working population in the future will be self-employed. What curriculum prepares people to cope with this?

At first, the idea of self-employment is seductive; people in control of their own lives, selling their services and skills in the market place, only working as much as they choose. Originally, many of the people taking and developing this 'option' did so voluntarily. Many of them were well-established experts in middle years who perhaps had taken an early retirement. They could immediately be subcontracted back by their previous employer amongst others. This first generation of peripheral suppliers to the hard core quite often had paid off their mortgages, had seen their children through their education into independence, and maybe even had a small pension to cushion them through leaner times, or allow them to take a holiday from time to time. So far so good.

But then other factors came into play. First, the market for independent consultants or very small companies began to get overcrowded. Those lucky enough to secure contracts began to take on more and more work, because they soon discovered that if they said they were unavailable, for whatever reason, the work would go to someone else. Those who started up later began to find that it was very hard to get a foothold in this precarious and very unstable market: but at least these older people were not destitute if the work did not come, though their morale and self-esteem may have suffered. But what has prepared these successful and less successful consultants for this pressurized life in which there is very little time to stand and think? Their own core of inner strength, motivation and intellectual capital will be their main resource, and even this will need sustenance and replenishment.

So much for the older generation of experienced company workers now working alone or in small groups. But what about the younger generation? I am thinking here particularly of the very many highly educated people who have heeded the advice of adults and taken Degrees, Masters, even Doctorates in an attempt to make sure they are qualified for high level work in this new knowledge based high-tech world. Many have taken further Postgraduate qualifications, in part because they could not get work and, in part, in the sometimes erroneous belief that this will get them a job. The overall increase in the numbers of qualified graduates in the last few years has been phenomenal: in 1987 when I joined the Employment Department, some 12–14 per cent of the age cohort obtained degrees. Now the figure is approaching 30 per cent and some would argue that it ought to be 50 per cent. The CBI (1994) has recently come out with a target of 40 per cent by the year 2000 as a minimum. It sees Higher Education as 'a prime source of highly skilled people, a key contributor to a dynamic economy and central to the future competitiveness of UK business'. I agree, but there are transitional difficulties.

This group of highly qualified young people now face at least two sets of major problems. First, they may have degrees but it does not follow from that they are capable people with marketable sets of skills, despite the efforts of the Enterprise in Higher Education initiative, which I set up in 1987 on behalf of the Employment Department. The flight into 'higher degrees' may in fact have handicapped, not enhanced, their employability in the short term.

But a much more serious problem is that there is not much employment to be had, particularly at the higher level: this is still a hard fact to swallow, considering the fact that there are still skills shortages in some high level jobs. But, never mind, these highly qualified young people can, surely, set up their own small businesses, or work as consultants/servicers of the remaining small core organizations? Or can they?

My observation is that in the long term it will pay to be a graduate, and my views are shared by Sir Christopher Ball (1992). But in the short term the going for these young people is extremely tough. If they are self-employed at this stage in their lives, then all too often (as we know from Maslow's hierarchy of needs, 1970), they do not have sufficient basic security from which to develop their full potential. What is missing for them? Unlike the older generation of self-employed entrepreneurs, this younger generation lacks many 'benefits' of employment: for example, pensions, holidays, sick leave, relative security of tenure, maternity/paternity leave. No work, even for a few weeks or months, means no money. And this vicious circle means that it becomes very risky to buy a house, have a family, take out a personal pension plan, or take a holiday. And certainly there is neither the time nor the money to buy into the formal education system.

Obviously some people do very well, but for all too many life becomes a series of short-term contracts, with all the insecurity which goes with that life style. It becomes impossible to turn down an opportunity for work in order to take a much needed holiday. It is a treadmill. Sometimes such people's insecurity is also exploited: wages may be relatively low and long hours can be demanded. If people do not like the conditions under which they work, then they do not have to be kept on. There are plenty of other people ready to take up the contract. These conditions are not conducive either to learning, or to the release of creativity or full potential.

But this is not all. Not only do these people not have any of their basic needs for security met, they are also isolated. They do not belong to an organization, and though they may well have some support through professional organizations, through their peer group or through some social/ sports activity, basically they are not going to get the benefits, which many of us have taken for granted in the past, of belonging to an organization. Such benefits include companionship, stimulus, cheap meals, challenges, use of shared amenities, training, fun, and even something to complain about! (Remember Elliott Jacques', 1955, seminal work on the organization as a defence against anxiety.) Yes, we all know that organizations create their own set of problems, such as inertia, bureaucracy, power games, paralysis by analysis, but for many people working virtually alone can be very lonely and very time consuming. Having to do all your filing, book-keeping, marketing and reprographics becomes tedious and inimical to creativity. Yet, in this scenario, it is not always possible to employ others to do this.

In addition, people who have not worked in organizations may also find they are constantly re-inventing wheels for themselves. This can be stimulating and exhilarating, but it is a slow process. It is almost as if organizations were now having to re-invent themselves *ab initio*. Re-engineering the organization with a vengeance! It is probably this complete recreation of the concept of organization which is needed in the long term, organizations based on different assumptions from those which now hold sway. But the transition, the chrysalis stage, can be worrying. Most people feel very insecure when they cannot see the light at the end of the tunnel or the butterfly emerging from the chrysalis.

Yet even more frightening is the fact that I have been discussing here the plight of the highly educated. What will happen to those people who have not had the advantage of an extended education? How will they cope in a jobless world? How will they cope particularly if they have already been labelled as educational failures? To build a permanent under-class is a recipe for disaster. My feeling is that this trend cannot continue indefinitely and that eventually totally new forms of organization will emerge. Then the whole cycle may well repeat itself — though my hope would be that the organizations of the future would be based on entirely different premises from the power and line cultures of the past.

So, back to the question: what kind of curriculum will help people of all kinds and levels of intelligence to survive and thrive in this very uncertain world? Current national concerns, not surprisingly, are about raising standards of achievement, meeting national training and education targets, catching up with our world neighbours, particularly those in the Pacific Rim. 'Learn 'em harder and harder': with an implicit assumption that 'failing' can be eradicated by better, tougher teaching. If only it were as simple. Some people respond to carrots, others to sticks, but most people need recognition, confidence, and some kind of security if they are to learn optimally. We forget this at our peril. These 'human factors' apply regardless of brainpower or background. Whatever systems we introduce to improve our collective performance, we need to ensure that they enable everyone to learn more, better and faster, and to be able to apply that learning to improved performance. We need also to enable that learning to continue through life, to be recognized and celebrated, to be put to the benefit of the nation, the community and the people themselves. These are not only in themselves beneficial, but also motivating factors.

In the emerging new world, the individual rather than the organization becomes the mover, the provider and the pusher of learning opportunities. The role of education and training systems changes from teacher to facilitator, supporter, counsellor; peer group stimulus and support grows in importance; educational institutions will be increasingly customer-focused if they are to remain in business. People, not organizations, will be the paymasters, and mostly they will neither want nor be able to pay very much. They will move back into 'self-help' groups where learning resources rather than large organizations are used to bring about intellectual and personal growth. Individuals who want to get on will be addicted to learning, but they will want that learning to be accessible, flexible and good value for money. They will not pay for poor teaching or time serving.

Whatever kind of curriculum will cope with all this? It could be that the idea of a curriculum is itself out of date. Think of all those years anguishing about what should be in the national curriculum. The concepts of transferable core skills, still being pursued in the new national curriculum, are also included in the CBI requirements for graduates for the twenty-first century (CBI, 1994). They include personal and interpersonal skills, communication, information technology, application of number, problem solving, and modern language competence. These skills were originally piloted through TVEI (1983–1994) and then extended to Enterprise in Higher Education: it is good to see that they have survived all the chopping and changing. However, it seems to me that a new order of core skills is beginning to emerge, not to supplant or replace those former core skills but to add to them some overarching qualities that the learner-worker of the future will need to develop. These are the development of intellectual curiosity, the motivation to do better, the confidence to admit learning needs, the determination to find out more, the will to share joy and pain with others, the ability to translate ideas into practicality.

How do we learn all that? Not entirely from our parents and upbringing, though these are key factors: more needs to be done to help parents with this very important role and the RSA project, *Parents in a Learning Society* (1994), is one small but significant step towards this. Most of us do not learn from being in a passive and totally dependent culture; the break-down of large organizations may well help to shake people out of this childlike dependency into mature adulthood. People learn when they take responsibility for the management of their own learning, a fact well recognized by the FORD EDAP scheme and the Rover Learning Business: in both of these companies the employees themselves decide what additional learning they want to undertake. They are clearly 'learning organizations' which fit well with the vision for Human Resource Development propagated in a recent Eurotechnet publication (1993):

> In the learning organization, the process of learning is permanent not intermittent, holistic not segmented, problem centred, context related and includes all members of the enterprise. The learning organization brings the strategy, structure and culture of the enterprise itself into a learning system. Management development is transformed into a self-learning self-management process. The transformation of the whole system for greater competitiveness is the goal!

This is the kind of approach we need to apply to creating a learning society in which lifelong learning becomes a reality. There are encouraging signs that this is beginning to be understood. A recent ESRC document (1994) setting up a £2m budget for research into *The Learning Society* makes the same point:

> While the need to create a 'learning society' is becoming widely recognized, the tremendous increase in learning required for a labour process based on conscious involvement, and a society of citizens active in their working and democratic lives to be a learning organization does not just mean more training, the whole organization culture has to change.

In other words, a paradigm shift from training to learning, and learning for all. My own concern is whether present mechanisms to enable people who have left full-time education to continue to be lifelong learners *really* exist. However, the emphasis in the White Paper on *Competitiveness* (DTI, 1994) on incentives and mechanisms to enable mature people to return to learning is encouraging. A whole section on lifetime learning promotes career development for all, tax relief and Investors in People: whilst for schools there is a new general Diploma, vocational courses, a vastly improved budget for careers guidance, and modern apprenticeships. The extension of the idea of Learning Credits bodes well. There is, however, a long way to go before every adult in the country actively and consciously feels that they are a 'learner'.

When I was responsible for TVEI, I took great care to build the concept of continuous learning for continuous improvement into our thinking. When we thought and spoke about the curriculum, we were not focusing entirely on the secondary school curriculum but had lifelong learning in mind. The kind of requirements of the curriculum which we were providing are summarized in this speech:

- giving young people opportunities to continue in further and higher education
- ensuring that all young people are equipped to cope with change
- increasing the number of people who are successful learners and therefore want to go on learning throughout life
- bridging the academic–vocational divide
- building a more flexible and responsive education system
- using modern technologies in the classroom so that they more readily mirror the realities of life after school. (Jones, 1990b)

Motivation, a sense of direction, recognition of success module by module, a record of achievement, these are vital ingredients for effective learning.

So the curriculum of the here and now and of the immediate future needs to be tough on technical detail, tender on suitability to individual needs, demanding of each person one further step in growth, rejecting of tell and sell, and strong on do-it-yourself. As managers in industry are now shifting to become leaders and facilitators, so teachers at whatever stage or age need to become facilitators, learning supporters, providers of guidance and counselling, builders of confidence and demanders of higher standards. The shape of things to come is still impossible to determine: 'that is of no importance', as le Petit Prince said to the Flower (St Exupéry, 1945). The principles of a learning person, a learning community and a learning society have never changed. And that is where the stability and the continuity comes from in this uncertain world of ours.

References

BALL, C. (1992) *Profitable Learning*, London, RSA.
BRUNEL MANAGEMENT PROGRAMME (1994) *Organisational Trends*, unpublished.
CBI (1994) *Thinking Ahead: Ensuring the Expansion of Higher Education into the 21st Century*, London, CBI.
DTI (1994) *Competitiveness: Helping Business to Win*, London, HMSO.
ELIOT, T.S. (1954 edition) *Chorus 1 from the Rock*, London, Faber & Faber.
Employment Department (1987) *The Enterprise in Higher Education Initiative*, London, HMSO.
ESRC (1994) *The Learning Society: Knowledge and Skills for Employment*, Brief for project.
EXUPÉRY, A. de (1945) *Le Petit Prince*, London, Heinemann.
GRAHAME, K. (1908) *The Wind in the Willows*, London, Methuen.

HANDY, C. (1994) *The Empty Raincoat*, London, Hutchinson.

HANDY, C. (1989) *The Age of Unreason*, London, Century Hutchinson.

JACQUES, E. (1955) *Social Systems as a Defence against Persecutony and Depressive Anxiety in new Directions in Psychoanalyses*, London, Tavistock.

JONES, A. (1984) *Counselling Adolescents: School and After*, London, Kogan Page.

JONES, A. (1985) 'Tomorrow's schools: open or closed?', RSA Cantor Lecture.

JONES, A. (1990a) 'Key features of USA and far eastern study tour', Unpublished report to the Employment Department.

JONES, A. (1990b) 'Future agenda', Address to IMTEC International Conference, Oxford.

MASLOW, A.H. (1970) *Motivation and Personality*, New York, Harper & Row.

Ministry of Education (1963) *Half Our Future*, London, HMSO (The Newsom report).

MONTAIGNE, M. de (1953 edition) *Essais*, Paris, Editions Garnier.

OHMAE, K. (1990) *The Borderless World*, New York, Harper Business.

PASCALE, R.T. and ATHOS, A.G. (1985) *The Art of Japanese Management*, London, Penguin.

RABELAIS, F. (1955 edition) *Gargantua & Pantagruel*, London, Penguin Classics.

RSA (1994) *Parents in a Learning Society*, London, RSA.

Secondary Heads Association (1983) 'A view from the bridge', in A. JONES (1987) *Leadership for Tomorrow's Schools*, Oxford, Blackwell.

SENGE, P. (1990) *The Fifth Discipline: The Art and Practice of the Learning Organisation*, London, Doubleday.

STAHL, T. NYHAN, B. and D'ALOJA, P. (1993) *The Learning Organisation for Human Resource Development*, Eurotechnet, Commission of the European Communities.

THUROW, L. (1993) *Head to Head*, Nicholas Brealey Publishing.

Chapter 8

A Learning in Organizations Model

Alan Jones

Introduction

Over the past four years or so much has been written in academic and professional management literature on the concept of 'the learning organization' — for example, Hayes, Wheelwright and Clark, 1988; Kanter, 1985; Pedler, Boydell and Burgoyne, 1988; and Senge, 1990, 1994. Some companies have also publicly declared themselves to be a 'learning organization'. However, in the writer's view much of what has been written about, and practised in, organizations lacks any rational or clear understanding of what a learning organization is in terms of how learning is to be defined, evaluated, or managed. Rarely, have the organizations, or the theoretical literature, presented any definition as to what is meant by 'learning'. Most seem to view training and development, which produces change, to be the hallmark of a learning organization.

Much of what is considered to be a theory of a learning organization is simply anecdotal rhetoric. Senge, and others, have produced little by way of empirical evidence to support their claims that a learning organization is about such things as 'mind-shifts', 'transformation', 'team leadership', and 'visioning and missioning'. No account is taken of the time it takes people and organizations to learn. Nor is there any emphasis on learning styles, characteristics, or processes which best support learning in organizations. Last, but by no means least, there is little questioning as to whether concentrating on learning will, in fact, produce change and transformation. Indeed, the often-made assumption is that learning equals change, whereas in fact this is not always the case.

At best the concept of the learning organization, as currently understood and propounded, seems capable of acting as an initial rallying call throughout an organization to cascade mission and vision statements, but provides little clue as to its usefulness, other than perhaps to superficially knee-jerk the organization into considering training and development. Few organizations seem prepared to radically reconsider the ways in which they view learning and its development. It remains controlled. The visioning, missioning, and empowering tactics adopted by many organizations can only be regarded, by and large, as a softer form of manipulative strategy for organizational compliance.

In few organizations is there scope for rejection, reflection, or revision of these top-down delivered activities, something Kanter (1984) observed in her organizational change studies. So, there is a need for a model or schema by which an organization can begin the 'journey' and go in a learning 'direction'. This chapter seeks to provide some pointers using some of the evidence from the organizations in which the writer has worked, and lessons from adult learning theory. First, however, there is the need to consider how to evaluate learning. In many organizations learning is viewed in terms of training inputs and behavioural outcomes and these seem to be of limited value.

Learning in Organizations

If specific objectives are achieved, learning is assumed to have occurred, irrespective as to whether activities have been worthwhile or understood. Little account is taken of contextual variables such as employee morale and the political nature of the organization at any given time. It is usually an activity or an event which is evaluated, not the processes and long-term outcomes for each of the people involved (Guba and Lincoln, 1981).

How to evaluate learning which results in understanding is an issue most organizations evade in their obsession to produce quantifiable measurement outputs. In turn, organizations produce systems, such as employee appraisal schemes, to support the controlling nature of the organization with its focus on assessment. Rarely do organizations concentrate on the worth or value of an activity — that is, 'evaluation'. In so doing, they lose a valuable resource by ignoring the less quantifiable aspects of learning.

How is Learning in Organizations to be Analysed?

Learning is a word which we all too often use too casually and with indifference but as Cullingford (1990, p. 2) notes:

> To study and understand learning is to enter that no-man's land between thinking, as a capacity, and development, as a process of change. Learning is both constant and changeable; it depends on moods and on general attitudes. . . .

To assess whether learning in organizations has taken place it is possible to ask:

- What learning has or has not taken place?
- Why has it taken place or not taken place?
- When has it taken place?
- How has it taken place?

Most organizations concentrate on such simple questions and management literature certainly attempts to quantify learning in such prescriptive ways. However, learning of all kinds goes on in organizations and to attempt a rigorous assessment of it in terms of specific outcomes may be the wrong approach (Tenbrink, 1974; Eisner, 1976; Brookfield, 1986; Cullingford, 1990). To assess learning, and to respond to the type of questions posed above, clouds the real issue. Cullingford (1990, pp. 229–30) further notes:

> Learning is a complex matter. It is . . . hard to prove or measure. . . . we should not sacrifice our understanding for the sake of a notion of what is 'empirical', or sacrifice truth to statistical formalism. . . . we know what we actually learn through our emotions, through associations and habits, as much as we do through readiness to meet the demands of being . . . tested.

When learning is measured by organizations rarely do they have an understanding of what it is they are measuring. When they do, they may well only be measuring activities as part of an organizational control system. Organizations also tend not to anchor their measurement activities in terms of explicit learning theories, against types of learning which best suit individuals, or in relation to specific learning domains or levels of learning. And rarely do organizations focus on the depth of 'understanding' that is achieved, the 'worth' of a particular event or activity, or the time needed for learning to occur which leads to understanding.

Of course, there may be occasions when it is not necessary for employees to understand what they are doing or the processes involved, providing they can complete the task required of them. However, as the adult learning literature demonstrates, depth of understanding produces a greater degree of creativity, flexibility, adaptability, and links their application more readily to other contexts. In the writer's experience few organizations ever define what they mean by learning and measure it in a fragmented, haphazard fashion. This results in a muddled view of learning and its evaluation. As Brookfield (1989: 262) observes:

> . . . the infrequency of systematic evaluation . . . is the absence of an evaluative model that derives its criteria and procedural features from the nature of the adult learning process.

Alan Jones

The Assessment or Evaluation of Learning

The two most recent organizations the writer worked with included a training organization and a utility company. Both tended to use quantitative methods of 'measurement' or 'assessment'. As with many other organizations senior managers regularly spoke of how they 'evaluated' learning in terms of measuring and assessing competencies. Major formal training initiatives formed the backbone of the learning process in the utility company, while in the training company, job-centred development informed how training and personnel development was undertaken. But in each case the impact was evaluated in terms of outputs. In the utility firm, especially, it demonstrated itself in issues to do with quality and service measurement standards, intensive departmental personnel appraisal sessions, and formal training sessions.

This approach to measuring learning is not surprising when the British education and training system generally emphasizes such practice, not least in the measurement of outputs in terms of examination passes in schools and higher education. Current British vocational training and education is also burdened with policies and practices which emphasize the acquiring and assessing of competence, skills, and knowledge in a precise and defined way, although some educationalists and professionals in the wider employment arena are questioning such an approach. If organizations need greater employee creativity and flexibility then an emphasis on transferability of skills and measurable or quantifiable competencies may not be the most appropriate format for employee development. And, as Kanter (1985, 1989) has observed, if the most successful organizations are those which operate at the edge of their competence, then 'hard evaluation' is virtually meaningless because people are engaging with the unkown, not the knowable!

The Qualitative Aspects of Evaluation

The Oxford dictionary defines value as 'worth', 'desirability', 'one's judgment as to what is valuable or important'. Thus, in making an evaluation of learning in organizations the approach needs to take account of events, processes, and informal and formal activities which are of worth, value and importance to the people involved, and the organization as a whole. However, the two may not rest easily together if senior managers interests do not conform to those of employees.

Phrases such as 'measuring learning' and 'assessing learning' seem inappropriate when considering the learning process, or indeed the outcomes. Rogers (1986, p. 172) points to the distinction between 'evaluation' and 'assessment' when applied to the learning process and acknowledges that the two words are used too loosely and interchangeably. He concludes that **assessment** is:

... the collection of data on which we base our evaluation. It is descriptive and objective; if anyone else were to do it, they would come up with much the same findings.

and he defines **evaluation** as:

... a process of making personalised judgements, decisions about achievements, about expectations, about the effectiveness and value of what we are doing. It involves notions of 'good' and 'bad' ... ... it is based on our own ideology.

Brookfield (1986, p. 264) also offers a useful analytical summary:

... assessment is a value-free ascertainment of the extent to which objectives determined at the ... outset ... have been attained. Assessment of these objectives requires no value judgements as to their worthwhileness.

He goes on to define evaluation as: ... inescapably a value-judgemental concept. The word value is at the heart of the term.

These definitions are important because (a) they fit in well with qualitative processes and the empowered worker-participant idea, and (b) it puts a strong focus on what the individual learner, or what the organization itself, perceives to be measures of learning success.

The Role of the Evaluator-Consultant in Analysing Learning

Against this backcloth this analysis seeks to focus on the qualitative aspects of evaluation. This is not to say that the harder measures have no worth because they do, in some situations. However, in focusing on them they do not reveal 'learning (as) a complex matter' (Cullingford, 1990, p. 229). Thus, it is suggested that costing and training modes of assessment and the 'hard' measurement goal-directed and taxonomy (Mager, 1984) styles of analysis are of some use, but of limited value.

The development of a learning organization culture was firm-specific in the writer's recent studies — that is, the organizations each created their own paths and determined their own criteria, or lack of them. Deliberate use of a softer approach to evaluation has therefore been used to elicit from the data a learning in organizations model.

Finally, evaluating learning as a process, or in terms of outcomes, is always difficult because people learn in different ways, at different times, and according to their personal needs. When an analysis is therefore made of learning it may be undertaken at the wrong time, with the wrong expectations, and fail to take account of where someone may be at in the stage of their learning. The same is true for an organization as a whole, in the sense that an organization can be said to learn at all. Collectively, the people that make up an organization may need to go through a number of learning processes, over a given period of time, before they perfect what it is they are aiming to achieve. The process is iterative.

The Researcher-Internal Consultant Role in the Evaluation of Learning and the Creation of a Learning in Organizations Model

Hamblin (1974) notes that if an open-ended approach is adopted to evaluating on-going processes, such as learning, then it is:

> . . . hardly ever (possible to) set up a scientifically controlled research experiment which has a beginning, a middle and an end, and at the end of which we can confidently state that certain statements have been proved true and false. It is necessary to adopt a much more discursive, exploratory approach to evaluation, in which we are not trying to prove anything but simply to find things out.

Moreover, an outsider, as someone not so involved, may more readily detect the changes in 'moods' and 'general attitudes' on which, as Cullingford (1990, p. 2) reminds us, learning depends.

Patton (1980) concludes that to evaluate something in reality is to investigate not specific learning outcomes but the negotiation of relationships — the backwards and forwards of interaction as people go about their work and lives. This demonstrates the validity, value and worth of the learning process. Brookfield (1986, p. 263), Stufflebeam (1971), Scriven (1967), Lincoln and Guba (1985) have argued that for evaluation to be worth anything in the context of learning it has to be viewed as a judgment of merit, worth, and value by the researcher or other person making the evaluation.

Against this background the writer's research has sought to make an analysis to gain some 'illumination' which 'sheds light on' how a learning in organization model can be developed against what is known about adult learning theory and learning processes in general. In doing so, however, the most informative approach is to take a 'discursive, exploratory approach' in evaluating what organizations set out to do.

Summarizing Adult Learning Theory

This chapter began by highlighting the complexity of learning theory. This then makes the task of evaluating learning in quite specific ways difficult because there is no one systematic and general view as to what constitutes learning. As Rogers (1986, p. 42) notes:

> The world of . . . psychology is full of division and uncertainty
> . . . fraught with dangers and complexities. The language is often
> abstruse and there is no agreement as to the 'true' models.

Virtually all education and training provision in the United Kingdom is based on the didactic and pedagogical approach to learning. This approach has spilled over into organizations in general because this is the system with which people are most familiar. Rogers (1986) also re-iterates the point that learning does not equal or mean change. An individual can, for example, learn that what already exists, or what is said or done, is correct so that no change is needed. Reinforcement is also learning. Where learning does result in change it does not necessarily have to be in a behavioural sense. It could just as easily be to do with attitude, emotions or even be structural or physical.

A further issue is time. Little account is taken of the time it takes for learning to occur. Judgments are often made too soon, and events and activities abandoned too readily, because behaviourally predetermined objectives are used as evaluative criteria. When they are not promptly met abandonment occurs (Thiede, 1964; Stakes, 1981; Brookfield, 1986). Embedded learning requires time and needs to be evaluated as a process that rarely occurs across an organization as a whole. It occurs more in pockets, especially if it is being evaluated, say, in terms of merit, worth, or value (Guba, 1978; Guba and Lincoln, 1981; Lincoln and Guba, 1985). A Collins and Porras (1991) study supports this view and found that the top one hundred American companies rated soft evaluation of purpose and value as being as important as hard, quantifiable measures and demonstrates the foolishness of short-termism.

Adult Learning

Adult learning theory makes five assumptions:

(a) Adults seek autonomy and self-direction in learning.

(b) Adults learn through using their own and each others' experiences.

(c) Adults want to start learning when they experience a need to know or to do something in order to perform better in some part of their lives.

(d) Adults tend to be task-oriented or problem-oriented in their approach to learning.

(e) Many adults are far more motivated by self-esteem, increased self-confidence, and personal recognition than they are by such things as salary, promotion, status, or pay grade.

Using adult learning theory to review learning in organizations allows for a narrower and more appropriate focus, whilst at the same time providing the opportunity to develop labels and language which are not 'abstruse' and 'fraught with dangers and complexities'.

Towards a Model of Learning in Organization

1 Learning Patterns

The organizations studied by the writer reveal that in their approach to learning people seemed to learn best in an episodic way, being allowed to give input to their work and its development. Vague ideas about corporate visions failed to provide an holistic view of the organization for most people. When an activity was approached in a sequential way in a context which made sense to them, employees acted more positively. When they were also given time to develop and perfect the tasks required of them, then more embedded learning seemed to occur. The case studies produced from the research provide some good examples.

The development of a thirty-day coaching assessment scheme by one of the companies to replace its formal annual appraisal system had these features: it involved everyone in its development once introduced; it was modified through actual implementation of the scheme in the company; staff took greater interest in it because they realised they were also developing a potential new market place product; it was relevant to their needs and personal understanding; and it was refined over some months prior to its launch. In the past, the company had tended to get involved with too many product development schemes, few of which ever achieved target launch date. This new one did.

The firm's Communications Manager, with her personal interest in information technology and communication networks, is a further good example of learning development and progress. She was allowed to 'blossom' over a two year period and her learning involved a variety of styles and situations, including formal and informal learning, and learning with and from her husband who was a computer programming expert running his own private company. Her general interest was 'formally' recognised by the company which allowed her to develop it further by paying for her to take a part-time degree programme. This subsequently led her to apply her kowledge and newly developed skills to upgrading a company programme and developing it into a new computer one to replace a manual system.

The important ingredients here though illustrate again that success and development occur when someone is: given time; allowed to thoroughly immerse themselves in a topic which is of personal interest to them; links personal interest and the job; and which can be developed in an holistic way. The Communications Manager was able to move from a fairly concrete level of understanding to a much broader level of technical knowledge and expertise which was both theoretically and practically operationalized.

A similar example was discernible in one of the other companies studied. The company-wide focus on quality, and linking this to paying bonus only if systems operated at a one hundred per cent efficiency level, involved everyone in the organization. Reaching this quality standard was approached over time (twelve months) and in stages. It involved everyone in the organization, it was something all could relate to, and it was on-going and required people to regularly refine operational systems. The firm also introduced a new billing and finance department in which the delinquent payers were counselled. The counsellors had the authority to negotiate payment schemes with customers and this produced an additional £2 million in hitherto lost revenue. The telephone operators/counsellors adapted the scheme and their own work schedules and procedures as experience dictated.

Where the two organizations cited above did not allow people time to develop, or used an overly expansive approach to development based on activities such as the formal cascading of vision and mission, training programmes, or brought in external consultants to undertake short-term assignments, then confusion and resistance surfaced and demotivated people thus inhibiting learning. Where there was no sequence to events which enabled people to practise and develop their skills further resistance turned to disenchantment.

Much of what can be discerned in these brief snapshops of activity reflects much of what we know about how adults learn.

2 Learning Episodes

Rogers (1986, pp. 69–75) notes that, in general, the majority of adult learning theorists are agreed that learning can be evaluated against 'learning episodes' or characteristics which adults display. So, when reviewing general learning processes, content and activity in an organization a starting point is Rogers' (1986, p. 74) learning episode schema. This enables an organization to determine the extent to which it engages in episodic, holistic learning activity. It generally incorporates many learning theory approaches but concentrates on the process of natural learning activities for, as Herbst (1976) argues, looking at the processes of learning tends to reveal more exactly what survives as sustained learning and change.

3 Learning Stages

These brief examples reveal the importance of time in enabling an individual to move from a fairly basic level of understanding to the point where they perfect their knowledge and skill. The Communications Manager clearly progressed through a number of stages in her learning, as did the staff of the billing and finance department when they introduced their new counselling scheme. Again, these traits exhibit many of the things we know about adult learning.

Brookfield (1986), Rogers (1986) and Cullingford (1990) each stress how learning occurs in stages. Some people may go through a number of stages at more or less the same time, whereas others need longer periods of time and may need to pass through separate learning stages (Brookfield, 1986). Thus, stages of learning and the time needed to engage with them are an important aspect to learning, influenced perhaps by prior experience and prior learning on which new learning can be based. Rogers (1986, p. 141) concludes that the majority of psychologists agree that at all levels, and in all major types of learning, there are four stages or steps. He describes these as: **play, structured play, grasping,** and **mastery**. He goes on to define 'mastery' not as an end point in itself but as:

> . . . practice, not just learning but using, exploring material or process further, discovering more relationships and obtaining mastery over it. This in turn leads to new learning needs and intentions, new skills or concepts. The process is a dynamic ongoing one.

However, before something can be practised an individual, or an organization as a collective entity, has to be attracted to something and then motivated to get to know more about it. There then follows a period of play, and if what is being considered seems to be helpful or useful and worthwhile then an individual tends to go into the practice stage in the hope that this will lead to mastery. Thus, for the purposes of analysis a modified pattern of learning stages is suggested, comprising:

attraction. . . . motivation. . . . play. . . . practice. . . . mastery

These five stages correspond closely to the Royal Society of Arts 'Learning Pays' (1991) report which describes learning phases as 'foundation' (dependency stage), 'formation' (transitional stage), and 'continuation' (independency stage) and to which the writer (Jones and Hendry, 1992) added the stages of 'transformation' and 'transfiguration'.

To develop a learning-centred environment then, it is necessary to have a clear view of an individual's or group's stage of learning in the learning process and across each activity with which they are engaged. Few organizations ever do this. Where time is provided and a person is permitted to go through the learning stages then, by and large, mastery is achieved.

The Communications Manager case study example serves to illustrate this whereas when her firm set up a new three business unit structure and then abandoned it after only twelve months there was a clear illustration that one year was insufficient time for the new organizational structure to work. Too much was expected too soon from each unit head. They never got beyond the attraction/motivation/play stages of learning. Mastery was always beyond their reach.

The other firm with its numerous initiatives (quality, learning organization, business process re-engineering) simply created confusion. Just as staff were at the attraction and motivation stages of learning they were thrust into another venture which required them to start with something new and so produced the same result. As a consequence they were rarely allowed to master anything of the corporate lessons being given to them. What can be labelled 'learning frustration' set in.

In summary, as a learning in organizations model is developed the stages of learning, 'attraction, motivation, play, practice and mastery' emerge as the 'learning theory' aspect of the model.

4 Learning Processes

The Communications Manager case study example illustrates that as an individual she went through some of the same processes, as the new networks with which she engaged. Her personal, general interest in communications and information technology led her to want to know more. She was attracted and motivated by the theory and practice. She subsequently made enquiry as to how this interest could be developed, and engaged in the play and practice aspects of learning by taking a part-time degree course. The degree programme provided her with the time to develop her ideas and during this period she was able to share her new found knowledge and expertise with her colleagues and advise them on information technology applications in the organization's other activities — for example, the marketing arm established a computerized data base for the first time in the firm's history.

She demonstrated her mastery of computerized systems in her ability to advise the despatch and mailing department on computerized mailing systems, the front-of-house receptionist about computerized mail-voice telephone answering, and revealed her ability in 'exploring material . . . discovering more relationships. . . . new learning needs and intensions. . . .' when she was able to devise a new computerized time management programme to replace the hand-held system.

The organization now had a new level of expertise. The Communications Manager had been able to apply her new knowledge and skills in a specific context on the way to mastering them. She was then able to generate a new network of applications working with other people in the organization and had demonstrated that things could be done differently.

A further example from the same firm also illustrates the point. Two brothers were the main owners of the firm and, despite many setbacks, they persevered with their American operation, subsequently mastered it, and turned it from a heavy financial loss position into a profitable one. This took time, concentration, effort, and clear focus which led them to master emerging key skills for success in dealing with the US market. A new level of expertise was created.

In contrast the quality focus company was too busy attempting to create whole organizational change with the expectation that people wanted it, understood it, and would conform to it. The learning, such as it was, was director controlled. Because the directors considered something was worthwhile the staff had to do likewise. The numerous ensuing staff and communication audits sought to assess conformity. The language used by the board and the human resource department staff was always that of 'informing', to produce 'conforming' activity.

In this quality-led organization two female human resource department staff were given responsibility for creating the learning organization culture and they frequently emphasized the top-down approach to learning. Learning was in the minds and heads of management, whose task it is was to tell others what they needed to know and do. For example, they reported to the writer that:

> Ninety per cent of the staff feel that our new initiative is . . . on-going.

> . . . our learning organization work has achieved . . .

> Cascading events were held to inform people . . .

Briefing sessions were a regular part of daily life in the company but, all the passing on of information to secure compliance and allegiance, simply left people stressed and resentful. The observation by one senior manager that the firm had 'all these Jumbo jets in the air' is a vivid description of the chaos created by too many initiatives, with few ever being mastered. This company's activities further illustrate how learning was perceived by the directors as compliance. There had to be a use of 'corporate language', and 'overall management agreement throughout the organization for consistency' despite the fact that most managers had their own individualistic styles.

What then do these observations reveal about further developing a learning in organizations model? Research on adult learning processes (Brundage and Mackeracher, 1980; Darkenwald and Merriam 1982; Knowles 1980, 1984) reveal the need to create 'stopping-off' places in the learning process, or what Kornbluh and Greene (1989) refer to as 'provisional encapsulations'. These encapsulations allow individuals time to assess and practice what they have learned, understand it more clearly, and decide upon its relevance, success, and application, or whether to abandon it. The opportunity for abandoning something is also a crucial aspect in the learning process.

These resting places provide periods for reflection and permit time for new things to be learned, mastered, and brought to fruition. 'Provisional encapsulations' allow space to determine whether people are genuinely engaging in learning that is valuable and having effect, or whether it is simply confirming that nothing radical, important, or meaningful is taking place — what Lennerlof (1989) contrasts as 'learned influence' or 'learned helplessness'. This is important because few organizations readily permit individuals or groups to abandon or jettison what they do not understand, or feel is not worthwhile and appropriate. Instead, learning becomes an indoctrination process. This was certainly the case in the two organizations mentioned above. Change programmes in the two organizations proceeded on the assumption that everyone would engage with the ideas, processes, and activities being promulgated by senior management.

Linking Learning Stages and Learning Process

In developing the model further there is a need to link learning theory (stages) with what may be called the management of learning (process). Firstly, in the two learning stages of 'attraction' and 'motivation' individuals make up what, in the educational literature, are termed by Susan Jones (1994) as 'communities of enquiry'. This notion fits well with andragogical principles where adult groups develop, and are sustained by, enquiry and learning generated by the work they do and the particular interests they possess.

Secondly, if provisional encapsulations are needed in the learning process then this generally corresponds to the play and practice learning stages. In the periods of encapsulation individuals engage with practising what they have already been attracted and motivated towards.

Thirdly, the educational psychology literature (Cullingford, 1990) also focuses on 'communities of learning' in which individuals and teams continue to master their learning and develop it so that it is refined and progressed. In so doing, the community of learning then gets itself back, at various times, into becoming a community of enquiry when new things attract them and have to be learned.

Learning and Change

The two organizations mentioned above also wanted to link learning with change and this was a key feature of their activity. However, if an organization deliberately wants to engage learning with change then an extension of the model is needed which links learning theory and practice to the management literature.

Pettigrew (1992) notes that 'islands of progress' seem to be an important element in leading sustained change processes so that people get a clear and concrete grasp of the fact that their efforts are producing something which is worthwhile within a reasonable period of time. As Pettigrew observes:

> The need for major alterations. . . . (is) not met by analysis alone, nor even by major programmes of radical change. What stands out is the use of modest islands of progress. . . .

He further notes that communicating the realisation that something was working and shows signs of success is:

> . . . invaluable in sustaining the momentum of a complicated set of changes.

And adds that:

> The political implications of such actions are far reaching. Fixed, elaborate hierarchies act as a brake. The exploitation of often impermanent, less formal internal and external networks seem far better suited to managing the necessary changes.

March and Olsen (1989) make much the same point indicating that most institutions still succeed or develop without transformational or instant change processes. They claim that institutions need to allow the informal networks which people create to develop, and what they term 'extensive adjustment periods' (1989, p. 55) must be tolerated to enable 'diverse, conflicting, and inefficient solutions' to be weeded out. This is essential in their view because the quality of institutional dreams (visions and missions) have to be measured against the quality of the implementation of that dream and the two are quite distinct. They conclude that institutional dreams can be dangerous because they raise too great an expectation:

> We are driven to the question of 'efficacy' whether an institution produces in an imperfect world what it promises in an imaginery one and whether the failures can be remedied without undue cost. We ask whether pursuing a specific virtuous vision brings good citizens closer to, or more distant from, the good life. . . . Asking such questions establishes a framework for evaluation that is . . . broader than the usual one. . . . (March and Olsen, 1989, p. 129)

So, a further measure of a learning organization from a change perspective may be the extent to which the organization provides 'islands of progress' at the time of 'provisional encapsulation' which generate 'learned influence' (the realization that something is working). If an individual or a group determine that they are engaging with 'learned helplessness' – that is, further work is needed to create an 'island of progress' or that a particular encapsulation period is not leading to an 'island of progress' then remedial action can be taken or the activity abandoned.

Although the Hendry, Jones and Cooper (1994, p. 19) work on the creation of learning organizations does not specifically use the term 'islands of progress', it does illustrates how 'pockets of success' (islands of progress) in Courtaulds Aerospace Advanced Materials Division acted as catalysts to speed up and slow down learning at particular factory sites, and across the whole organization in terms of general management learning. The study also illustrates how success and progress of this kind are linked to the informal networks they term 'communities of practice'.

The study shows the importance of communities of practice which then begin to formalize themselves and become interlinked. In brief, communities of practice are the groups which form in any organization outside the job specifications and structures which the organization itself constructs to tell people how things should be done. People become experts in a particular skill or product line and tend to network with other groups, especially where the attitudes and work of one group closely link with that of another. Each rely on the other. In any organization there are many such 'communities of practice' and the way these form and re-form are:

> . . . the key to whole organizational change. Change at the single 'community of practice' level can create an internal laboratory for learning and change, and act as a model for other 'communities of practice' because most people . . . belong to more than one 'community of practice'. 'Communities of practice' represent the way work is really done, and are fundamental to whole organizational change. (Hendry, Jones and Cooper, 1994, p. 21)

This hypothesis is borne out by Beer (1990) and his associates who maintain that: change occurs in pockets of an organization not at the centre or across the organization as a whole; that embedded change and learning occur when there is a concentration on employee roles, responsibilities and relationships; there are particular parts of an organization that are more adaptable to change; and the key to understanding whole organization change is to concentrate on how individual parts collectively adapt on an incremental basis over time. They finally conclude that successful learning and change occur when individual expectations are seen to be as important as organizational ones.

Summarizing the Evaluation Criteria

In summary, the proposed evaluation criteria for looking at learning in organizations are the extent to which an organization deliberately:

- Exhibits an approach to learning and development based on 'andragogical' principles and practices and the processes by which these are brought about.
- Encourages 'communities of inquiry' which become at the same time 'communities of practice' which are allowed to surface in the organization and impact on it.
- Provides 'provisional encapsulation' which, in turn produce 'islands of progress' to generate 'learned influence' (preferably) or 'learned helplessness', in that people can be allowed to jetisson that which they feel and know does not work.
- Links values to business imperatives and operational issues and allows them to develop naturally.

The Final Stages for a Learning Organization Schema

Having provided periods of progress and times for encapsulation people have to go on to conclude the learning process and, where applicable, change processes. This is the mastery stage in the learning literature. Pettigrew, Ferlie, and McKee (1992) identify the need for organizations to produce 'sanctuaries of comfort' and the learning literature (Illich, 1971; Brookfield, 1986; Kenny and Reid, 1988) notes the need for 'communities of learning' which develop at the mastery stage of learning to permit refinement and further development of what has been learned. As the sanctuaries develop so the people making up such groups become the technicians in their area of expertise and establish themselves as the further researchers and developers. In undertaking these tasks they remain in their community of expertise but also spawn new communities of inquiry and practice. All of this occurs in an episodic manner over whatever period of time an individual or a particular group may need. The cyle of learning in organizations begins again. Figure 8.1 illustrates the complete learning in organizations schema. Its emphasis is on people working and learning together because:

> The more we understand the way in which any organization works the more we see the difference between the changes willed on us by the person in command and the actual changes in spirit and level of work. Organizations change as a consequence of changes in individual self-concepts. (Cullingford 1990, p. 220)

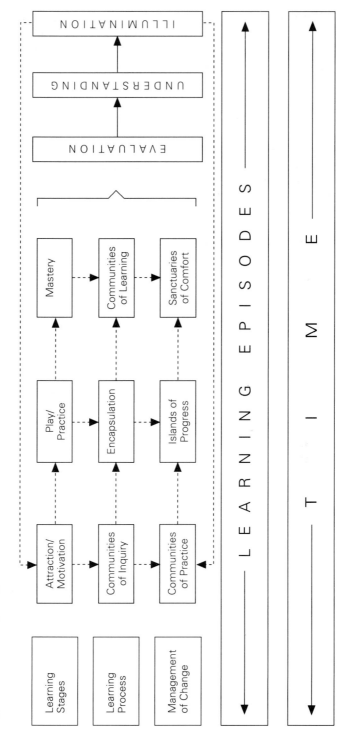

Figure 8.1: A learning in organizations model

Figure 8.1 represents the main criteria for creating a learning framework to develop, track, and evaluate learning in an organization. It also provides a clear assessment level in terms of the management of change in organizations and the influence learning has on the change process. The model emphasizes how learning and change can be developed and evaluated as short-term activities (episodes) which are also part of longer-term learning events. Once illumination occurs, the learner is led back to the beginning of the model as new circumstances demand that the newly found knowledge, skills, developed relationships, or organizational structures require still further development.

The model allows for all learning to be assessed in terms of value over time. Extended and short-term learning episodes can be evaluated against the value they bring to the individual and the organization. Employees are provided with in-built, systematic periods of time to reflect on learning processes and events to bring their learning to complete fruition. At each stage of learning development the model allows for individuals and groups to establish specific learning development agendas. What emerges therefore is not so much a model of what a learning organization looks like but rather a model for effectively analyzing learning in an organization, hence the use of the label 'learning-in-organizations' model.

Conclusion and Summary

The 'learning-in-organizations' model developed in this chapter has emerged inductively from the writer's assessment and review of the learning organization literature, adult learning theory, and the management of change literature. The model seeks to combine adult learning theory with ideas about the learning organization and the evidence which has emerged from the data collected from the writer's own empirical work. The model's aim is to allow the complexity of learning to surface in a way which provides a qualitative approach to understanding how people develop in organizations.

References

BEER, M., EISENSTAT, R.A. and SPECTOR, B. (1990) 'Why change programs don't produce change', *Harvard Business Review*, **68**, 61, pp. 158–66.
BROOKFIELD, S.D. (1986) *Understanding and Facilitating Adult Learning*, Milton Keynes, Open University Press.
BRUNDAGE, D.H. and MACKERACHER, D. (1980) *Adult Learning Principles and Their Application to Program Planning*, Toronto, Ministry of Education, Ontario.
COLLINS, J. and PORRAS, J. (1991) *Organizational Visions and Visionary Organizations*, Research Paper 1159, Stanford, California, Stanford University Graduate School of Business.
CULLINGFORD, C. (1990) *The Nature of Learning*, London, Cassell.

DARKENWALD, G.G. and MERRIAM, S.B. (1982) *Adult Education: Foundation and Principles*, New York, Harper & Row.

EISNER, E.W. (1976) 'Educational connoisseurship and criticism: Their form and functions and educational evaluation', *Journal of Aesthetic Education*, **10**(3–4), pp. 135–50.

GLASER, B.G. and STRAUSS, A.L. (1967) *The Discovery of Grounded Theory*, Chicago, Aldine.

GUBA, E.G. (1978) *Toward a Methodology of Naturalistic Inquiry in Educational Evaluation*, SE Monograph Series in Evaluation, no. 8, Los Angeles, Center for the Study of Evaluation, University of California.

GUBA, E.G. and LINCOLN, Y.S. (1981) *Effective Evaluation: Improving the Usefulness of Evaluation Results Through Responsive and Naturalistic Approaches*, San Francisco, Jossey-Bass.

HAMBLIN, A.C. (1974) *Evaluation and Control of Training*, Maidenhead, McGraw-Hill.

HAYES, R.H., WHEELWRIGHT, S.C. and CLARKE, K.B. (1988) *Dynamic Manufacturing: Creating The Learning Organization*, London, The Free Press.

HENDRY, C. and JONES, A.M. with COOPER, N. (1994) *Creating a Learning Organization: Strategies for Change*, Sutton Coldfield, Man-made Fibres Industry Training Organization.

HERBST, G. (1976) *Alternative to Hierarchies*, Leiden, Hand Van Beinum Foundation for Business Administration.

HERRIOT, P. (1992) *The Career Management Challenge*, London, Sage.

ILLICH, I. (1971) *Deschooling Society*, London, Calder and Boyars.

JONES, A.M. and HENDRY, C. (1992) *The Learning Organization: A Review of Literature and Practice*, London, HRD Partnership.

JONES, S. (1994) *The Human Factor*, London, Kogan Page.

KANTER, R.M. (1984) 'Managing transitions in organizational culture: The case of participative management at Honeywell', in J.R. KIMBERLY and R.E. QUINN, *Managing Organizational Transitions*, Homewood, Illinois, Richard D. Irwin, Inc.

KANTER, R.M. (1985) *The Change Masters: Corporate Entrepreneurs at Work*, London, Unwin Hyman.

KANTER, R.M. (1989) *When Giants Learn To Dance*, London, Simon & Schuster Ltd.

KENNY, J. and REID, M. (1988) *Training Interventions*, London, IPM.

KNOWLES, M.S. (1980) *The Modern Practice of Adult Education: From Pedagogy to Andragogy* (2nd edition), New York, Cambridge Books.

KNOWLES, M.S. and ASSOCIATES (1984) *Andragogy in Action: Applying Modern Principles of Adult Learning*, San Francisco, Jossey-Bass.

KORNBLUH, H. and GREENE, R.T. (1989) 'Learning, empowerment and participative work processes: The educative work environment', in H. LEYMANN, and H. KORNBLUH, *Socialization and Learning at Work*, Aldershot, Avebury.

LENNERLOF, L. (1989) 'Learning at work: Some basic findings', in H. LEYMANN, and H. KORNBLUH (eds) *Socialization and Learning at Work*, Aldershot, Avebury.

LINCOLN, Y.S. and GUBA, E.G. (1985) *Naturalistic Inquiry*, Beverly Hills, California, Sage.

MAGER, R. (1984) *Preparing Instructional Objectives*, San Francisco, Fearon Publishers.

MARCH, J.G. and OLSEN, J. (1989) *Rediscovering Institutions*, New York, Free Press.

Alan Jones

PATTON, M.Q. (1980) *Qualitative Evaluation Methods*, Beverly Hills, California, Sage.

PEDLER, M., BOYDELL, T. and BURGOYNE, J.G. (1988) *Learning Company Project: A Report on Work Undertaken October, 1987 to April, 1988*, Sheffield, The Training Agency.

PETTIGREW, A.M., FERLIE, E. and MCKEE, L. (1992) 'Shaping strategic change — the case of the NHS in the 1990s, *Public Money and Management*, **12** (3), July–September.

PETTIGREW, A.M. (1992) 'Managing Change for Competitive Success', paper presented to the Accounting Association of Australia and New Zealand, Annual Conference, 5–8 July, Palmerston North, New Zealand.

ROGERS, A. (1986) *Teaching Adults*, Milton Keynes, Open University Press.

SCRIVEN, M. (1967) 'The methodology of evaluation', in R.M. GANE, M. SCRIVEN, and R.W. TYLER, (eds) *Perspectives on Curriculum Evaluation*, AERA Monograph, **1**, Skokie, Illinois, Rand McNally.

SENGE, P. (1990) *The Fifth Discipline: The Art and Practice of the Learning Organization*, London, Century.

STAKES, R.L. (1981) 'Conceptualising evaluation in adult education', *Lifelong Learning: The Adult Years*, **4**(8) pp. 4–5, 22–23.

STUFFLEBEAM, D.L. *et al.* (1971) *Educational Evaluation and Decision-Making in Education*, Itasca: Illinois, Peacock.

TENBRINK, T.D. (1974) *Evaluation: A Practical Guide for Teachers*, New York, McGraw-Hill.

THIEDE, W. (1964) 'Evaluation and adult education', in G. JENSEN A.A. LIVERIGHT, and W.C. HALLENBECK, (eds) *Adult Education: Outlines of an Emerging Field of University Study*, Washington D.C., Adult Education Association of the USA.

Chapter 9

Towards the Virtual Library: Deconstruction and Reconstruction of Learning Resources in Higher Education

Alasdair Paterson

Once perceived as among the most conservative of operations — provinces of hush and dust — academic libraries everywhere are accepted to be in a condition of continuous change. Where that once unequivocal name *library* persists, the semantics are understood to extend beyond print on paper, beyond volumes on shelves, to include materials accessed through audio-visual and information technologies and their convergences; increasingly, in academic institutions, the preferred title of *library and information service* or *learning resources centre* makes more explicit the change in emphasis, in role. University librarians no longer think of themselves as exclusively (or in many cases, significantly) people of the book, and their public image has developed beyond that of the scholar *manqué*. They are managers: of a building, of staff, of collections, of services, of systems, of everything the word library has implied, but above all, of information.

Information, in these ebbing years of the century, certainly takes some managing. Never has so much information been produced around the globe and never has such a small proportion of it been represented on the shelves of the average research library, whether the information comes in units as large as 'Middlemarch' or as small as a mathematical equation. The productivity of world scholarship exceeds more and more the purchasing power of library budgets. Yet there is no piece of information, no recorded thought, no discovery to which one of our users may not want access; here at least survives something of that ambition to encompass all knowledge which lies at the root of the word 'university'. At the same time, the needs of undergraduates rarely stretch to the abstruse but do require primary and secondary materials which are as immediately and plentifully available as possible; a decline in student book-buying in recent years, for wholly understandable reasons, has increased the pressure in this sector. The boast of older universities that their teaching is research-led, that there are many benefits to undergraduates in being directed in their learning by someone who is an active, leading-edge researcher, translates in library terms into another competitive tug on resources, with academic researchers at the end of the day unwilling to sacrifice their information needs for the sake of those of student learners.

Peering into this information blizzard, particularly on the research side, academic libraries have developed 'access to information' policies as a less unaffordable alternative to building comprehensive collections on their own shelves, using remote databases (though still largely of bibliographic references rather than full text) and document delivery (typically photocopies of periodical articles obtained through the British Library Document Supply Centre) to continue to pursue the service objective of bringing in the right information within the least elapsed time at the least incurred cost. To put it another way, purchase 'just in case' has been replaced to a considerable extent by supply 'just in time' — although, as our efforts have gone into facilitating the discovery of what there is out there in the 'docuverse' (as it has inevitably been labelled), so too our academic users find themselves contending with a glut of information, a superfluity of the apparently relevant, endlessly renewed. I am reminded of Jorge Luis Borges' story 'Funes the memorious' (Borges, 1970), in which a young man, following an accident, suffers physical paralysis with an accompanying mental alteration which renders him incapable of forgetting anything. To recover every nuance of every day he has lived through (including every word of everything he has read) he views as a stupendous compensation, but unable to generalize, unable to categorize, unable to bring things to a conclusion and move on, he finally dies of congestion of the lungs.

What academic libraries have been through in recent years en route to the present situation is well logged in the Follett report, produced by the Joint Funding Councils' Libraries Review Group chaired by Sir Brian Follett (JFCLRG, 1994) — indeed the very existence of the report points to the concern of the academic community that present requirements and future developments on and off campus are being imperilled by a lack of library and information resources. The report itemizes the trends over the late 1980s and early 1990s:

- the reducing purchasing power of library grants;
- the continuing explosion in information in all formats;
- periodicals (the *lifeblood of research*, another circulatory metaphor of the kind which installs the library as the *heart of the campus*) as an area of accelerated inflation and publication but reducing purchase;
- remodelling of the academic year (modules, semesters and the imminence of the two-year degree);
- pressure on services and space.

In the face of this, 'access to information' seems a more sustainable policy, though American librarians, taking the business of predicting the future to its *reductio ad absurdum*, have estimated that in twenty years' time, if current trends continue, no academic libraries will be buying any books or journals — just lending them to each other! To cope meantime with these trends, we've instituted essentially short-term, ground-holding operations — annual rounds of periodical cancellations, attempts at protection of book budgets, space rationalization. In other words, we're waiting for the cavalry to arrive.

This cavalry is unlikely to be followed by wagons full of gold. Salvation lies in unpicking the tangle into which academia has, somewhat myopically, got itself. Rethinking the balance of teaching and research support expenditure must be part of that, as must be urgent attention to the disastrous ecosystem of scholarly communication which sees universities give away expensively-generated research to commercial publishers and then buy it back at annual inflation rates (I'm thinking of the past two years) of some 20 per cent. We expect the eventual solutions to be delivered by information technology, following some brisk exchanges on intellectual property, but as we scan the horizon anxiously for relief we're also aware that, here and now: electronic access is largely at the bibliographical level; access to electronically-stored full text is limited; and document delivery is expensive, less than immediate and experienced as a poor substitute for material on shelves.

Beyond all this, however, gleams the vision (mirage?) of the 'virtual library' — the world of comprehensive electronically-housed information deliverable directly to the scholar's own workstation on the scholar's own desktop, infinitely more searchable, demolishing barriers of location and time. For the student, multimedia will allow a liberating blend of core texts online, structured modules to work through, live or recorded videos of lectures, group interaction and shared or individual project development, monitoring by teachers online — all available wherever a terminal is (including study bedrooms and remote homes). Getting there, however, is going to be messy and the basic managerial challenge will continue to be the management of change, possibly glossed as the management of chaos. Networks such as the world-wide Internet and the British Joint Academic Network (JANET and now SuperJANET) promise the electronic global village, but problems of infrastructure costs, network standards and protocols, academic culture (in which prestige and readership still depend on print publication) and intellectual ownership (which blocks electronic sharing) are still considerable.

This period of deconstruction and reconstruction which lies (immediately and indefinitely) before us will see us move away from what we can't sustain and re-examine what it is that, as libraries, we can offer our institutions. But it means a transitional and expensive time — we can't summarily abandon the approaches and skills which will guarantee a university education and support a research effort, both of which will still in part rely on conventional, paper-based distribution of information, but we also have to move further into the world of networked information and confront the changes this will make for us and our users. Information will go on being produced at an accelerating rate, and technology will be vital not only in helping us access it but also in unpacking the bundles — periodicals, books — in which we have been accustomed to buy it.

Of course it would be futile to pretend that academic librarians are autonomous beings, with *carte blanche* to redesign their services without taking into account what the university is up to. Indeed, however library-centred the librarian's model of the academic universe, it must be conceded that there are planetary influences around and above us which determine much of what we do — and a music of the spheres, usually in the form of a series of unharmonious questions, we strain to hear and act on. Will we see more students priced out of higher education? How far will the unit of resource be driven down? Will the long-heralded separation of universities into divisions, into research and teaching universities, or within universities into research and teaching departments, take place? Will higher education become more important nationally than other, competing budget heads? Will there be new, mould-breaking ways to access higher education? And what is the purpose, what is the ultimate benefit in all this? The answers to these will greatly determine how a library and information service discerns its role.

Certainly, universities are currently suffering under a regime of 'more with less', which throws tremendous pressure on academic services. How many more, how much less? The CBI canvasses that:

> The Government's approach should be fundamentally revised so that the UK aims for a minimum graduation target of 40 per cent rather than a participation target of 33 per cent of young people by the year 2000. Significant increases in higher education participation by mature people should also be expected. (CBI, 1994)

Even from the present library perspective, as student numbers of all kinds grow, so books are heavily competed for, space and seating is at a premium and the likelihood that research students will not find research collections in their topic on the shelves increases. At the same time teaching staff/student ratios lengthen and the logic of student-centred learning demands more overtly that academic libraries become guarantors of a university education, which is increasingly a matter of the individual learner and their needs. Librarians find themselves acting more and more as advisors, demonstrators of technologies and information tools, instructors in information skills, in self-help. The stimulating Fielden report on human resource management in academic libraries (Fielden, 1993), a pendant to the Follett report, views this as the shape of things to come:

Professional staff will be expected to play a greater role in learner support . . . and their liaison role with academic departments will become central to their functions. Thus, a new form of convergence, which we call 'academic convergence' will gradually develop.

Universities are also in search of new markets and are responding to demands which impose a rethinking of their traditional role; they are now looking to increase the part-time student base, to engage with learning activities in local regions and to address distance learning. All of these have implications for information and information technology resources. Here we lag a little behind the USA, which allows us to profit by example. What we are still labelling 'non-traditional' students (mature, part-time or evening) are already so numerous in the USA as to be talked of in higher education circles as the 'New Majority'. Problems of scarce time and inconvenient distances to travel are severe for this group and for those teaching and providing services for them; solutions which make creative use of technology are allowing colleges to improve access and also to tap new areas for potential expansion of student numbers.

Very much an example of innovative practice (I select one from many) is the University of Maine's welding together of a regional Community College. Barriers to conventional distance learning in Maine are particularly acute, with a sparse and dispersed population of potential *Roads Scholars* further disadvantaged by heavy snow and the threat of any winter drive ending with a moose on the hood. The backbone of the Community College is therefore an electronic one; it assists TV, computer and phone linkages, it delivers learning, allows teacher–student and student–student interaction, permits interrogation of on-line library catalogues and facilitates the movement of resources such as library books around the system. Beyond the several University of Maine campuses are an array of colleges, schools and other centres where students can access university education. This model, with its broadcasting classrooms, electronic texts, shippable libraries and on-line essay-marking, sounds alienating; unexpectedly, students report a greater feeling of personal attention, of one-to-one, than in a campus dominated by mass lectures and overcrowded tutorials, while the important peer contact takes place with other local students with similar experiences.

An explicit part of progress in innovative teaching on US campuses is a whole staffing tier, largely missing in older British universities, dedicated to instructional support. Such staff, going by a variety of titles (such as instructional designer, educational technologist) are the lynchpins of developments in their respective campuses: investigating new technological possibilities; available to suggest or jointly author software solutions for faculty teaching problems; able to coordinate and communicate IT-based innovations across campus; concerned to overcome the barriers to the spread of educational technology. Library staff, already moving into the more active learning support areas described, find themselves participating in the cross-campus teams which result from this approach, helping to generate multimedia teaching packs and other CAL applications, assembling, packaging, distributing, assisting, managing.

All of this is slowly being translated into the British context, with some local variations. For example, in some British cities companies have won cable TV franchises which commit them to taking optical cable, capable of carrying telephone, digital and video signals, past every house within the city boundaries, potentially allowing any student in a hall of residence or in a bedsit to connect up, interrogate the library catalogue and the emerging banks of full text and graphics/video from their own bedside, indeed move into the huge learning resources of the Internet without coming near the library or the university. Unsurprisingly, universities are in earnest dialogue with these providers, and this is one way in which the virtual library could be enabled. Not just for those in search of degrees either — the opportunity for fuller university involvement with the learning needs of its region, at school, at home or in the workplace, for qualification or for self-development, is very exciting. The question of who is, or who could be, a student, is once more up for redefinition, and the learning assets of the university have the potential of being open to all — indeed, if a clustering of local further education institutions around a degree-validating university develops as a pattern in future years, with a matching partnership between libraries and learning resource centres, the resulting pool of knowledge and resources makes the most ambitious programmes feasible. The Maine model is suggestive, but clustering as envisaged above offers more empowerment to the individual learner — and, let it be said, to universities in search of a leadership role. Learning resources in such a context would be based, not just on those owned by the hub university and the associated institutions, but on the world of networked information into whose more than somewhat tangled luxuriance both have already cut (rather different) paths.

It's possible to infer from what I've said of the activity, that the approach of the academic library is invariably dependent on that of the university. This is not entirely true. Firstly, academic libraries have always seen advantages in a cooperation which sometimes seems to conflict sharply with institutional competitiveness; local and regional information plans, inter-lending schemes, joint purchases, access for each other's academic staff and (in vacations) students, all show a belief that such activities enhance the availability of information on a national and regional basis, and ultimately benefit one's own institutional members. Secondly, academic libraries have struggled hard to ensure an expenditure in support of teaching and learning as well as research; in institutions which are research-led, the claims of undergraduates for adequate study materials are often drowned by the shouts from their departments for better research collections, particularly more periodicals, and it is the library which tries to rectify institutional myopia to what is after all its bread and butter, under-graduate teaching and learning. This makes strategic alliances between library managements and student officers more frequent than might be suspected. Thirdly, academic libraries have not shut their doors on the local community; access to university collections, if not the right to bor-row, is available to all, usually free; borrowing rights are available for modest annual fees and sometimes, for special categories such as teachers, waived altogether. This is experienced by university students particularly as an extra competitive pressure on seating and stock availability, but the public access principle is broadly maintained. The advent of the virtual library of course offers liberation from the limitations of a paper-based resource, from the competition for physical seats and physical copies, and one would expect the benefits of this to be shared by the locality, the city and the region — yet in another way wider access is threatened.

Connectivity is one thing, intellectual property rights another. Li-brarians, authors and publishers have historically struggled to balance common sense and fair dealing (slippery terms) through several parlia-mentary stabs at copyright legislation; now computer technology, with its almost infinite potential for distributed access, its superlative ease of copy-ing and searching, brings new disequilibriums. Publishers are very appre-hensive of the electronic book and journal, not least because they have no way at present of calculating a realistic figure for selling access (and an unknown potential multiple access) to electronic files — whereas they have learned to live with, factor in and to an extent control photocopying and library lending of print editions. The outcome is a much more strin-gent control. To buy a site licence for an electronic database (even where this is possible and affordable) is to accept limitations at the building, site, or institutional membership level. Where only *bona fide* members of the institution can access on-line data, the situation is actually worse than in the *ancien regime* of print, where anyone with access to the shelf (or to the national inter-lending system) can read the book; the electronic media which enhance the potential of wider networking of information also offer the potential for monopoly and pricing structures which could make the virtual library another temple of the elite. As I have written elsewhere:

> How much information will remain in the public domain and be accessed according to social need, and how much the prerogative of those who can pay? In the middle ages, to be poor in a worldly sense was also to be poor in information; you pieced together what you could of world history and the articles of your faith from the bright wall-paintings of the parish church, while the

priest intoned the Mass in an unknown language. Our efforts as librarians must be to prevent any comparable impoverishment in our information-rich age; if history does repeat itself in this respect, it will be both as tragedy and as farce. (Paterson, 1989)

For library staff, therefore, the next ten years will be enormously challenging — not least the need to stay alert to commercially-induced impoverishment of available information and individual information users, to the seeds of a dystopia. Print culture will be alive and kicking throughout this period, and we will have to use a familiar blend of house-keeping skills and financial ingenuity to sustain this. At the same time, the building blocks of the virtual library will begin to fall into place and we will have to make decisions about what new services to integrate; eventually this will change into deciding which traditional products and services to stop providing as the virtual library switches on a few more lights. There will be ongoing training and development, and an increasing role in training our users, indeed teaching core modules in information skills, for a familiarity with a large information provision system such as a progressive academic library, and with text-based information on-line, will form a necessary component in the accomplishments necessary for life in the twenty-first century. Our 'just in case' purchasing and storage will be overtaken by the publishers, with their backlists on electronic files, looking after the 'just in case', and us having things printed out or electronically transmitted, in whole or in part, 'just in time'. We may find ourselves involved in administering textbook rental schemes, negotiating individually or in consortia with commercial publishers to digitize texts or to produce tailored textbooks drawn from a number of pre-existing sources — one American publishing house already offers a customized course textbook service based on its extensive digitized backlist, allowing a pick-and-mix of sections, chapters, pages. . . . Later, we may take on the roles of sellers and distributors of our universities' own campus-produced material in electronic format. As accessing and using sources — or later as sellers and distributors of our own campus-produced material in electronic format.

As accessing and using information leaves the physical library behind, so too will librarians move out into the wider campus, pursuing transformed roles. Inescapable too will be the movement within institutions from the *information technology* strategies that most now have in place, basically infrastructure and hardware-based, towards an *information* strategy, seeing the processes of accessing, collecting, storing and using information in a holistic way; so, as problems with copyright and networking standards are overcome, as technologies converge, as electronic information is mapped and tamed, all libraries will inexorably become the Library.

References

BORGES, J.L. (1970) *Labyrinths,* London, Penguin Books.

CBI (1994) *Thinking Ahead: Ensuring the Expansion of Higher Education into the 21st Century*, London, CBI.

JOINT FUNDING COUNCILS LIBRARIES REVIEW GROUP (1994) *Report,* HEFCE

JOHN FIELDEN CONSULTANCY (1993) 'Supporting expansion: A report on human resource management in academic libraries for the Joint Funding Councils Library Review Group', Bristol, the Higher Education Funding Council for England.

PATERSON, A. (1989) 'Trends in medieval librarianship: Medieval to modern times', *An Leabharlann/The Irish Librarian*, Second Series, **6**(1), pp. 17–34.

Chapter 10

Structures and Funding

Tony Cann

Introduction

Our place in the world, our future as a nation, the success and happiness of our population depends on the UK becoming a learning society. The problem we face is that it is not satisfactory to make slow progress. The rest of the world does not stand still. Recent changes, such as the opening of eastern Europe and China, on top of developments in other parts of Asia and other parts of the world, make the need to develop as a high added value, technically based economy more urgent. I see it everywhere, every day. Medium technology products manufactured in under-developed countries flood into Britain under western brand names, and I know international textile companies whose most productive factories are in China. Others are manufacturing in eastern Europe where the wages are a sixth of the UK levels, and are planning to manufacture a few miles to the east in western Russia where the wage levels are one sixth of those in eastern Europe. Our competitive position now depends on high added value products and on our ability to compete with other high added value economies. Yet we talk only about catching up on their current achievements — while they too continue to move forcefully to even higher levels of productivity and skills, and the talk is at the general level of aspiration, not the specifics of action. It is of catching up, not leading.

The need for a learning society to convert and compete is not just urgent. It is a matter of economic life and death. It is a matter of social success or disaster. It is survival. Why, oh why, does it take so long to realize? It revolves round structures and funding issues. John Ruskin said, 'What we say or what we think is of no consequence. The only consequence is what we do.' We are not really doing enough, quickly enough. Why not?

The Need for Leadership

My fundamental observation is that we need consistent leadership and policies which give cohesion and are founded on integrity. We have a stable government but during five years as Chairman of a Training and Enterprise Council (TEC) I have been responsible to five different Secretaries of State. All have been brilliant, fine people. Each, however, has come with their own emphasis. Can effective leadership evolve from this system? It is made worse as the civil service, which serves the government, also enjoys the game of short-term musical chairs and, though outstandingly capable people, civil servants seldom possess particular expertise. It is like driving a high performance motor car on a race track. If you are trying to drive the car round the track at very high speed you need to understand the car and know the track in depth. TECs have tried to supply the system with knowledge of the car and the track and driving ability to give better results. It does not solve the leadership problem, but as many civil servants could, and do, act entrepreneurially, and can manage if trained, they could spend time on the track learning about it. They need first-hand experience at local level, for example, by secondment to TECs, preferably well away from atypical London. Similarly there are many people like those who have joined the Training and Enterprise Council Boards who spend time off the track helping the leadership.

The inconsistencies within Departments of State are made worse by major inconsistencies between them. The government machine seems to act like a number of uncoordinated separate groups. Conventional wisdom says that one Department of State should be responsible both for education and training. However, their approach is currently so different that an absorption of one by the other would either cause paralyzing alienation, or set back the small grinding progress that has been achieved in the progress towards greater skills over the past few years. Rhetoric like 'fusing the best of both departments' is not convincing. Had such fusion been possible it would have happened before now.

Understanding what policies will work and creating focussed goals is key to achieving them. Leadership is also about accepting responsibility for achieving the goals. Responsibility for achieving a learning society lies with the leadership, but Secretaries of State do not remain in post long enough to be judged while civil servants officially protect their ministers. Hard objectives are often avoided, forward targets are nebulous, and those adopted are progressively softened. The National Education and Training Targets (NETTS) for example were almost forced on Government, and it is not clear that the dates for their full implementation are being pursued with rigour. Who will take responsibility for their fulfilment? All this is made worse by the short-termism of the system. White Papers occasionally stray into the area of long-term strategic goals, but policy is more often determined by the three-year treasury planning cycle. So the effect is to avoid commitment to results in the knowledge that ministers will not be in place long enough to be accountable.

The White Paper *Competitiveness: Helping Business to Win* (Cm 2563) issued in May 1994 was welcome in that it attempted to create an overall strategic thrust. However, in effect it simply attempted to explain past policies in a retrospective apologetic way, avoiding priorities, and offering very little that was really new. It is a patchwork quilt of apologies. There need to be apologies if our current competitive position is so low. The conclusion is that we need a step change in skills creation not the gentle tinkering offered.

What leadership structures might we adopt nationally? Government has to delegate the responsibility to executive organizations while setting its goals. The key positions are held by the funding bodies and Investors in People (IiP). The funding bodies have control of money, but need goals more specific and visionary than the securing of 'sufficient and adequate provision' specified in the White Paper *Education and Training for the Twenty-first Century* (Cm 1536, 1991) and they need wider formalized consultative mechanisms. The Investors in People initiative has already achieved some success. By the end of 1994 there were over 10,000 organizations committed to it representing more than 16 per cent of the employed workforce, and nearly 1,200 already meeting its requirements (Cm 2563, page 41). It has taken hold as a vehicle for positive change. But the use of an independent organization to deliver national objectives is new — Investors in People UK was established as such only in 1993 — and is as yet untested. IiP UK needs teeth to strengthen the role of the Chief Executive and staff.

I have spent some time discussing the questions of leadership and responsibility as these are crucial in obtaining effective structure, focus, consistency and cohesion. An element in obtaining focus is integrity which I define as honesty of intention carried through with consistency into action. This precludes saying one thing and then acting as though it is something else. It precludes saying, for instance, that the skills of the workforce are critical and then failing to follow through with programmes and funding which supports the creation of skills in the workforce. It also precludes: claiming that new businesses are vital and then not encouraging those most likely to create successful businesses; claiming that coordinated business links are vital for local economic development, but only providing short-term funding for them; saying that employer initiatives are key to helping the education system, but at the same time withholding funding from them. A typical example is the change to Single Regeneration Budgets operated through Integrated Regional Offices proposed from 1995. A good idea in itself, but likely to cause waste through discontinuties and the unwillingness of government to think through the detail. All actions, or non-actions, of this sort create confusion, lack of confidence and defocus.

Converting Leadership to Results

If we can get consistent, coherent leadership with integrity we can achieve focus with urgency of implementation. We now need to convert this to results. But what results? The most important requirement is to pursue the National Education and Training Targets (NETTS) with the utmost seriousness. They are:

Foundation learning

1 By 1997, 80 per cent of young people to reach NVQ 2 (or equivalent).
2 Training and education to NVQ 3 (or equivalent) available to all young people who can benefit.
3 By 2000, 50 per cent of young people to reach NVQ 3 (or equivalent).
4 Education and training provision to develop self-reliance, flexibility and breadth.

Lifetime learning

1 By 1996, all employees should take part in training or development activities.
2 By 1996, 50 per cent of the workforce aiming for NVQs or units towards them.
3 By 2000, 50 per cent of the workforce qualified to at least NVQ 3 (or equivalent).
4 By 1996, 50 per cent of medium to larger organizations (200+ employees) to be 'Investors in People'.

We are making progress towards these targets, but the dates approach rapidly. The White Paper *Competitiveness: Helping Business to Win* (Cm 2563) reports 61 per cent of 16-year-olds reaching NVQ 2, or an equivalent standard, by 1993. So we have to add another 19 per cent — an increase of 30 per cent — in four years. At NVQ level 3 the progress is better. The same document reports 26 per cent of 17-year-olds are now achieving two 'A' level passes and predicts 50 per cent of 16–17-year-olds will be studying for GNVQs by 1996–1997. This not only suggests that this NETTS target will be reached but that, importantly, the balance will tip away from the long-standing over-emphasis on academic 'A' and 'A/S' levels. This leaves the learners aiming at NVQs where the most urgent needs are for better quality Youth Training opportunities and for far better part-time provision for young people at work. This is where we hope the proposed emphasis on 'Modern Apprenticeships' should have good impact.

What results do we expect from higher education (HE)? We need first to distinguish between breadth and depth and then decide where each is needed. HE at present represents a certain level of attainment, but does not guarantee breadth. The traditional honours degree is intentionally specialist; it may, but does not have to, provide breadth as well. The take up of GNVQs has shown how qualifications of breadth and work relevance as opposed to 'A' level of depth and academic relevance are seen by our young people (and also by industry) as meeting their aspirations. Their real value lies in their being not an end in themselves, but that they lead to NVQs at level 3 as in the concept of modern apprenticeships and/ or to HE and professional qualifications. The same principle applies to degrees; their attainment is one of the way-stations of lifelong learning. Within HE, the vocationally orientated and more broadly based degrees of the former polytechnics have helped to balance the specialized and academically orientated degrees of the longer-established universities, but the balance is not yet right. The introduction of modular degrees may help us forward.

But to contain our thinking within the degree-shaped mould is to accept an unnecessary constraint. Learning does not come in degree chunks. In a modular system there is no magic in the last chunk, particularly today when the knowledge shelf-life is reducing. We need as many people to be continuously updating and learning as possible. I would prefer 15 million to be learning 3 hours a month than 3 million learning 15 hours. The learning milestones in the form of qualifications and units towards them are, however, important. Achieving them encourages learners to travel further. Milestones are the prerequisites to going to higher levels of skills and learning, and better GCSE results lead to more 16–19 achievements and automatically to more HE. All also lead to more GNVQ 3s and NVQ 3s and to levels 4 and 5.

Learning within Employment

The enormous development of learning within employment will be a result of increasing the skills of those already in employment. A trend over the past years has been that organizations are becoming smaller. They too are realizing that they need to focus. Non-core activities such as transport, cleaning and catering are now being contracted out. Companies are also realizing that smaller units cannot afford the same overheads as larger units, and the same training departments, but also the fact that contracting out is more efficient. What companies need is an infrastructure of training supply. They want this in a very relevant form, at the times they want it and often on their premises. Reducing demarcations between people, the use of teams and multi-skilling means that it is becoming more and more feasible to make provision in economic groups on employers premises, even for small groups. It will be open to colleges and private providers to make this provision.

The question is will the impetus come from individuals or from the organizations in which they work? With 25 million people in work and about two out of three working in about 100,000 organizations, each employing more than twenty-five people, we can quickly influence a large proportion of the 100,000 and their 16 million people. It will be much more difficult to influence the 9 million working in about 2 million organizations or who are self-employed. We must also find ways for these 100,000 organizations to create a pull-through effect on the remaining 9 million individuals. Investors in People is the right vehicle to influence these 100,000 organizations and, in fact, when the NETTS target is reached — where 50 per cent of organizations employing 200 plus people (and some smaller ones too) become IiP — we will be well on the way to becoming a learning society, as this will mean over 20 per cent of the employed workforce are learning with work-related training plans. IiP is much more than giving all people in an organization a training plan relevant to work as it requires the preparation of both a strategic and a business plan to be shared with all employees. The effect is therefore double. It not only forces planning, but it creates the skills to carry out the plan. The effect of IiP is even more than this because it motivates all employees to develop their ability to meet the organization's goals. Unlike the top-down administrative approach of British Standard 5750, IiP is essentially bottom-up and gets to the heart of what makes organizations really succeed — all of its employees. In times of massive change, IiP is a standard that helps organizations cope successfully with change. IiP is the key element — the main support beam — for a learning Britain. Everybody needs to get behind it. It is the most promising development for many years. Provision of all kinds needs to be focussed by it and towards it.

Provision of Learning

The provision of learning in a learning society is an enormous and complicated task. The organizational changes and the cultural changes we have indicated are considerable. The cavalry is, however, at hand in the form of modern communications technology and we must invite the cavalry in. We must not wait until they are supporting other countries and are at our gate. We are at the brink of a new era of learning using technology. Video conferencing will soon allow interactive lectures and tutorials over any distance. In Blackburn a company will, as routine, have a lecture and tutorial from a specialist in Los Angeles. Individuals will be able to call up one of 10,000 training videos and dial up information, articles and books from CD ROMS at the push of a button. Interactive video will allow people to test competences. Simulations and virtual reality will allow experience. The possibilities seem endless and exciting. The explosion in the market, in which a substantial proportion of learning is likely to be open, and database learning will provide income to originators of material.

145

It will slash accommodation and travel costs and offer increased effective-ness. The support structure will still be important, but with video conferencing this need not necessarily be local.

Learning can be, should be and ought to be fun. Shopping used to be a chore, now it is regarded as a leisure activity. So will be learning. It is happening now as learning becomes more learner-centred. The function of the teacher is changing to one of an enabler, confidence builder and mentor. The environment will change too. People don't like shopping in unattractive environments. Nor do they like learning in environments suitable to school children. These are the results we need. How can they be achieved? Much will depend on the colleges of further education.

With GNVQs available, in addition to BTEC Diploma and other relevant but not job-specific courses, the attractiveness of colleges to young people can only increase. Their work with adults seeking to strengthen their general background should grow too. But accepting this, my interest in this chapter is primarily to focus on meeting the more defined needs of those in employment.

Over recent years the development of more relevant vocationally orientated courses has only moved ahead slowly and the provision and attainment of true vocationally competent qualifications has probably re-duced. Too many institutions are unsure of the future and are trying to do everything and competing locally in all areas. So the temptation to develop courses which reflect an ability to teach them rather than the needs of the market becomes strong. Provision has always to be based on clearly identified learning needs in different areas. Colleges have consider-ably improved their marketing skills in the past few years, but more still needs to be done. The requirements of those in employment change rapidly. Only by staying close to the markets can colleges respond to them effec-tively. One solution might be for colleges, using technology, to offer access to courses elsewhere creating what might be access points to 'virtual' colleges. Some might suggest that a solution is smaller, specializing col-leges, but the alternative could be in larger institutions giving more critical mass and supported by greater staff flexibility in terms of fewer perman-ent staff and greater numbers of part-time staff or staff working full-time on short contracts.

The situation was made worse by a payment system which assumes all part-time provision to require 30 per cent of its full-time counterpart. This may carry an aura of good sense, but one international comparison shows its weakness. The German part-time model is of 480 hours a year for three years. We would see these as full-time courses, and they are so recorded in the Department for Education (DfE) international statistics. The German model in fact achieves in three years the equivalent of a UK two-year full-time course which is funded in the UK at less than a third of the full-time provision. In practice (and reinforced by the recession) provision for young people, 16–19, has become divorced from work and runs the risk of appearing less relevant from industry's point of view. The new Further Education Funding Council (FEFC) tariff whereby 450 hours of supported tuition is considered a full-time course will hopefully make the provision of better and fuller part-time provision possible. It is a significant step in the right direction.

It will be important to focus on the different types of provision (academic, semi-vocational and truly vocational) with measures of overall attainment in each area. All three have embedded core skills. For instance, currently the NETTS simply talk about two 'A' Levels, NVQ 3, or equivalent. We need to designate targets for the different elements if we are to change the balance. This seems to be the pattern in other countries and would enable us to see clearly where we are going.

Regional Management of Colleges

Regional management of colleges has always been weak in England and Wales. (In Scotland they do things better, and in Northern Ireland there are different circumstances again.) The organizing principle for the size of TECs could usefully be the ability to maintain contact with 500–1000 organizations. Regional management ought also to play a greater part in the funding of educational institutions. It is not a question of whether (or not) the central bureaucracy can devise efficient funding methods, but the responsiveness to unprogrammable local conditions that is missing from present arrangements. The new Integrated Regional Offices (IROs) — which at the moment have no Department for Education (DfE) involvement — are the first faltering steps to regional control and accountability and are to be welcomed. If a few more regions of the UK had the flexibility given to the Scottish Office a few more schools and colleges might have similar levels of educational attainment. Effective regional structures will also increase in importance as Whitehall takes more power to itself. For instance, it will be impossible to manage 25,000 schools effectively from the centre and good regional structures will be needed. It can be argued that the current regionalization of the UK creates groupings that are too large, and sub-regions such as TEC areas or local government areas are more sensible. Size has to be related to purpose. For instance, TEC areas are related to the ability of the TEC to liaise effectively with the local private sector organizations. The average TEC can relate well to, say, 500 organizations which does, in fact, in my area, East Lancashire, cover half the working population.

Only since the incorporation of colleges in 1993 have college managers been fully responsible and accountable. Despite a fairly long tradition of internal autonomy, incorporation is a huge extension of authority and accountability. Some additions to management staffing have been essential, but the dangers of over-large bureaucracy are real. Even more important is the quality of management with provision for relevant management training brought constantly up to date. The availability of College Governors with ability and expertise is also a key issue. Some colleges are still groping to work effectively at this level, though as yet it is too early to judge how many will succeed. The aim must be to have effective governing bodies setting appropriate strategies to meet the learning requirements of their areas.

The future growth of colleges in the FE sector ought to be enormous. This is because if we are to create a learning society the biggest market will be those in employment. Although currently half the enrolments of FE colleges are adults, as a proportion of what they do this is not reflected in the income adults bring. This is because the adults mostly follow part-time courses. This represents a penetration of the adult population of only three or four out of a hundred. The critical need to reach the National Education and Training Targets itself implies at least 2–3 million new learners following NVQ 3 courses, and if the Investment in People target is met some 3 million or more working adults will have evaluated training programmes, some of which will be following programmes leading to NVQ 3. Overall it is not far-fetched to see that by the year 2000 there will be around 5 million additional regular adults following learning programmes. As the principal local provider FE colleges will benefit from a good proportion of this group. A recent report by the FEFC inspectorate looking at Denmark and Sweden indicated that half of their adult population are learning in their college system.

Colleges will need to be more focussed to achieve growth from this area and will have to offer vocationally relevant part-time provision suitable to those in work in terms of location and timing. Currently the provision is half full-time and half part-time with the income 80 per cent for full-time and 20 per cent for part-time. In the future if NETTS, especially IiP, are a reality and as a learning society develops, we may in FE colleges move to 80 per cent part-time and 20 per cent full-time provision with colleges' income being more than half from part-time provision. Failure to grasp this opportunity will be disastrous because it will reduce the relevance and importance of FE colleges in the area of vocational learning.

It is clear then that the importance of 16–19 provision must not make us blind to adult needs. Much of the life-time provision will be post 16–19 or post NVQ 3, GNVQ, or 'A' Level/BTEC etc. This provision needs to expand on a local and/or part-time basis. It also needs to expand in novel ways, including distance and open learning systems. The FE college where I am a Governor has had success in promoting courses where an increasing proportion is achieved through distance learning, and the time in the standard college classroom format is reducing. Other colleges report similar developments.

The whole process of young people moving all over the country is itself expensive, but moving part-time learners to scattered provision is unbelievably so. At a time when one in three young people are moving to HE it is amazing that large local areas of the country have hardly any HE provision. This applies often in our industrial heartlands where HE provision is concentrated in vast amounts in the big cities often leaving conurbations of half a million where HE students have mostly to travel outside the conurbation. HE provision will therefore need to be more local, but it must not be at the expense of local FE. Once again, access to some HE can be on a 'virtual university' model using the facilities of colleges of FE to provide the technical connections with teaching at some distance away.

An Investment for the Future

We need as a nation to decide how we are going to pay for a learning society. This must be considered as an investment for the future. Time is not on our side. We need to move quickly. There are two sources of the needed investment. These are taxes and private sector finance. The UK prides itself on low taxes (though company taxes are the highest in Europe). We pride ourselves on being wage competitive. The necessity therefore to move to higher added value is apparently made less urgent. European social policy does add costs to industry, but increases the motivation to move to higher productivity and added value. We compensate for our low productivity and training by a higher proportion of the population working longer hours and shift work. All impede the necessity to increase skills. It is not always lack of educational resources which reduce vocational training, but sometimes the way we use, and for what we use them. We filter many of our most capable people and educate them in non-vocational areas and they turn out not very vocationally useful. We train a small proportion of the less capable in vocational areas and they are not very vocationally useful either. A recent National Institute of Economic and Social Research study comparing the productivity in the UK and Holland showed 26 per cent higher productivity in Holland and deduced it was due to greater skill levels. However, Dutch employers spent less on training than the UK employers! The fact was that the Dutch state had already provided much more relevant vocational provision.

We spend considerable resources on the 16–18 age group, but it is not just college costs and fees. It is also child support, income support and travel costs. If more learning was vocational and work-based with the money used to facilitate this we could have very high quality vocational provision and the youngsters would earn their keep in a relevant occupation. We need to use the considerable available resources to this end.

Current Youth Training provision gives some resources to employers, but basically only pays for the 'off the job' provision. Over the years the real contribution to help employers, apart from the off the job element, has gone from £27 in 1981 (£54 in 1993 value) to almost zero today. Taking all the factors into account recession, reduced funding, the pull of the 'A' Level/HE route, and the financial bias towards full-time study it is no wonder that work-based traineeships have reduced. The sadness is that the work-based part-time route on the German model of 480 hours per annum for three years is not only just equivalent to two years full-time, but its effectiveness is considerably better as it is interlaced with work. Also, because of this interlacing the German model provides more effective monitoring.

The arguments oscillate on the different methods of financing students. There is much talk of loans being repaid by a graduate tax. All young people to, say, 25 need to have a substantial learning programme. Is training a graduate in electronics that much more worthwhile than a young unskilled person training for a BTEC? Every young person should learn — our problem is that we are not utilizing the capability of two-thirds of the labour force. If every young person has the right to learn why is there a graduate tax? Surely this should be universal state provision.

Finally, there is the financial responsibility for training people in work. Clearly collectively this has to be the employers responsibility, but how do we make it collective? We need to benefit employers who provide training and penalize those who do not. We also want to kick-start the system to get results quickly. This means getting IiP going quickly. A simple solution would be to add a very small amount to National Insurance, say, 0.25 per cent and give 2 per cent return to IiP companies for a limited period of, say, five years. This would give a great boost to Investors in People, but could cause problems too. The standard would have to be very controlled for quality and continuously developed. TECs might have difficulty in serving all those companies which want to go through the process. These are the problems of success, not of failure, and we can organize ourselves to overcome them. A fiscal incentive would provide the leverage for continuous improvement of the standard over time. We might even consider 1 per cent off employers contributions and 1 per cent off employees. Such a scheme would be neutral from the tax point of view, but be positive in increasing productivity and gross domestic product.

Structures which reflect clearly defined purpose create leadership and focus and allow effective management and local enterprise. We need to plan our structures not to cope with yesterday but to cope with tomorrow and benefit from its technological possibilities. Clearly funding, not so much in terms of additional money but in terms of how it is applied, is a key motivator. We will have to use this motivator to get our goals in a competitive timescale. Perhaps thus we will not get a steep change but a *step* change in vocational training. We need not just to tilt the system towards the vocational, but to stand the system on its head. So will follow greater competitiveness as a result of the productivity increases achieved by a highly skilled workforce.

Chapter 11

Learning — A Qualified Success?

John Hillier

The role of assessment and examinations in learning has always been the subject of some controversy. It is interesting to read, for example, in the early history of the City and Guilds of London Institute, one of the first examining bodies, of the consternation of many of those involved when it was found that craftsmen who were otherwise completely competent in the trade in which they practised were unable to answer fairly simple questions about the scientific theories on which that trade was allegedly based (City and Guilds of London Institute, 1993). Similarly, the early history of the Royal Society for the encouragement of Arts, Manufactures and Commerce (Foden, 1989), another examining body, shows much discontent about the effect of somewhat pedestrian examination questions on the processes of learning that were produced in schools. A good deal of the education satirized so effectively by Charles Dickens was the result of this approach to examination.

Examinations of one kind or another are such an integral part of education in this country now that it is easy to forget that they are a comparatively recent introduction and that their role in many other developed countries is of considerably less importance. For example, in the German DUAL system, often held up as one of the finest examples of a vocational education and training system, three and a half years of vocational education and training are the subject of only one eight-hour examination. One compares that with the amount that is done in, for example, the General Certificate of Secondary Education where more than sixteen hours of examination may be devoted to the results of two years of secondary education. It is clear that examinations have a significance in British education that is unparalleled almost anywhere else in the world. It is equally clear, however, that the faith placed in the external examination in this country is not always justified. There have been many research studies indicating, for example, that the same examination marked by different markers (Newstead and Dennis, 1994) may produce widely different results. A recent study by the British Psychological Society, for example, has shown that marks might vary between 50 per cent and 85 per cent on one essay marked by six different markers. This in degree terms represents a spread between a first class honours degree and a third class honours degree. Equally, it has frequently been demonstrated that the relationship between an examination result and what it is supposed to predict is sometimes very shaky. For example, many studies have shown that the correlation between 'A' level results and degree results is very low; this is surprising given that 'A' levels have almost the solitary purpose of predicting success in higher education.

It is of course easy to see why the externally set and marked examination is so seductively attractive. It is apparently independent; all students are judged apparently against the same standards by markers who have no connection with the processes of learning that have led up to the assessment. Less publicized, but equally important, it is seemingly a very cheap way of assessing large numbers of people at the same time. It also apparently exists independently of the education and training courses which lead up to it, although close scrutiny quickly demonstrates that this is far from the truth.

Anyone who gives close study to the programmes that lead up to GCSE and 'A' level in this country will know that enormous amounts of teaching time and effort go into the scrutiny of question papers; the spotting of likely questions; their administration — either as tests, or as mock examinations; and marking and debating the results with students. It would be no exaggeration to say that as much as 50 per cent of any given 'A' level course could be devoted to efforts directly connected with passing the examination. This may well make a mockery of the extensive syllabus which is provided given that only a very small part of it will ever feature in the final examination. The phrase 'what you test is what you get' characterizes much education and training. It can be seen as a problem — witness the comments of the Royal Society of Arts referred to above — or it can be seen as an opportunity. To capitalize on the opportunity, however, involves integrating the process of assessment with the process of learning in ways which in much modern education have yet to be fully explored.

Before examining how such an integration can be brought about, it is necessary to devote some time to consideration of the question of what should be assessed. This may seem an obvious question, but for many years in this country it was implicitly agreed that what should be the subject of assessment was that which was determined by the teacher as being necessary for whatever purpose the assessment was carried out. Thus, for example, for many years it was considered vital for the proper study of English language and literature for there to be a high level of achievement in the study of the Latin language and literature. Up to the 1960s, entry to a degree course in English language and literature was contingent upon 'A' level success, or its equivalent in earlier times, in Latin. However, since this requirement has been gradually dropped over the last thirty years it is hard to discern any diminution in the quality of candidates, study or work, in this field.

It is easy to understand, and perhaps entirely logical, that in examinations which are designed to facilitate progression through an academic route, it should be those responsible for the higher levels of academic achievement who determine their content. Thus, university professors, in general, have played a leading part in determining the content of 'A' level, and in the past, 'O' level syllabuses. It was only in the 1980s that it started to become clear that where examinations were used as indicators of success in employment, these decisions about syllabus and assessment might be flawed. The Review of Vocational Qualifications carried out in 1985 (Manpower Services Commission and Department of Education and Science, 1986) indicated widespread dissatisfaction among employers about the results of the education and training processes being carried out on their behalf in schools and further and higher education, and considerable disenchantment with the reliability of success in academic examinations as a predictor of success in the workplace.

The government therefore decided to set up a new approach to assessment for work. The National Council for Vocational Qualifications was set up in 1986 with a brief to find out from employers what was required for effective performance at work in jobs at all levels and in all sectors of the economy; and to develop a framework of qualifications based, not on what people needed to know, but on what they were required to do, to what standard and across what range of circumstances, in work. Thus for the first time in this country, control over what is assessed was removed from teachers and educators and given to those who are required to make a living, or provide services, based on the results of education and training systems. Employers were not, of course, the only voice in the process. Trade unions and people responsible for education and training have played a significant part. But in the eight years of development that have followed, employers have played the leading role in defining the standards of competence on which the new system of qualifications for work, National Vocational Qualifications (NVQ), is based.

This has not been an easy task. In 1986 there was no common way in which employers could state their requirements of their employees. Some occupations had had qualifications of various kinds for many years — written examinations for craftsmen, for example, were first introduced by the City and Guilds of London Institute in the 1850s. Other sectors of employment, accounting for almost half the adult workforce, had no relevant qualifications in existence at all and had been forced for many years to rely on the inaccurate predictions provided through academic examinations. Even in occupations at the highest levels of competence, the same pattern could be discerned — there was no common pattern of qualification in management, arguably the largest single category of high level practitioners in the country. In the engineering sector, to take another example, fifty-three professional bodies had separate autonomous control over the process of qualifying an ever-shrinking population of professionally qualified engineers. The NVQ framework now covers 85 per cent of the working population, with approximately 600 new qualifications and their creation in this short space of time represents a major achievement for the employers, trade unionists and others, who have contributed to their development. It is also a tribute to the Government, which over that period, has been unswerving in its commitment to the development of a new framework of qualifications for work and has consistently seen it as an important contribution to improving the international competitiveness of the British workforce.

A further important change has been the recognition that it is no longer sufficient to learn and qualify in the early part of a career and then seek to make a living out of that process for a further forty or fifty years. Patterns of employment within organizations, and changes in work demands, organization structures and employment prospects mean that no individual now can count on following the same occupation throughout a working life. Indeed in many cases people will experience two or three employment changes — sometimes voluntary, often involuntary. It is therefore necessary to have a system of learning and qualification which is available throughout a working life. While the rhetoric of this is now well accepted, the institutional arrangements for delivering it are at a very early stage of development. One of the principal characteristics of the NVQ system is that qualification is not dependent on attending a particular institution, or following a particular process of learning, or taking a particular amount of time to acquire the necessary competence. All of these features are vital if the system is to be accessible to adults throughout their working life. They do, however, predicate a system of vocational education and training which is suited to this purpose and we are far from having such a system yet. Far too many institutions, and this includes those provided directly by employers as well as those funded by the government, are still working on outdated and inflexible models revolving around academic years and terms, and many of them have yet to embrace fully the needs of their customers for education and training to be available not just throughout the working life, but throughout the working year, throughout the week and throughout the day.

Another important question that emerges in capitalizing on the opportunities that systematic assessment against clearly defined standards provides, is how and by whom such assessment can be carried out. The academic notion that assessment is in some way distinct from the process of learning, although as we have seen, scarcely ever carried out in practice, produces some scepticism about assessment processes which are integral to the learning process and therefore carried out by the same people who are responsible for the learning process. It would be naive to pretend that there are not legitimate concerns, about teachers or instructors, or indeed employers, who are judge, jury and executioner for the trainees and candidates under their control. Many factors can interfere with an independent assessment in such circumstances and these worries are compounded when financial benefit to the institution, or to the individual teacher or instructor, may be contingent on success in the assessment. Reliable systems of moderation and verification are therefore essential and this in turn means that the bodies responsible — in many cases bodies who have traditionally seen themselves as examining bodies — need to review their purpose and method of operation. They have to provide systems which ensure that national standards are applied impartially and fairly wherever they are used and that checks and balances exist to ensure that each assessor is operating the system in a way which is consistent with all of their colleagues who may number many thousands up and down the country. This is a challenging task for awarding bodies and most, quite naturally, have taken some time to come to terms with its full implications.

Systems of assessing competence, particularly when carried out in the workplace can appear more expensive than traditional examinations. Whether this is actually true requires considerably more research than has yet been possible. We have already noted above, the many hidden costs in the traditional examination system and the extent to which preparation for the examination may overwhelm the programme of study. Equally, it is becoming clear that the assessment of competence in the workplace, if properly integrated within employers' normal systems for assessing the performance of their employees, can be conducted in an extremely cost-effective way. It is also encouraging to see that employers who have experience of it now recognize that the set up costs, which can of course be considerable, are well worth it in relation to the economic benefits that flow from a properly qualified workforce. A recent survey by the Confederation of British Industry (CBI, 1994) has indicated most encouragingly that employers see overall benefit in a properly qualified, competent, workforce and do not see the initial costs as a reason for not proceeding.

Whatever the merits of different approaches to assessment and examination, it is important to recognize that there are a number of different purposes that they may be designed to serve. Most early examinations — and many academic examinations still in use — are designed essentially to discriminate between the achievements of a given group of candidates. Indeed in the early stages they were often referred to as competitive examinations. This means that some candidates pass and others fail, and while both the educational process and the examination is of considerable value to those who pass, it is of no value at all — and may even be a positive disadvantage — to those who fail. Clearly, the higher the proportion who fail, the less useful the activity overall will be. There are circumstances, however, in which this kind of examination is essential. Where there are more applicants than places, for example, in higher education establishments, or, in other contexts, in employment, then the use of the examination as a discrimination device is clearly essential. Indeed some of the earliest competitive examinations were developed for entry to the Civil

Service, and some of these are still in use. Unfortunately, since only those candidates who pass the examination are accepted, either for the education programme or employment, it is impossible to judge the predictive validity of the examinations, since this would require accepting some of those who failed in order to see how well they performed in education or in employment. The few studies there have been of this kind tend to indicate that such examinations have a poor validity record. It would be tempting, although completely unfair, to say that the performance of the Civil Service over the last 150 years bears eloquent testimony to this!

More recent recognition that the competitive examination produces a high level of wastage in the sense that those who fail gain nothing of value from the process, has led to the development of a different concept; namely, that it should be possible to recognize the achievement of all candidates, rather than simply those who exceed an arbitrary standard. This implies two important differences from the competitive examination principle. Firstly, the use of criterion-referenced assessment, which in turn involves clearly and unambiguously stated standards of achievement against which each candidate's performance can be judged. By definition, therefore, the assessment process does not involve comparing one candidate with all of the others (norm referencing), but comparing each candidate against the standard required. There is now little argument that this is the most appropriate approach for assessments which are designed to reflect people's competence at work; after all, who is interested in being operated on by a surgeon who has demonstrated only that he knows around 40 per cent of what needs to be known to be a competent surgeon. Happily, in other areas of competence where qualifications have been reformed on the NVQ model, it is possible to determine whether or not an individual has met all the standards required to become a competent practitioner. For example, every new entrant to the hairdressing profession in the UK is now judged against clearly defined, industry-wide standards. It is too early to judge the overall effect on the nation's coiffure, but it should be possible to detect an overall raising of standards over time.

The second difference is that it is essential not to rely solely on one assessment at the end of a process of teaching or learning. To recognize the achievement of every candidate it is necessary for the assessment to be done on a modular, or unit, basis so that those candidates who, by choice, or because of their ability, are unable to complete the entire qualification, can get credit for what they have achieved. This contrasts with the situation in 'A' levels where currently, according to the Office of Standards in Education (OFSTED) figures, 30 per cent of the candidates fail to achieve a standard that has any practical or commercial value in that it does not secure either employment or access to higher education; and this having spent at least two years of their young lives in pursuit of what has turned out to be unattainable. Unit based qualifications and the modular learning programmes that often accompany them do present some difficulties, however. It is clearly possible, although not desirable, to divide a subject in such a way that the sum of the parts is less than the whole. It is necessary to structure very carefully the units of assessment to make sure that overall understanding of an occupation, or a subject, is not jeopardized by the assessment structure and it is often necessary, therefore, to look at assessments which are integrative — that is, bringing together various strands from various parts of what has been learnt — as well as assessments which relate solely to particular units of achievement. In that way, the best of both worlds in assessment can be achieved.

Assessment that is both unit based and criterion referenced may be more expensive than assessment which is norm referenced and based on a single terminal assessment event. Such arguments, however, may be deceptive. The measures considered necessary, for example, by the School Curriculum and Assessment Authority to monitor and maintain standards in GCSE and 'A' level currently take some £42 million per year of the tax payers' money. This necessary quality control expenditure is entirely concealed from candidates, educational institutions and the awarding bodies who administer the qualifications. The comparable figure for the NVQ system, which embraces currently roughly the same number of candidates, is around £8 million per year. Much of the reason for this difference lies in the much greater emphasis on quality *assurance* which is possible in a criterion-referenced system. The initial expenditure in developing and agreeing clear and unambiguous standards, pays off handsomely in the later stages of the process.

For all the advantages of a criterion-referenced, unit-based system, such as has been developed for NVQs and GNVQs, it is still vital to establish in the minds of users and candidates the real value of such an approach. Public perception in the UK still rates the competitive examination more highly than a system in which it is possible for everyone to succeed, albeit in different measures and at different levels. And there is clearly also considerable inertia in the education system: for some good reasons, such as capitalizing on the many years of experience of operating the systems with which they are familiar; and for some not so good reasons, such as an unwillingness to expose themselves to a more rigorous and wide-ranging approach to assessment — particularly since it rapidly becomes obvious that a change in an assessment regime has to be reflected in approaches to teaching and learning and that effect can often be revolutionary.

Much is spoken and written these days about empowerment. Making clear to learners precisely what is expected for success in every aspect of what they are learning, can be a very attractive and motivating prospect for them, but it also involves dispelling much of the mystique that has surrounded teaching and the construction of syllabuses and programmes. Open statements of this kind allow students and candidates to judge for themselves the effectiveness of the learning processes to which they are subjected. It allows them and others to determine objectively whether or not success has been achieved. All of these aspects can be very threatening for those in the teaching and learning professions and, while it is exciting and stimulating to see that many have risen to this challenge, there are still many — and sadly significant numbers in higher education — who have yet to feel the stimulus. This in turn means that educational institutions have yet to fully adapt to the kinds of flexible and customer driven approaches which new systems demand and facilitate. All too often still, education is arranged around a timetable, devised around the agricultural year and church feasts in the Middle Ages (and sometimes still uses methods first developed at around the same time). The concept of the 'empowered learner' has yet to take root widely in the education system. The messages of total quality and customer orientation have taken over twenty years to become embedded in manufacturing industry in this country, although, thankfully, those aspects of manufacturing which survive have now embraced them fully. There is a great need to transfer this understanding into the management and operation of education. All of those who have been through the process in manufacturing and service industries recognize how difficult and demanding a process it is, and that simply embracing the rhetoric and expressing appropriate sentiments in brochures fall well short of the serious and fundamental organizational and individual changes that are required.

Bringing about the necessary changes in the provision of education and training though, is only a part of what needs to be achieved. The central problem of getting the public perception to equate professionalism and competence with qualifications will be a long struggle. Except in a few regulated professions there is no real tradition in this country of the equation of qualifications with competence. Indeed the concept has often been devalued as witness the many certificates, allegedly of competence, to be found on the walls of even the most incompetent motor vehicle repair workshop; or the use of wholly inappropriate academic qualifications to demonstrate the expertise of the proprietors of bogus quack medicines. There is a need to gain public acceptance of the idea that the concepts which they respect in the highest professions — the law, medicine, engineering and accountancy, for example — are being extended throughout the working population and that, over time, it will become necessary to be qualified in order to gain employment, secure promotion, or sell your services to the public. Whether or not a system of legal licensing should be introduced is a somewhat different matter; this is probably an area in which it is better for the law to follow public opinion rather than lead it. In other words, introducing compulsory licensing too soon, when either the qualification system itself is insufficiently robust, or insufficient numbers of people are appropriately qualified, would quickly bring the law into disrepute. Once the system is judged robust enough, and sufficient numbers of people are qualified, it would be a comparatively simple matter to bring the law into line with the reality.

The question of the use of qualifications as licences to practice — which is much more widespread in other countries than in the UK — leads us to some consideration of the various roles that qualifications may be called upon to play. We have already considered the use of qualifications in a competitive sense as part of a gate-keeping process in education or employment, but other uses are also possible. At the simplest level, qualifications are sometimes used to signify attendance at a particular process of education or training. Indeed, in the much admired German DUAL system, the certificate awarded for the general education component is precisely that; there are no final examinations and the certificate is awarded simply to reflect attendance at the necessary classes. This use leads to a further use to which qualifications are often put. They may be used as triggers for systems of funding or reward. At the simplest level, a certificate of attendance may be used to justify the payment of fees for a training programme or course. At a more complex level, systems of payment for providers of education and training may be related to the achievements of their students in terms of qualifications. Such systems are already in use in government training programmes in the UK and are gradually coming into use in funding methods for further education. Whilst it is entirely logical that payment to providers of education and training should be related to the achievements of their students, there are also some disadvantages. For example, the attachment of potentially large sums of money to students' success or failure can result in unacceptable pressures being brought to bear on those who are responsible for assessment. This is most obvious in systems of assessment where much responsibility is devolved to those in the institution, but it can also happen in systems which are externally assessed, where it may lead, for example, to candidates not being entered for examinations in case they might fail them, and at the extreme, to persons other than the actual candidate presenting themselves for assessment. A further application along these lines is the use of qualifications as a determinant in pay systems. This has been established many years in some branches of the armed services and in the police and fire services. Its more widespread use in employment can, however, also produce unacceptable strains on the qualifications system. In turn this means that the approaches to quality assurance, whatever system of assessment is being used, must be robust enough to withstand the pressures that funding regimes may unintentionally bring to bear on them.

All of these financial developments may simply mean that the two mottoes 'what you test is what you get' and 'you get what you pay for' are becoming synonymous and this in the end may prove a helpful development. If it means that cash is directed towards identifying and meeting the needs of individual learners and recognizing all their achievements, then it can only be beneficial. In the end, we get the assessment regime that we deserve and we get the teachers and programmes we deserve as a result of that. Much has been learnt in this country in the last ten years about the interaction between assessment and learning and what started in the early 1980s as a brave experiment in developing an assessment driven curriculum model is rapidly becoming a system of qualifications for work and for preparing for work, which is envied and copied worldwide; but there is no room for complacency. We have developed and implemented very quickly a system which is radically different from much that has gone before (although echoes and resonances with work on learning and behavioural objectives going back many years can be detected). A long period of continuous improvement and development will be necessary in order to fully exploit the potential of what now exists.

References

CBI (1994) *Quality Assessed*, London, CBI

CITY and GUILDS (1993) *City & Guilds of London Institute — A Short History*, London, the City and Guilds of London Institute.

FODEN, F. (1989) *The Examiner*, Leeds, Leeds Studies in Adult and Continuing Education.

MANPOWER SERVICES COMMISSION AND DEPARTMENT FOR EDUCATION AND SCIENCE (1986) *Review of Vocational Qualifications in England and Wales*, London, HMSO.

NEWSTEAD, S.E. and DENNIS, I. (1994) 'Examiners examined', *The Psychologist*, May.

Chapter 12

Towards a Strategy for Lifelong Guidance to Support Lifelong Learning and Work

A G Watts and Stephen McNair

The Death and Resurrection of 'Career'

The notions of 'lifelong learning' and of the 'learning society' are linked to radical changes which are taking place in the concepts of 'learning', of 'work' and of 'career'. The changes are evident both in the words we use, and in the ways we use them.

Under the traditional model, we have tended to refer to learning as being synonymous with education, and to work as being synonymous with employment. Education has conventionally been viewed as preceding employment, and as providing — directly or indirectly — a preparation for it. Individuals have then entered (if they were fortunate) a career. This has been viewed as a structure which has provided predictable opportunities for systematic promotion through a series of posts of increasing responsibility and status.

Within this model, the decisions about individuals' progression have largely been made about them rather than by them. The education system has operated as a kind of graded escalator which has relentlessly carried forward those who succeed in surmounting the various hurdles it has presented. Students who have passed their 'O' levels/GCSEs have gone on to take 'A' levels in their most successful subjects; those who have passed their 'A' levels have gone on to degrees; those who have secured first-class degrees have gone on to postgraduate work. At the point at which students 'fail', they have been ejected from the education escalator and sought transfer to the employment escalator. Thereafter, employers have decided whether and when individuals should be promoted. 'Career management' has referred to the management of careers not by the individual but by the organization.

This picture is, of course, a caricature. The reality was always much more complex. But the model is sufficiently accurate to be recognizable. The words that are used — education, employment, career — tend to refer to entities outside the individual: to educational institutions, to employer organizations, to career structures. But the words, and the concepts, are now changing. The emerging model refers less to education than to learning. It refers less to employment than to work. And it uses the word career in a very different way.

The shift of attention from education and employment on the one hand, to learning and work on the other, is significant in three respects. The first is the breadth of the terms. Learning takes place in many settings, not just educational ones. It covers informal as well as formal learning. It includes not only education but also training: it does not deny the distinction between them, but it encourages them to inter-penetrate one another. Similarly, work covers employment and recognizes its crucial importance, but covers other work too: self-employment, for example, and all the household work and voluntary work, not to mention shadow-economy work, which sustain communities and enrich their quality (Watts, 1983, chapter 9).

The second respect in which the shift is significant is the nature of the terms. Education and employment tend to describe institutional structures: they are, in that sense, bureaucratic, industrial-society concepts. Learning and work, by contrast, are essentially about processes, and are owned by individuals: they are more potent concepts for a post-industrial society.

The third significant shift is in the relationship between the respective pairs of terms. Education tends to be seen as preceding employment. But learning and work cannot be seen in that way. One works to learn; one learns to work. They are symbiotic: they depend upon one another. Both are continuing processes. In the post-industrial world, a society that wishes to work must be a learning society.

Alongside these shifts is a parallel change in the nature of career. The traditional concept of a career as a structure — of a career in engineering, or a career in ICI — is dying. In its place is emerging a new concept of career as a process, to describe an individual's lifetime of learning and work. The career is now owned by the individual, just as learning and work are.

One of the effects of the new concept of career is to open it to all. The traditional concept was, by definition, limited to the few who were able to secure access to the structural positions that provided progression. The emerging concept, however, is not limited to steps up hierarchical ladders. Progression in learning and in work can take place through lateral and horizontal as well as vertical movement; it can occur within positions; it can be effected outside organizational structures altogether. It therefore offers opportunities of 'careers for all' (CBI, 1989b), particularly if progression can be supported so that career becomes more than mere biography.

These various shifts reflect changes in the 'psychological contract' (Argyris, 1960; Herriot, 1992) between the individual on the one hand,

and education and employment systems on the other. Employers are less prepared to take responsibility for long-term commitments to individuals. Many are seeking to reduce their core workers, and to operate in more flexible ways through a growing contractual fringe and through the use of part-time and temporary workers (Handy, 1989). More and more employees are based in small and medium-sized organizations rather than in large organizations. The notion of a 'job for life' is dying. Educational institutions, too, are increasingly viewing individuals not as captive students but as independent learners. The growth of such concepts as flexible learning, open learning, modular courses, accreditation of prior experiential learning, and credit accumulation and transfer, all reshape the institution as a resource for the individual to use in more flexible ways. Individuals are moving more frequently between educational institutions, between employers, and between the two. Their relationships with these institutions are open to more regular negotiation and review.

These trends are partly responses to the relentless pace of social change. Organizations now have to adapt much more rapidly than in the past both to political pressures and to market forces. Shorter-term contracts with individuals can give organizations greater flexibility; the regular renegotiation of these contracts can make organizations more responsive and open to innovation.

From the individual's perspective, the change is both a threat and an opportunity. It could mean that individuals are more open to exploitation; that they find it more difficult to secure progression both in learning and in work; that their periods of education and employment are fragmented, and interspersed with wasted periods of unemployment. On the other hand, it could mean that they are able to exercise more choice and control over their own progressing lives, and to develop in more autonomous ways.

In the national interest, it is critical that the opportunity rather than the threat be realised. As is argued elsewhere in this book, Britain's economic future, and its social harmony, depend upon a massive improvement in the skill levels of its people. To achieve this requires new forms of structural support for individuals within the changing organizational structures. Simply withdrawing the old organizational supports without putting anything in their place is to court disaster: trusting the market to deliver the public good is blind faith. The supports needed are of various forms: they include basic income support as well as incentives to learn. One of the most important, we contend, is guidance.

Towards a National Guidance Strategy

Within the traditional model, the role of guidance services has been very limited. Since choices have been determined largely by social forces, and by selective processes within education and employment, guidance services have tended to be confined to acting as a kind of switch mechanism at the transition from education to employment. They have accordingly tended to be marginal in position and low in status.

Within the emerging model, on the other hand, the role of guidance is potentially central and pervasive. If individuals are constantly to develop their learning and their work, and regularly to negotiate their relationships with educational institutions and employers, then guidance needs to be available on a continuing basis. It is a key means of empowering individuals within this negotiation process. It is the lubricant of development within the emerging model: activating and channelling the individual's energies, and enabling the education and employment systems to respond to, and draw from, those energies.

Guidance can be provided from many sources, formal and informal. The informal guidance from family and friends can be very influential, and indeed valuable, but it is not sufficient. It is informed by close knowledge of the individual, and possibly of particular opportunities. It tends, however, to be based on limited and sometimes erroneous information on wider opportunities, to be instinctive rather than skilled and to be biased by the ties of relationship. It needs to be supplemented by more formal guidance from more dispassionate and professional sources.

Our view is that a national strategy is needed for lifelong guidance in support of lifelong career development in learning and work. Guidance needs to be embedded both within education and within employment; in addition, guidance needs to be available from a neutral base. What is needed, in short, is a strategy based on three prongs:

- *Careers education* as an integral part both of schools and of post-compulsory education, offering regular opportunities for pupils and students to explore the relationship between what they are learning and their career development.
- *Career development* as an integral part of all employment provision, offering trainees and employees regular opportunities to review their current work, their future aspirations, their skill requirements, and ways of meeting these requirements.
- *Access to neutral careers guidance* at points when individuals wish to review possibilities for movement between educational institutions, or between employers, or between the two.

Existing provision is probably most strongly developed in the careers education prong. Careers education and guidance in schools was defined in the initial version of the national curriculum as a cross-curricular theme, not from age 14 but from age 5 (NCC, 1990); the review of the national curriculum by Sir Ron Dearing (1994) underlined the importance of careers provision and in principle provided more space for provision to be made for it in Key Stages 3 and 4. In further education (FE), careers education elements are increasingly being incorporated into courses concerned with broad forms of vocational preparation, and into access provision for adults; and the new funding arrangements for FE attach considerable importance to guidance at entry to, during, and on exit from, learning programmes (FEFC, 1992). Within higher education (HE), most universities have well-established careers services, and the concept of 'personal transferable skills' has facilitated the growth of careers education elements within the curriculum (Watts and Hawthorn, 1992).

Provision in the career development prong has in the past been much weaker, but is now growing rapidly. The Government's Investors in People (IiP) programme, alongside the emerging structure of National Vocational Qualifications (NVQs), is providing strong support to appraisal schemes, and the like, which incorporate guidance elements. In addition, employers are increasingly including access to guidance as part of outplacement packages.

Cross-cutting education and employment is the National Record of Achievement (NRA), which includes attention not only to recording of past achievement but also to action planning. The NRA is now in extensive use in schools and colleges, and is also being introduced by some employers. It potentially provides a basis for lifetime learning and progression.

Much work is still needed to develop these two prongs. In relation to careers education in schools, for example, the position of the cross-curricular themes is structurally weak and has received little support from government agencies. Again, career development structures within employment are still very limited, particularly among small and medium-sized companies: much more needs to be done before help with career development becomes a reality for all or even most employees. The building blocks, however, are in place.

The potential advantages of guidance services within education and within employment are twofold. First, they have more continuous contact with the individuals based in their organization, and so are able to deliver more sustained guidance than any external service could do. Second, they are likely to be in a stronger position to influence their organization to alter its opportunity structures in response to individuals' needs and demands, as revealed through the guidance process.

At the same time, developing guidance services within education and within employment is not sufficient. Many people spend significant parts of their lives outside education and employment structures — because they are unemployed, for example, or engaged in child-rearing. Again, guidance services within particular organizations do not usually have a sufficiently broad view of opportunities outside that organization. Moreover, the organization can have vested interests in the outcomes of the individuals' decisions, which can make it difficult to provide guidance that is genuinely neutral. Her Majesty's Inspectorate (1992), for instance, have criticized the tendency in some schools to bias guidance at 16 to encourage students to stay on — with the capitation advantages this brings to the school — rather than to move on to learning opportunities elsewhere. In further and higher education, departments can have an interest in students' modular choices. Employers, too, are likely to be reluctant to encourage valued employees to explore opportunities in other companies, or indeed particular options within their own organization.

It is therefore crucial that, alongside guidance within education and employment, there should also be access to the broader and more impartial perspective which a neutral guidance service can bring. This is however the most difficult area in policy terms. Instead of being embedded within wider provision, it is likely to require separate funding. This raises the questions of where such services should be located both physically and organizationally, and how they should be financed.

Securing Access to Neutral Guidance

The main source of neutral guidance in Britain has traditionally been the Careers Service, which since 1973 has been a mandatory responsibility of Local Education Authorities (LEAs). It has offered guidance free of charge to individuals in full- or part-time education, other than higher education; it has also been available to young people for a period of time after leaving education. Such a service has never, however, been extended comprehensively to adults. An Occupational Guidance Service was set up for adults in 1966, but was not widely publicized, and was dismantled in 1978. Educational Guidance Services for Adults have been set up in some areas, and some Careers Services have developed services for adults, but these initiatives have usually been based on fragile short-term funding.

The case for public funding of guidance services is a strong one. Such services can play a significant role in fostering efficiency in the allocation and use of human resources, and social equity in access to educational and vocational opportunities. In market terms, guidance can be viewed as a market-maker (McNair, 1990): a means of making the learning and labour markets work more effectively. It does this in three main ways: by informing and supporting the individual decisions through which the market operates; by reducing market failure — e.g., drop-outs from education and training, and mismatches between supply and demand in the labour market; and by contributing to institutional reforms designed to improve market functioning (Killeen, White and Watts, 1992). In these terms, it can be viewed as a public good, which merits public funding even under a market-oriented government antipathetic to social-welfare provision. There would therefore seem to be a strong case for expansion of guidance services to cover adults as well as young people.

There have however been different views about whether this should be a single integrated service or a network of services catering for different target-groups. There have also been different opinions about where such services should be located. The CBI, which has been very influential in raising the public profile of guidance, has itself adopted three very different positions on this matter: having initially argued that the Careers Service should be transferred from LEAs to Training and Enterprise Councils (CBI, 1989a), it subsequently appeared to support the notion that it should be managed by LEA-TEC partnerships, and then announced that the TECs should not be directly involved in guidance delivery at all (CBI, 1993). The National Commission on Education (1993) recommended the setting-up of Community Education and Training Advice Centres (CETACs), developed out of the existing Careers Service, which would operate as citizens' advice bureaus for all information on education, training and careers, both for young people and for adults. It saw these centres as receiving their funding from, but operating at arm's length from, new Education and Training Boards which would replace Local Education Authorities.

At the same time, however, both the CBI and the Government have been sceptical about whether a comprehensive guidance service need be wholly funded from public funds, and have been interested in exploring the extent to which market principles might be applied to the provision of guidance itself: in other words, the extent to which a market in guidance might be established. The underlying notion here is that the claimed benefits of the market — that it, ensures greater responsiveness to consumer choice, and greater efficiency because the benefits of competition — should be as applicable to guidance as to other activities (see Watts, 1991).

In practice, the application of market principles to guidance provision has so far taken a number of different forms. In relation to the Careers Service, the Trade Union Reform and Employment Rights Act 1993 removes the Careers Service from the control of LEAs and gives the Secretary of State for Employment powers to implement the services as he or she sees fit: in England these powers are being used to invite competitive tenders to run the Careers Service for the still limited statutory client group in particular areas. At the same time, the Government has launched two initiatives — Gateways to Learning and Skill Choice — which provide support for TEC-managed pilot schemes involving 'guidance vouchers' directed particularly at non-statutory adult client groups. Some of these schemes are aimed particularly at the unemployed and are fully-funded; others are targeted more at those in employment, and include greater emphasis on matched financial contributions from individuals and/or their employers.

Within these initiatives there are three very different applications of market principles at work. The reorganization of the Careers Service in England is based on the notion of raising standards through competitive tendering for monopoly public contracts, offering public services that are free to specified users. Some of the voucher schemes are based on continued public funding for guidance which is disbursed not direct to the services but to the users: under this model, quality is enhanced through responsiveness to user demand. Both of these models are variations of quasi-markets (Le Grand and Bartlett, 1993), representing limited applications of market principles to continuing social welfare provision. Other voucher schemes, on the other hand, seem to be based on the notion of a temporary public role in pump-priming a real market, in which the user will pay and public funding will progressively be withdrawn.

It is clear that there are major difficulties in setting up a real market in guidance (PACEC, 1993). Some of these difficulties could be regarded as transitional problems, concerned with getting people to pay for services which in the past have been free. Others, however, are more enduring. In particular, it is clear that those who arguably need guidance most — the unemployed, the unwaged and the low-skilled — are in the weakest position to pay. Moreover, if employers rather than individuals pay for guidance, this is likely to prejudice the neutrality of the guidance that is offered. In short, it is clear that a market in guidance will not of itself deliver adequate take-up and adequate quality (in terms of neutrality in particular) to meet the public interest in guidance as a market-maker. At the same time, it is possible that some appropriate mix of public provision and market provision *might* be viable in this respect. It might also offer the possibility of breaking through the public funding restrictions which have so far prevented the development of a guidance service that would be available comprehensively to adults as well as to young people. Since under current government policies this is the only viable option that is likely to be politically credible, attention needs to turn to the forms which such an option might take.

One possible model would be to make some foundation guidance provision accessible to all. This will meet the public interest in delivering universal access to guidance at a basic level, and will also develop awareness of guidance needs and of guidance services, so creating a stronger market for enhanced guidance provision. The foundation provision could comprise three elements: an open-access information centre; brief diagnostic guidance designed to identify guidance needs; and signposting to guidance services where these needs might be met. Thereafter, individuals able to pay for enhanced guidance could be expected to do so, while publicly-funded adult guidance vouchers could be targeted at groups where the ability to pay is low and/or the public interest in take-up is high (TEC National Council, 1994; Watts, 1994).

A strategy along these lines would need to be carefully monitored to assess the extent to which the public interest in guidance as a market-maker was being met. Guidance vouchers are still experimental. Their administrative costs need to be balanced against their potential benefits both as a marketing device and as a means of empowering individuals in their relationships with guidance services. In addition, the benefits of competition between guidance services need to be balanced against the benefits of collaboration, particularly if progression and continuity in guidance support are to be achieved. More evidence is needed, based on more carefully designed experiments than the present ones, before a firm judgment can be made. This is important if future policy decisions, involving extensive public expenditure, are to be founded on empirical evidence rather than on ideological assertion. In the meantime, attention is also needed to define quality standards for guidance provision. This will give the market in guidance the best chance of compatibility with guidance as a market-maker. It is therefore to the issue of quality that we now turn.

Quality in Guidance

The diverse traditions and histories of the various services have produced a legacy of practice which is richly various, but patchy and inconsistent. There has been, to date, no common agreement across the full range of guidance providing agencies about how to define, measure and assure quality: the absence of clear and agreed definitions of the boundaries of guidance has not helped matters.

If one considers guidance as a market-maker, the quality of guidance has a direct bearing on the effectiveness of the learning and labour markets. It helps to ensure that potential learners and employees understand the opportunities available, and supports them in negotiating, directly and indirectly, with educators, trainers and employers to ensure the best possible match between demand and supply. In the same way, an efficient market in guidance requires definitions of quality in guidance which potential customers can understand, in order to enable them to make rational choices between rival suppliers. If the customer has better (or more intelligible) information about price than quality, the former will inevitably drive the latter down.

But the notion of quality is an elusive one. The replacement of planned systems with market-led ones in many areas of public service has stimulated a growing interest in the use of industrial and commercial models of quality assurance. Policy makers and managers have sought models which might help to explain how quality can be defined (and by whom); how it can be recognized and measured; and how it can be assured and improved. This process has proved difficult in many areas of public service, and while there may be agreement about the basic principles that quality is a matter of 'fitness for purpose' and that the service should be responsive to customer needs, the application of these principles is far from simple. In the case of guidance, the notions of customer, need and purpose are all problematic, as is the definition of the service itself. Quality assurance systems will have to find ways of responding to these dilemmas if they are not to result in damage rather than improvement to the service. There are at least four areas where quality assurance systems will need to be particularly sensitive. They concern the nature of the customer, the complexity of the service, the difficulty of measurement and the importance of ensuring continuous development and improvement.

The Nature of the Customer

Commercial models of quality assurance stress the notion of the customer. The tradition in many areas of guidance has been to place the individual recipient of guidance in this role, despite the fact that he or she has rarely been expected to pay for the service directly, and thus lacks the purchasing power which is the principal means of negotiating in a market economy. Experiments with vouchers have sought to rectify this, but to date guidance has usually been paid for directly by employers, educational institutions, or local or central government — each of which is therefore, in some sense, a customer of the service. All share a concern to maximize the match between opportunity (in learning or work) and individual potential. All will, from time to time, wish to encourage individuals to make particular choices: educators and trainers because the economics of providing education and training require that appropriate numbers are recruited for particular kinds of programme; government in order to prepare to meet long-term labour market skills needs as yet unperceived by individuals, or to reduce the numbers of people unemployed; and employers to meet the needs of the business by guiding individuals into (or out of) particular career routes. In all these cases, guidance is part of the process of negotiating a match between supply and demand, involving varying degrees of pressure and resistance.

There has, however, been increasing support for the notion of an individual-centred system. It is significant that the CBI, speaking on behalf of employers generally, argued the classic liberal case for individual choice in the education and training market in its report *Towards a Skills Revolution* (1989b). The argument is that individuals do not willingly make irrational choices, and that the collective economic interest will be better served by the combined effect of well-informed individual decisions than by attempts by employers or government to steer or direct. Since it is in the interests of both individual and employer that the choice be both well informed and 'owned' by the individual, the employer should exert influence through better information, not through coercion. A significant development of this principle in the late 1980s was the growth — led by the motor industry — of Employee Development schemes, which placed funds for training in the hands of the individual employee. These schemes appear to produce a dramatic growth of commitment to learning. After an initial period of turbulence, while the unfamiliar notion is absorbed, individuals do indeed seem to make rational choices, often very much more closely aligned with the employers' needs (whether for new skills or radical restructuring) than might be anticipated. This suggests a growing agreement that, whoever is paying, the prime customer is the individual recipient, although government is not always so willing to leave power in the individual's hands.

The Nature of Guidance

Quality assurance systems will also need to recognize the complexity of guidance itself. Guidance is not a simple product. Rather, it is a process of negotiation, in which neither the need nor the outcome is clearly defined at the beginning. Choices about guidance or indeed about learning and work are more like negotiation with an architect to build a house than like buying fish or furniture. They involve an outcome which neither party can visualize clearly at the beginning, and with a complex mix of short- and long-term implications, some of which will only be understood after irrevocable decisions have been made. The 'product' of learning or guidance is a new individual, changed by the process itself, and all these changes — economic, social and emotional — carry risks, as well as benefits, for that individual.

The people who understand this most clearly are, of course, the professionals who deliver guidance to individuals. Whether this is a careers teacher, a careers officer, a personnel officer, a college admissions officer or tutor, or an adult guidance worker, the central purpose of the professional is to interpret the client's necessarily inarticulate expression of need and support him or her through the processes of negotiation to meet that need. The professional does this on the basis both of theory and of previous experience of similar situations, and will always have more experience of the service, its potential, its ways of working and its outcomes than any single client. This professional power raises important questions of professional ethics, which have exercised the Advice, Guidance, Counselling and Psychotherapy Lead Body. In many fields, government has been anxious to develop ways of resisting 'producer capture' by professional interests. Nevertheless, quality assurance systems which fail to recognize that guidance professionals are more than simply a supplier in the market will inevitably distort and damage the service available.

The Problem of Measurement

The value of any process lies in its outcomes. But as Killeen, White and Watts (1992) have demonstrated, the outcomes of guidance are notoriously difficult to define and to measure adequately. One crucial reason for this is that the primary benefits of guidance for learning and work are long-term and endlessly changing. The same individual, asked about satisfaction with the guidance provided, is likely to give different answers at different times. Most people go through a period in the early stages of a new job or learning programme where they wonder whether they have made a mistake; many experience a period of elation at the end of a learning programme, which dissipates later. Other approaches to outcome measurement have been tried, especially in government programmes, where the government concern to reduce unemployment has resulted in crude notions of outcome which undermine the principle of impartial client-centredness discussed above. Outcomes like securing paid employment are easy to measure, but may not be the most appropriate long-term solution. Simple, and easily understood, measures of quality are thus very likely to mislead. If they are used as the basis for policy decisions, they may cause damage to the real quality of services or to individuals.

The Stimulation of Improvement

Many theorists of quality in the commercial world have stressed the importance of continuous improvement, proposing that individuals will, given the appropriate environment, wish to improve, and to deliver a high quality service (Bendell, 1991). Management must ensure that quality assurance systems do not destroy that inherent motivation. The key to this is leadership with clear and consistent purpose, a sense of ownership by all staff, and recognition of achievement rather than punishment of failure. While this does not imply the absence of objective criteria for performance, it places emphasis on stimulating continuous improvement, rather than the achievement of minimum thresholds. Significantly, this approach will be very familiar to most professional teachers and trainers.

A Way Forward

It follows that quality assurance systems for guidance will be complex. They will need to recognize the complexity of defining guidance and the views of its many customers; they will need to reflect the difficulties of assessing quality; and they will need to understand the importance of securing continuing commitment by all those who work in the service. We propose that this implies a system based around two key elements. The first is the creation of a community wider than the guidance professionals, where quality issues can be debated and developed, and the notion of quality shared, rather than an imposed framework of rigid criteria. The second is the establishment, by that community, of an agreed framework of principles, within which diverse practice can exist, and debate continue at a variety of levels. Progress has begun on both of these, although much work remains to be done.

The notion of a community is a response to the diversity of interests, agencies and practices involved in guidance, as funders, providers or beneficiaries. All are concerned to maximize quality, and each needs the opportunity to learn from the others. For this reason, the RSA and CBI in 1994 established, with the consent of government, the National Advisory Council for Careers and Educational Guidance, with the development of quality high on its agenda. Its purpose is to bring all the interests together to support a collective approach to defining and developing services and quality, across the many professional boundaries within the field.

An important parallel development was the creation in 1992, by the Employment Department, of the Advice, Guidance and Counselling Lead Body (subsequently expanded to become the Advice, Guidance, Counselling and Psychotherapy Lead Body). The Lead Body's role is to draw on the expertise of all relevant agencies to define a set of occupational standards which describe the competence of workers in the field. Its membership is drawn very broadly, and its debates are seeking to establish common ground across this range. Its remit, however, relates only to the national reform of vocational qualifications and does not include the quality of the services themselves.

The notion of a framework of principles is important in order to allow different agencies to operate without undue constraint, and to allow communication at a range of levels, from individual users to professional researchers. The first attempt to do this was carried out by the former National Educational Guidance Initiative, which worked with a broad group of professionals to produce a discussion paper *The Quest for Quality in Educational Guidance for Adults* (Rivis and Sadler, 1991). This paper proposed a framework of twenty elements against which any guidance agency could be assessed. The elements included some features like client-centredness and confidentiality to which any agency claiming to provide guidance would be expected to adhere, and others like information systems and feedback activities where standards would be locally set. Some were defined as absolutes, which must be present, while others only required a clear definition of what was, and was not, offered. In each case, the paper made suggestions about the kinds of evidence which might demonstrate acceptable quality.

This approach allows discussion of quality in guidance at a variety of levels. The framework helps to set the boundaries of professional debate about definitions, evidence, and standards, while allowing the individual user to understand what is being offered. The notion of 'impartiality', for example, is open to wide debate: professionals will wish to know how impartiality is expressed in practice, and to see appropriate evidence; some clients will be satisfied by being assured that this is the case, while others will wish to use the framework to probe the service providers in more depth.

This framework is in a very early stage of evolution, and there is much room for debate about its structure and content. Nevertheless, the principle — of creating a set of categories which enable people from very diverse backgrounds to communicate about quality, and to recognize what kinds of questions are relevant, what is essential, what optional, and what will vary according to context — is very important. A society organized around learning and work, rather than education and employment, will need such collective ways of understanding quality. If these collective processes can lead to effective strategies and instruments, guidance will then be equipped to play its crucial part in ensuring quality in learning and work themselves.

References

ARGYRIS, C. (1960) *Understanding Organizational Behavior*, Homewood, Illinois, Dorsey.

BENDELL, T. (1991) *The Quality Gurus*, London, Department of Trade and Industry.

CONFEDERATION OF BRITISH INDUSTRY (1989a). 'Towards a skills revolution — a Youth Charter' interim report of the Vocational Education and Training Task Force, London, CBI.

CONFEDERATION OF BRITISH INDUSTRY (1989b) *Towards a Skills Revolution*, report of the Vocational Education and Training Task Force, London, CBI.

CONFEDERATION OF BRITISH INDUSTRY (1993) *A Credit to Your Career*, London, CBI.

DEARING, R. (1994) *The National Curriculum and its Assessment: Final Report*, London, School Curriculum and Assessment Authority.

FURTHER EDUCATION FUNDING COUNCIL (1992) *Funding Learning*, Coventry, FEFC.

HANDY, C. (1989) *The Age of Unreason*, London, Business Books.

HERRIOT, P. (1992) *The Career Management Challenge*, London, Sage.

KILLEEN, J., WHITE, M. and WATTS, A.G. (1992) *The Economic Value of Careers Guidance*, London, Policy Studies Institute.

LE GRAND, J. and BARTLETT, W. (1993) *Quasi-Markets and Social Policy*, Basingstoke, Macmillan.

MCNAIR, S. (1990) 'Guidance and the education and training market', in WATTS, A.G. (ed.) *Guidance and Educational Change*, Cambridge, CRAC/Hobsons.

NATIONAL CURRICULUM COUNCIL (1990) *Curriculum Guidance 6: Careers Education and Guidance*, York, NCC.

NATIONAL COMMISSION ON EDUCATION (1993) *Learning to Succeed*, London, Heinemann.

PA CAMBRIDGE ECONOMIC CONSULTANTS (1993) *Research on the Labour Market Need for Advice and Guidance Services*, Cambridge, PACEC (mimeo).

RIVIS, V. and SADLER, J. (1991) *The Quest for Quality in Educational Guidance for Adults*, Leicester, Unit for the Development of Adult Continuing Education.

TEC NATIONAL COUNCIL (1994) *Individual Commitment to Lifetime Learning*, London, TEC National Council.

WATTS, A.G. (1983) *Education, Unemployment and the Future of Work*, Milton Keynes, Open University Press.

WATTS, A.G. (1991) 'The impact of the "new right": Policy challenges confronting careers guidance in England and Wales', *British Journal of Guidance and Counselling*, **19**(3), pp. 230–45.

WATTS, A.G. (1994) *A Strategy for Developing Careers Guidance Services for Adults*, Cambridge, Careers Research and Advisory Centre.

WATTS, A.G. and HAWTHORN, R. (1992) *Careers Education and the Curriculum in Higher Education*, Cambridge, CRAC/Hobsons.

Chapter 13

A Strategy to Achieve Lifelong Learning

Tony Webb

Introduction: The Key Messages

Anyone reading the preceding chapters of this book will be struck by three continuous themes which are shared by virtually all the contributors.

The first is the need to achieve the learning society or — as the Confederation of British Industry (CBI) has put it to highlight the economic imperative — 'to sustain the skills revolution'. Anyone looking for a divergence of view on this issue will be disappointed.

The second theme found in most contributions is the need to focus on the individual. The key to the learning society is to get the individual to take the lead and become responsible for her or his learning. There seems to be fairly broad agreement that top-down pressures from government, from employers and from the providers will not on their own do the trick, though this was not something which came through so strongly in the National Education Commission's vision and goals, which David Bradshaw summarizes in Chapter 1.

The third theme is the important role that the National Education and Training Targets (NETTs) and the Investors in People (IiP) standard have to play in the achievement of the skills revolution. One is struck by how much has been achieved over the last ten years, especially in terms of putting in place the appropriate education and training infrastructure. While more still needs to be done, the message that emerges is that we must perhaps concentrate most of our attention on getting the key actors — providers, employers and individuals — to use the system to deliver the outcomes that are needed. As Jon Ainger and Roy Harrison say in Chapter 3 'Britain still requires a quantum leap in skills if we are to compete at the highest level . . . learning is the key to Britain's future'.

Finally, only the chapters, by Christopher Ball and Tony Cann, make relatively frequent reference to ideas such as efficiency and value for money. This point is taken up later.

This concluding chapter seeks to do two things:

Tony Webb

1   First to draw conclusions in policy terms on the strategy that
     needs to be followed to achieve lifetime learning.
2   Second to suggest what should be the outputs of the education
     and training system in the year 2000 that we should now be seek-
     ing to achieve.

A Strategy for Lifelong Learning

If we are to continue to make progress and build on what has been achieved,
then we need a strategy for learning. Not only should the strategy need
to be explicit, but it will need to have won the support of all the key
players in the education and training field. They include, above all, the
individuals who *are* Britain. A consensus must be formed around the
strategy which is strong enough to persuade the politicians or indeed any
other grouping not to divert from its implementation.

Though it will surprise some, the evidence suggests that such a strategy does exist, even if it is hidden from the view of many involved. There
are seven fronts on which we must work if we are to sustain the skills
revolution, become a learning society and see the development of a culture
of lifelong learning:

* set national learning targets
* achieve coherence
* empower individuals
* create a social market
* establish a national qualifications system
* enhance local delivery
* spread best practice

Action has been taken in all of these areas already, though more needs to
be done.

1 National Learning Targets

The National Education and Training Targets (NETTS) were originally
proposed in the CBI Report *Towards a Skills Revolution* (CBI, 1989) and
agreed and published in 1991. Some people were surprised that the NETTS
were originated by employers, yet perhaps the best known business adage
is that if you cannot measure it then you cannot manage it. Or, put more
sharply, if you don't know where you are going, it is difficult to be
confident you will reach your destination.

Now we do know where we are going. We have the National Advisory Council for Education and Training Targets (NACETT) which

178

was set up by the Government in March 1993, as an independent body containing a majority of employers, with the main roles of monitoring progress and of advising ministers on policy to achieve the targets.

The targets provide a focus for education and training policy and many — but not all — relate to learning outcomes rather than inputs or processes. Some observers believe they have already proved their worth by leading to achievements beyond those which would have happened if the targets had not existed. While this is difficult to prove, it is not an impossible hypothesis. Further, the attempts to monitor the targets have highlighted the paucity of available data, especially on vocational achievement.

NACETT has already performed a valuable role by ensuring there has been a steep improvement in the quality of information needed to monitor effectively the progress towards the targets and is even now consulting on revised targets to be put in place by 1995 and which will have a common achievement year of 2000. Outside the policy field, there is still a big awareness gap amongst those involved in the provision of education and training that prevents the targets having their maximum impact. Hopefully, widespread consultation and changes in their presentation will help to put this right.

The concept of NETTs has had bipartisan support from all the political parties. They have become an established part of the education and training infrastructure. With the advantage of hindsight it is perhaps surprising that it took so long for the idea of national targets to be both advocated and adopted.

2 Coherence

'Lack of coherence' may be an overused phrase in much education and training literature, yet history provides several examples where policy on education has not appeared to be developed in tandem with policy on vocational training — and vice versa. Many believe that these instances would not have occurred if there had been just one government department responsible for education and training policy. That may or may not be true, but there have also been, in the past, elements of incoherence within the policies of each of the two major departments — Education and Employment — let alone between them.

But we must look to the future, not the past, and much has been done in recent years to put the Government's education and training policy on a more coherent basis. The learning provision of the 16–19-year-old age group is the one area that continues to stand out as needing most attention. Yet even here the main issues are now being tackled.

First, the introduction of General National Vocational Qualifications (GNVQs) as a third 'route' for this age group (and others) represents a major development. These new qualifications provide not only for the transition from education to work, but also at the higher levels, for entry to higher education. There are GNVQ units which provide for the 'core skills' that employers value so highly, and the modular structure facilitates the learning process. There is some scope for GNVQs or core skills elements to be taken both by academic 'A'- and 'AS'-level students on the one hand and by those following the work-based National Vocational Qualification (NVQ) route on the other, though this scope is not yet as wide as it should be. GNVQs have yet to prove themselves in practice and the greatest risk is that, given the immense school, college and student demand for them, standards will be variable and the qualification will become discredited. That must not be allowed to happen.

Coherence at the 16–19 stage will also be promoted by the decision of the Government, announced in its White Paper on Competitiveness in May 1994 (DTI, 1994), to consult on the introduction of financial learning credits for all 16-year-olds, not just those opting for employment or training. The present intention (September 1994) is to follow the consultations with a Green Paper and to pilot the scheme. Currently the arrangements for funding a 16–19 provision are like the proverbial dog's dinner. Students face a variety of funding pathways — by the local education authorities for LMS schools; by the Funding Agency for Schools for grant maintained schools and City Technology Colleges; by the Further Education Funding Council for Further Education and Sixth Form Colleges; and by TECs, LECs and employers for those following the work-based route. Learning credits could provide a coherent financial framework which, it has been argued, is an essential element if real parity of esteem between the different learning routes is to be achieved.

3 Social Market

Competition provides the biggest stimulus for businesses to change what they are doing and how they are doing it to the benefit of the economy. What is needed is for similar pressures to be brought to bear on education and training providers to supplement their own efforts to adapt to changing circumstances.

Many employers in this country and the USA got heavily involved in manpower planning in the 1960s and 1970s, and burnt their fingers rather badly in trying, and largely failing, to predict their future skill needs. It was not just employers who got it wrong but governments as well. As a result, the way employers look at developing the competencies of their employees has changed dramatically. What employers are looking for now are employees who have a broad range of transferable skills and are flexible enough to adapt quickly to acquire new competences as circumstances change ever faster. What is more, employers are increasingly looking to providers who can deliver the necessary training on a just-in-time basis.

Pressures for increased public expenditure continue to grow with longer life expectancy, advances in medical science and practices, and an increase in the environmental consciousness of the electorate at large. It is not obvious that there is going to be any significant reduction in these pressures over the next few years. At the same time many observers believe that political parties seeking to get elected will not succeed in doing so if higher taxes are a prominent part of their programmes. The twin pressures for more public spending yet no tax increases have led to an urgent drive by governments in all the western democracies to find more efficient and effective ways of getting increased value from public expenditure. One such approach is to seek to bring the benefits of competition to enhance public sector services.

Unfortunately the concepts of the social market and market testing have become embroiled in debates about political dogma, which has politicized the process and made it appear an argument between extremes. The reality is different. The social market can deliver considerable benefits in terms of better performance without requiring anyone to be a 'slave to the market'. Indeed, such a system is 'social' in so far as it responds to the individual's and society's needs, and 'market' in that it introduces necessary, yet controlled, competition to stimulate improvements in performance.

Public sector education and training provision is of course a service and it cannot be measured in cash terms alone. Nevertheless, the provision needs to be effective in terms of outputs — such as how many people benefit and to what levels — and, at a time when public finance is in short supply, efficient in how it uses the resources at its disposal.

In his 1992 Social Market Foundation pamphlet 'Fighting Leviathan', Howard Davies identified ten common features of an effective social market. Perhaps the five most crucial ones are:

(i)   a *financial framework* that ensures *accountability* and *rewards performance;*

(ii) a set of *clearly defined and measurable outputs* as public services no less than business ones need to be explicit about what they are trying to achieve;

(iii) a *purchaser-provider* split so that those responsible for purchasing the service and controlling its quality, and those responsible for providing this service, should not be the same people;

(iv) a *variety of different providers* to compete against one another and thus keep standards high; and

(v)   *reliable data on performance* so that well informed choices can be made by the purchasers. (Davies, 1992)

Experience tells us — the Technical Vocational Education Initiative (TVEI), the Work Related Further Education (WRFE) budget and the Enterprise in Higher Education Initiatives (EHE) to give just three examples — that financial incentives can have a marked influence on education and training provision.

The introduction of financial learning credits would help create a social market for 16–19 education and training as well as empowering students, enhancing motivation and increasing coherence. While the Further Education Funding Council (FEFC) has done an excellent job in seeking to develop a funding methodology that provides incentives to colleges to enhance their efficiency, the methodology used fits in very well with the concept of financial learning credits and could easily be delivered through them.

4 Individual Empowerment

There is increasing recognition that if a learning culture is to become the norm in the UK, we need to find ways of encouraging individuals to take responsibility and control for their own learning. This theme comes out in many of the previous chapters in this book. As Sir Christopher Ball has so graphically put it, many people see education (and training) as something which is 'done to them' rather than something which they have played a part in doing themselves.

It has surprised many that perhaps the strongest call for the empowerment of individuals in their learning has come from employers. One of the main themes of the CBI report *Towards A Skills Revolution* was that individuals needed to be put first:

> It remains a priority to create a new culture in which the school leaving age ceases to be an end to education and in which the development of skills and knowledge continues throughout working life.

A recent Institute of Management (IM) survey has identified empowerment as one of the three major challenges facing managers in the next decade (IM, 1994).

It has been suggested that the dramatic increase in the numbers of young people at age 16 staying on in full-time education or obtaining structured training in employment leading to the acquisition of NVQs — a CBI policy objective for all those taking the work-based route — from 48 per cent in 1986 to an estimated 80 per cent in 1993, has meant that 'motivation' is not an issue. The practical experience of employers recruiting young people is that it is still a minority of young people who leave school sprinting to embrace the culture of lifetime learning. Motivation and the winning of commitment remains on the agenda.

Empowerment is the key to achieving the widespread acquisition of the learning culture. Employers are increasingly realizing it, and beginning to reap the benefits of releasing the untapped potential of individuals in terms of higher skill and competence levels and improved individual and organizational performance. The financial learning credits initiative could be the vehicle for spreading the learning culture, yet educators are apprehensive of their students explicitly becoming their customers. They are not alone. You just have to talk to employers who are recruiting young people and have been faced with potential young employees armed with training credits and wanting to know what types of training are available to them, to realize what a major change is being implemented. At the same time, one also realizes what a desirable change it is.

The empowerment and credit debate has already had one beneficial impact. This is the substantially increased investment in careers education and guidance, especially for young people, that has taken place over the last few years. Still further increased expenditure on careers education and guidance was announced in the Competitiveness White Paper in May 1994 (DTI, 1994). It is now recognized that high quality careers education and guidance can actually save the tax payer money by ensuring that less young people are taking education or training options for which they are not best suited. Tony Watts and Stephen McNair identify in Chapter 12 of this book, an emerging strategy for lifelong guidance to support life-long learning and make the point that learning, work and career are now increasingly owned by the individual rather than the organization.

5 National Qualification System

A national system of vocational qualifications is a key element of the skills revolution. Qualifications have a number of functions to perform including recording the achievement of knowledge, skills and competence, and providing a ladder for progression. Other important roles are to provide the vehicles for lifetime learning and, by ensuring rigorous, frequently updated and broad standards, qualifications contribute to upgrading skills and achieving the competent and adaptable workforce that is essential if the UK is to be competitive in world markets.

David Bradshaw, in the opening chapter of this book, identifies one of the sharpest differences between employment and education being that the former is about getting the job done, while the latter emphasizes the acquisition of knowledge, much of it divorced from its applications. John Hillier (Chapter 9) explains how competence-based qualifications differ from norm-referenced, academic ones and why the former are favoured by growing numbers of employers. A CBI survey of its members, *Quality Assessed* (CBI, 1994), found that well over nine out of ten employers saw advantages in the introduction of the NVQ and Scottish Vocational

Qualification (SVQ) system with its competence-based and employer-determined standards. The CBI survey — and others — have identified a number of obstacles that stand in the way of the take up of NVQs and put forward a range of recommendations to make the system more user friendly for both employers and individuals.

For those of us impatient about the hesitancy with which employers are taking up NVQs, it is worth remembering that the German system took many decades in its formation. It is essential that standards contained in NVQs are high and relevant and that the quality of assessment is beyond reproach. Whether NVQs should eventually become a legally required licence to practice, as John Hillier suggests, is likely to become increasingly debated. That debate should not be allowed to get in the way of the efforts to get the full NVQ framework in place as soon as possible. It would be a tragedy if political uncertainty should undermine the development of the NVQ system.

Ken Richardson, in Chapter 5, refers to the importance of organizing vocational training in the workplace and the introduction of the NVQ system will undoubtedly make on-the-job training more respectable again. This is already happening and it will provide a major challenge to the private and college providers. While the new regime for colleges will see an increase in their responsiveness to customer needs, they will do well if they can effectively meet the developing demand by employers for what was termed earlier in this chapter as 'just-in-time' training. More generally, there has been a substantive change in the balance of training demanded by businesses in the last few years, with a relative switch away from the initial and induction training of their new recruits, towards the up-skilling and multi-skilling of their current employees.

6 Local Delivery

One of the major defects of the UK training infrastructure has been the fact that while there have been mechanisms to take forward initiatives at the national, and to a lesser extent, the sectoral level, many valuable initiatives in the vocational education and training field have passed smaller firms by. Given that according to the *Training in Britain* study (DE, 1989), nine out of ten small firms do not train, this has clearly been a matter of major concern to policy makers and governments.

The establishment of the employer-led, locally based Training and Enterprise Councils (TECs) in England and Wales and Local Enterprise Companies in Scotland (LECs) has been a bold political initiative to fill this gap. The fact that 1,200 local leaders of industry have agreed to serve on these strategic bodies gives an indication of the increasing importance businesses attach to education and training.

While there has been some uncertainty about the balance of the work of TECs, in relation to training on the one hand and economic development on the other — and between the training of the young and unemployed and the training of the employed — the establishment of the TECs and LECs has been a major development, and is already beginning to yield benefits in terms of relating training more closely to local employer needs. TECs are not direct providers of training — they contract out the provision — and there has been a significant fall in the unit cost of the TEC training schemes, mainly Youth Training (YT) and Training for Work (TFW), as more business-like approaches have been applied to the contracting process. TECs and LECs also run the Youth Credits schemes and are responsible at the local level for the delivery of the new Modern Apprenticeships and Accelerated Modern Apprenticeship sectoral schemes. They also award the Investors in People standard.

The expansion of the TEC National Council has given the TECs an enlarged central unit which should enhance significantly their efficiency when operating collectively at the national level. There are also signs that the spread of best practice is being conducted in a more methodological way, though the TEC National Council has not yet established a centrally controlled team of experts that can visit TECs and suggest ways of improving performance.

With the establishment of such a radically new approach to training at the local level, it is inevitable that teething problems should occur. Many of these relate to the administrative burdens imposed on TECs by their sponsoring government departments and the Treasury, but others relate to an earlier lack of willingness by TECs to adopt common systems in dealing with their customers and, particularly important, their suppliers. These issues are being tackled, though some TECs continue to be jealous to preserve their independence and local identity. The common national framework for the delivery of Youth Credits, for example, still gives too much weight to local, rather than national, considerations.

There are other tasks too. One issue which remains to be resolved is the resourcing of TECs. The CBI has suggested that TECs should have a single budget and be free to use that in the way they think best to deliver the required outputs. The move towards three-year licences should help TECs plan ahead more confidently and enhance their dealings with suppliers. Concern about shortages of resources has led a very small number of TECs to get involved in direct service delivery, in competition with other providers. This is a mistake. As far as is reasonably possible, TECs need to be confident that, given their strategic role, they can continue to look with confidence to sustained taxpayer funding. The CBI has suggested that there is a case, which needs to be studied in detail, for TECs and LECs being resourced by a funding council rather than by the relevant government departments.

Another key issue that TECs and LECs need to resolve is to establish their local accountability. At present TEC and LEC Boards are not elected and are judged by some observers as suffering from a 'democratic deficit'.

It is important that TECs and LECs should continue to be business-led with a clear employer majority if they are to continue to win full business support and involvement. If that position changes, there is a serious possibility that business leaders will vote with their feet. This would seriously weaken the authority of TECs with the local business community. In practice, there is much TECs and LECs can do to enhance their accountability to the local community and, in this context, it is encouraging that the TEC National Council has taken up a CBI recommendation to develop a code of best practice for local accountability.

The main indicator of the success of TECs and LECs in the end will be the extent to which they have been able to involve employers, especially those from small firms, previously untouched by the skills revolution. It would be nothing short of a calamity if TECs and LECs, as employer-led bodies, were not given time to prove themselves. In this context it does no harm to remind ourselves that the youngest TECs are only just 4-years-old.

7 *Spread of Best Practice*

Any strategy for education and training must involve the spread of best practice. This is all the more important given the very substantial changes taking place in the institutional framework and in the responsibilities of the delivery agents, particularly higher education institutions, colleges and schools. Steps are being taken to ensure this happens. The work of OFSTED and the four-yearly inspection of schools is one such example. Another is the inspection activities of the Further Education Funding Council which have led to the production of an excellent series of reports on further education colleges, identifying areas where performance can be improved. It would be beneficial if a body such as the Audit Commission were charged with generally overseeing efficiency and effectiveness studies in the education field. The Audit Commission has been excluded from inspection activities for individual institutions in these areas, but it could perform a valuable role with general studies on particular education efficiency issues.

The Investors in People (IiP) standard is proving an extremely effective device for enhancing the training performance within organizations. Organizations gaining the award know they are following a systematic approach towards the training and development of their employees. Very few organizations have achieved this standard without benefiting from the 'journey' and there is already strong evidence that changes in practice, especially but not exclusively in the field of the evaluation of training, will bring substantial benefits to employees and employers alike. One of the most encouraging features is that the standard relates to all organizations, and bridges the divide that has sometimes existed between business, public sector and other organizations.

Currently administered by TECs and LECs, the IiP standard is the 'jewel in the crown' in terms of potentially assisting in the up-skilling and multi-skilling of all those in work, and generally ensuring that the training performance of organizations matches that of the best. Tony Cann, in Chapter 10 of this book, identifies the standard as the right vehicle to deliver the lifetime learning targets. After a slow start, the take-up of the standard is accelerating quickly. While it is unlikely that the National Lifetime Target of half of the organizations employing over 200 employees achieving the standard by the end of 1996 will be met, the IiP standard remains the most effective vehicle for enhancing the training of those in employment. It is important that high standards continue to be applied to the assessment process. The consequences of the credibility of the standard being undermined would be very damaging.

The IiP standard has been identified as a possible exemption mechanism if a national training levy were introduced. Irrespective of the view one might take of a statutory levy system, the question needs to be asked of whether the standard could stand up to the pressure that might be put on it? Whatever happens, the standard must not be undermined.

Education and Training in the Year 2000

If the full support of all the key players were gained for the seven-point strategy, what would the education and training system look like in the year 2000?

Despite the encouraging developments referred to earlier in this chapter, and by Jon Ainger and Roy Harrison in Chapter 2, the UK remains well down the world league table in education and skills. A tremendous effort is required from all concerned if the original national targets, set in 1991, are to be met, let alone the new ones that will be put in place in 1995. Furthermore, our main competitors are not standing still and many are setting themselves ambitious targets. South Korea aims to have 80 per cent of their young people qualified to higher education entry standard by the year 2000. Closer to home, France has an equivalent target of 75 per cent.

If the education and training system in the year 2000 is to contribute fully to helping UK businesses compete effectively and thus generate the national resources required to bring improved public sector services and higher living standards, then the following outcomes, relating to the seven point strategy, are required.

1 National Targets

The revised national targets set in 1995 will have been met. This means that in terms of skills levels, the UK will have roughly caught up with many of our main competitors.

New targets will be in place which, if met, will enable the UK to take the lead in the international skills league by the year 2010.

2 Coherence

A coherent system of 16–19-year-old provision will be in place, characterized by relevant criterion-referenced qualifications and core skills, 100 per cent use of the National Record of Achievement and action planning, together with a single financial framework based on learning credits.

There will be a clear financial framework so that all involved — government, business, parents and individuals — understand their respective responsibilities in the funding of learning.

Ninety-five per cent of adults will believe that relevant education and training can be of benefit to them and their employability, and will take a pro-active role in seeking lifelong learning.

3 Individual Empowerment

Enhanced careers education and guidance will be available at regular intervals, not only to all young people but also to adults.

Voluntary individual training accounts will be used by all adults who want them.

Taxpayer-funded learning credits will be the basis of the funding of all 16–19 learning and the taxpayer contribution to higher education funding will be through the 'student'.

As a major source of higher level skills, 40 per cent of young people will be successfully qualifying through the higher education system.

All the unemployed will have automatic access to appropriate learning opportunities.

4 Social Market

As indicated above, taxpayer-funded learning credits will be in place for all 16–19-year-olds and the taxpayer's contribution to the funding of higher education will be directed through the student.

All institutions providing education and training will be as responsive to change and the needs of their customers as the best businesses in the toughest markets.

5 Effective Qualification System

The national curriculum, including technology as a core subject, and careers education, will be fully embedded in schools and supported by all but the most blindered teachers.

A uniform and coherent national learning qualifications system will be in place, embracing both education and training at all levels. The system will be characterized by defined outcomes or competences, transferable core skills, credit accumulation, transfers between academic and vocational routes, and breadth encouraging self-reliance and flexibility.

Assisted by a competence-based qualifications system, effective and continuous training, regular appraisal and performance related pay, the quality of UK teachers and lecturers will match that of any other country in the world.

Seventy per cent of managers and supervisors in both the public and private sectors will have relevant competence-based qualifications.

6 Local Delivery

TECs and LECs will have earned the full support of local businesses and all other partners in the local community.

TECs and LECs, as employer-led bodies, will have become fully effective strategic governors in their localities and the preferred delivery mechanism for all national learning initiatives, both public and private, at the local level.

Assisted by Business Link, and other TEC and LEC initiatives, 50 per cent of small organizations with ten or less employees will be involved in training.

7 Best Practice

Eighty per cent of organizations employing more than ten people will have achieved the IiP standard and will systematically evaluate their education and training.

Half of the one hundred largest UK-based businesses will have become recognized 'learning organizations'.

Statutory intervention will no longer be a training policy issue.

The European Community will look to the UK education and training system as the main source of best practice and innovation.

Change will be regarded by all organizations and 90 per cent of employees as an 'ally' to progress and enhanced performance rather than a threat.

Conclusion

We have travelled a remarkable distance towards becoming a learning society over the last decade. With the advantage of hindsight, the progress made has been far in excess of the expectations of ten years ago. Credit is due to many for this advance. Yet there remains much more to be done and, if the skills revolution is to be sustained, the journey of progress should never end. The danger of complacency must be avoided, but it is encouraging that few of those involved in policy development are remotely satisfied with where we are. They recognize that still further major improvements in our education and training performance are essential for our future competitiveness. Continuous improvement must become an integral feature of our education and training system. It is no longer a dream to believe we can become a learning society; it is within our grasp.

References

CBI (1989) *Towards a Skills Revolution*, London, CBI.
CBI (1994) *Quality Assessed*, London, CBI.
DAVIES, H. (1992) *Fighting Leviathan: Building Social Markets That Work*, London, The Social Market Forum.
DE (1989) *Training in Britain*, London, HMSO.
DTI (1994) *Competitiveness: Helping Business to Win*, London, HMSO.
HM Inspectorate (1992) *Survey of Guidance 13–19 in Schools and Sixth Form Colleges*, London, DES.
IM (1994) *Management Development to the Millennium*, London, IM.

Notes on Contributors

Jon Ainger joined the Education and Training Directorate of the CBI in January 1994. His policy responsibilities include training for young people, careers guidance and special needs. He is a member of PETRA, the European Committee of initial vocational training.

Sir Christopher Ball is Director of Learning at the RSA (Royal Society for the encouragements of Arts, Manufacturers and Commerce). He was formerly Warden of Keble College, Oxford (1980–88) and Chairman of the Board of the National Advisory Body for Public Sector Higher Education (1982–88). He is the author of a number of books and reports on learning and has advised and lectured on education and training, and the relationship between learning and the workplace in more than a dozen countries in the last five years.

David Bradshaw OBE is Researcher to the RSA's Learning Society Exchange, Editor of its Newsletter *Synapse* and an education consultant. He was a college principal for nineteen years, a member of the Board of the National Advisory Body for Public Sector Higher Education and Honorary Secretary of The Association of Colleges for Further and Higher Education from 1983–88.

Tony Cann CBE is currently Chairman or Director of a number of companies in engineering, textiles, electronics and distribution in the UK, USA and eastern Europe. He is also Chairman of East Lancashire Training and Enterprise Council, and one of two North-West representatives on the TEC National Council, a member of the National Advisory Council for Education and Training Targets, a member of the Further Education Funding Council and a Ministerial representative for the North-West Council for Sport and Recreation.

Roy Harrison has been Head of Training Policy at the CBI since June, 1991. He worked in the personnel, education and training functions of British Coal for 29 years, finally as Principal of BC's Management Staff

College. He was a member of BTEC's Engineering Advisory Board and is a member of NVVQ's NVQ Accreditation Committee and of the Council of the National Advisory Council for Careers Education and Educational Guidance.

John Hillier joined the National Council for Vocational Qualifications as Director of Accreditation after many years of working in the glass, steel and tobacco industries and has been its Chief Executive since 1 August 1991. Under his direction, NCVQ met the Government's target that the NVQ framework should cover 80 per cent of the employed population at levels 1–4 by December 1992 and has successfully introduced GNVQs in over 1,000 schools and colleges.

Alan Jones is Senior Research Fellow at the Centre for Corporate Strategy and Change at the University of Warwick Business School. He trained and has worked both as a teacher and as a management consultant, and is the main author of a number of publications on the theme of the learning organization and adult development in the workplace.

Anne Jones is Professor of Continuing Education at Brunel University. After qualifying and working as a teacher, social worker and school counsellor she spent seventeen years running secondary schools in London. Then, for four years, she directed the Department of Employment's Education Programmes. She is the author of numerous books, an established broadcaster and a council member of several distinguished bodies, notably the RSA.

Stephen McNair is Associate Director for Higher Education of the National Institute of Adult Continuing Education (NIACE) and Further and Higher Education Adviser to the Employment Department. He previously worked as a teacher and administrator and was for eight years the Head of the Unit for the Development of Adult Continuing Education (UDACE). He is a member of the Executive Committee of the National Advisory Council for Careers and Educational Guidance.

Alasdair Paterson is Librarian at Exeter University. He entered the library profession after distinguished studies at Edinburgh and Sheffield Universities and his previous posts have been at the university of Liverpool, Cork and Sheffield, and he was a member of the Sheffield 2,000 group.

Naomi Sargant has combined a professional life as an educator and social researcher, with a commitment to opening up educational opportunities for adults. She spent twelve years as a market and social researcher at the Gallup Poll before joining Enfield College of Technology as head of marketing teaching. She was founding Senior Commissioning Editor for Educational Programmes on Channel 4 for eight years, a member of the Advisory Council for Adult and Continuing Education and has written widely on the education of adults, and the use of the media for education.

Ken Richardson worked in industry and spent several years in the RAF before taking a first degree in Biology and Psychology and then a PhD in neurobiology with the Open University's Brain Research Group. He became Research Officer to the National Child Development Study at the National Children's Bureau before returning to the Open University as a Lecturer (and then Senior Lecturer) in the Psychology of Education. His current research is on conceptual development and cognition in context.

Tony Watts OBE is Director of the National Institute for Careers Education and Counselling, which is sponsored by the Careers Research and Advisory Centre in Cambridge (**CRAC**). A joint founder of CRAC, he has written a large number of books and articles, has carried out many projects for government bodies, and has acted as a consultant to a number of international organizations including the European Commission, OECD and UNESCO.

Tony Webb was appointed Director of Education and Training at the CBI in July 1986. He started work at Gallup Poll doing commercial market research. He joined the CBI's Economic Directorate and eventually became Deputy Economic Director. His areas of responsibility included industrial policy, taxation, price control and local government finance. Since he became Director of Education and Training, the CBI has produced a number of important reports including *Towards a Skills Revolution* (1989), *World Class Targets* (1991), *Routes for Success* (1993), *Making Labour Markets Work* (1993) and *Thinking Ahead* (1994).

Index

'A' levels 9, 20, 45, 143, 144, 147, 148
    failure rate 157
    maintaining standards 158
    predictive power 67, 153
    syllabus content 154
abstract knowledge 73
academic learning 23–4, 69, 75
academic libraries
    access to information 132, 133
        electronic 133
        local community and public access 137
    changing role 131, 134, 138
    competition for resources 131–2, 134, 136–7
    Fielden report 134–5
    Follett report 132
    intellectual property 133, 137
    new markets in higher education 135–6
Accelerated Learning (AL) 79, 80
Accelerated Modern Apprenticeships 43, 185
access 48
accreditation 164
added value 2, 4, 20, 21, 140
Adult Learners' Week 1994 59
adult learning theory 116–18
adult training see lifelong learning
Advice, Guidance, Counselling and
        Psychotherapy Lead Body 172, 174
Advisory Council for Adult and Continuing
        Education (ACACE) 49–51, 52, 55, 60
Ainley, P. and Corney, M. 52, 53
America 2000 18
apprenticeships 34, 43, 143
Argyris, C. 163
Arup Partnership 20
aspirations 1
assessment 114–15, 153
    criterion-referenced 157, 158
    modular 157–8, 164
    purpose 156–7
    reliability and independence 155–6
    use in reward or funding systems 160
Audit Commission 45, 186
automation 2, 4
autonomy 117

Ball, Sir Christopher 12, 19, 24, 25, 58, 60, 65,
        91, 105, 182
Banham, Sir John 15
BBC (British Broadcasting Corporation) 6
Beer, M., Eisenstat, R.A. and Spector, B. 125

behaviourist psychology 86–7
Bendell, T. 173
Bennett, R., Glennerster, H. and Nevison, D.
        18
Berryman, S.E. and Bailey, T.R. 9
bibliographic services 132, 133
Blake, Quentin 80
bodily intelligence 81–2
Boeing 99
Borges, Jorge Luis 132
brain function 80–81, 88–90
Branson, Richard 30
Briggs, Katherine 85
British Library Document Supply Centre 132
British Standards 5750 145
Brookfield, S.D. 113, 115, 116, 117, 120, 126
Bruer, J.T. 87, 91
Brundage, D.H. and Mackeracher, D. 122
Brunel Management Programme 103
Bruner, J.S. 73
BTEC (Business and Technician Education
        Council) 56, 146, 148

cable TV 136
Callaghan, James 38
Campbell, Mike 22, 31
Canada 98
Canon 99
car production 4 see also Ford; Nissan; Rover
        Cars
Career Development Loans 61
career progression 163–4
careers guidance 165–6
    neutrality 167–70
Careership 41
Carraher, T.N., Carraher, D.W. and
        Schliemann, A.D. 73
Cassels, John 53
CBI (Confederation of British Industry) 47, 185
    A Credit to Your Career (1993) 168
    Quality Assessed (1994) 42, 156, 183
    Thinking Ahead (1994) 18, 28, 105, 107, 134
    Towards a Skills Revolution (1989) 24, 41, 45,
        57, 163, 171, 177, 178, 182
CD ROMS 145
Ceci, S.J. 67
cerebral cortex 80, 89
change, organizational 102–9, 123–5 see also
        learning organizations
China 140

City and Guilds of London Institute 152, 154
City Technology Colleges 180
cleaning staff 5–6
cognitive psychology 86–7
Cole, M. 73
colleges of further education 146
  provision of higher education 149
  regional management 147–9
Collins, J. and Porras, J. 117
communications technology 98, 101, 145
communities of enquiry 123
communities of learning 123
communities of practice 125
Community Education and Training Advice
  Centres (CETACs) 168
companies: organizational change 102–9, 123–5
competence 154, 157, 159
competitive advantage 2, 15, 16, 18, 19, 20, 39,
  41, 140
  Pacific Rim 98–102
competitive examinations 157, 158
computer-assisted learning 100, 145
computer manufacturing systems 99
computer skills 5, 7
conceptual skills 27–8
Confucian societies 20, 30
Constable, J. and McCormick, R. 40
construction industry 35
consultancy 4, 104, 115–16
consumer spending 15
continuing education 20, 29
  Advisory Council for Adult and Continuing
    Education 49–51
  definition 52
Cook, M. 67
cooperative behaviour 70–71, 97, 99
Coopers and Lybrand 39
copyright 137
core curriculum 38, 39
corpus callosum 80
Courtaulds Aerospace Advanced Materials
  Division 125
credit accumulation 164
Credit Accumulation and Transfer Scheme
  (CATS) 61
credits, financial *see* Learning Credits; Youth
  Credits
criterion-referenced assessment 157, 158
Crosland, Anthony 48
Crowther, G. (Baron Crowther) 47
Csikszentmihalyi, Mihaly 87
Cullingford, C. 112, 113, 115, 116, 120, 123,
  126
curriculum 9, 38, 39
  core skills 107
  information and communication technologies
    98, 101
  rote learning 96
customer-focused education 107, 159, 171–3,
  183

Darkenwald, G.G. and Merriam, S.B. 122
Darwinian theory 66, 69, 70, 74
databases 132, 137, 145
Davies Howard 16, 33, 181
Dearing, Sir Ron 165
Denmark 148

Department for Education 147
Department of Education and Science (DES) 51,
  52, 55, 56–8, 154
Department of Employment 35, 39, 44, 47, 54,
  57, 62, 184
Department of Trade and Industry 108, 180
DeVille Working Group 40
Dickens, Charles 152
disembedded thinking 73–4
disposable income 1
distance learning 135
document delivery 132, 133
Donald, M. 72
Donaldson, M. 73
Dryden, Gordon and Vos, Jeannette 82–3, 89

Eastern Europe 140
Economic and Social Research Council (ESRC)
  22, 108
economic change 1–3, 93
economic decline 1, 14
Economist, The 89
Edelman, G. 90
Educating Cities movement 14
Education Business Partnerships 45
Education Reform Act 1988 38, 42
educational research 24
educational standards 94
  pastoral/academic split 97
educational system *see also* learning
  aims 13–14
  assessment of learning potential 66–9
  bias against adult learners 54, 56
  customer focus 107, 159, 183
  'drop-outs' 18–19, 20
  'great debate' 38
  learning strategies 9–10
  links with industry 37, 38
  measuring outcome 95, 97–8
  National Commission on Education 11–12
  Pacific Rim 100, 101
  single chance theory 82–3
  teamwork 10
  traditional progression 162–3
  transfer of learning 9
Edwards, D. and Mercer, N.M. 68
Eisner, E.W. 113
electronic access 133
electronic publishing 137, 145
Eliot, T.S. 95
élitism 68
empirical research 24
Employee Development schemes 171
employers
  investment in training 39–40, 44, 56, 59
  predicting future skill needs 180–81
  provision of training 144–5
  work-based traineeships 150
    learning credits 183
employment changes 8, 155, 163–4
employment market 3–4
  change in education 9–12
  general trends 8
  inter-person services 3, 5–6
  routine production services 3, 4–5
  structural instability 2
  symbolic-analytical services 3–4, 6–8

Employment Training programmes 60, 62
empowerment 158, 182–3, 188
encapsulations 122–3, 125
enfranchisement 75
engineering 3, 6–7, 10
    qualifications 154–5
English language 26–7
Enterprise in Higher Education 105, 107,
    182
entitlement 60–62
episodic learning 119
ethnic minorities 59, 60
Eurotechnet 108
evaluation 114–15, 126
examinations 152
    criterion-referenced assessment 157, 158
    hidden costs 153, 156
    predictive power 67, 152–3
    purpose 156–7
    reliability and independence of examiners
        155–6
    traditional progression 162
    use in reward or funding systems 160

facial appearance 66
Faure, E. 14
Fielden report 134–5
financial provisions 59–60, 103–4, 149–51
Foden, F. 152
Follett, Sir Brian 132
Ford 57, 108
France 33, 187
Fulton, O. and Elwood, S. 67
Funding Agency for Schools (FAS) 42, 180
further education 27–8 *see also* colleges of
        further education
    careers guidance 166
Further Education Funding Council (FEFC)
        43, 142, 147, 148, 166, 180, 182,
        186
Further Education Unit (FEU) 38

Gardner, Howard 68, 81, 82, 90
Gateways to Learning 168
GCSE (General Certificate of Education) 33, 43,
        152, 153, 158
gender issues 59, 60
genetics 69–71
George, J. and Glasgow, J. 73
German language 79
Germany 33, 39, 146, 150, 152, 160
Girling, R. 8
global economy 1–2
GNVQs (General National Vocational
        Qualifications) 43, 45, 143, 144, 146,
        148, 158, 179–80
Goodwin, B. 70, 71
graduate employment 20, 28, 31, 104–5
graduate tax 150
grant-maintained schools 42, 180
Green, A. and Steedman, H. 33
Green, Michael 56
Guba, E.G. 117
Guba, E.G. and Lincoln, Y.S. 112, 117
guidance 164–7, 173–5
    neutrality 167–70
    quality 170–73

Hamblin, A.C. 116
Handy, Professor Charles 8, 14, 40, 75, 103,
        104, 164
Hayes, R.H., Wheelwright, S.C. and Clarke,
        K.B. 111
health and safety 6
Hendry, C., Jones, A.M. with Cooper, N. 125
Her Majesty's Inspectorate (HMI) 166
Herbst, G. 119
Herriott, P. 163
Heyck, T.W. 9
hierarchies 8, 103
higher education 9, 10, 21, 28, 43, 143–4
    careers guidance 166
    increase in qualified graduates 104–5
    libraries and learning resources *see* academic
        libraries
    modular degrees 144
    new markets 135–6
    Open University 47–9
    provision in colleges of further education
        149
    research-led teaching 131–2, 134, 136–7
hippocampus 89
Hoggart, Richard 50, 51
Holland 149
Holland, Geoffrey 53, 54, 55, 61
home-based workers 8, 10
Hong Kong 2
Houston, J. 82
human potential *see* learning potential
Humphrey, N. 90
Hyundai Electrics 99

IFF Research Ltd 55, 59
Illich, I. 126
IMD, World Economic Forum 33
indoctrination 123
Indonesia 2
industry: links with schools 37, 38
Industry Training Boards 34–6
Industry Training Organizations (ITOs) 43
information management 131
    access 132, 133
        electronic 133
information processing 86–8
information technology 98, 101
innovation 99
Institute for the Future (IFF) Research Ltd 55,
        59
Institute of Management 182
Integrated Regional Offices (IROs) 147
intellectual property 133, 137
intelligence
    multiple 81–2
    personality types 85–6
interactive videos 145
Internet 133, 136
inter-person services 3, 5–6
interpersonal intelligence 82
intrapersonal intelligence 82
investment patterns 15
Investors in People 20, 29, 44, 57, 108, 142,
        145, 148, 150, 177, 185, 186
    careers guidance 166
Investors in Training 41
IQ 65, 67, 82

Jacques, Elliott 106
JANET (Joint Academic Network) 133
Japan 2, 33, 39, 40, 99, 100
John Fielden Consultancy 134–5
Joint Funding Councils' Libraires Review Group
     132
Jones, A. 97, 98–101, 109
Jones, A.M. and Hendry, C. 28, 120
Jones, D.E.L. 49
Jones, Susan 123
Joseph, Keith 51, 53
Jung, Carl 85

Kanter, R.M. 111, 112, 114
Kenny, J. and Reid, M. 126
Killeen, J., White, M. and Watts, A.G. 167,
     172
knowledge in context 72–4
Knowles, M.S. 122
Kolb, David 83, 84, 85, 87–8
Korea (South) 2, 99–100, 187
Kornbluh, H. and Greene, R.T. 122

labour costs 2
Labour Party 60, 61
Lafleur, B. 19
Langlois, J.H. 66
language teaching 79, 88–9
Latin 153
leadership 140–2
league tables 42
learned helplessness/influence 123, 125
learning *see also* educational system
   Accelerated Learning 79
   brain function 80–81, 88–90
   economic benefits 18–20, 30–31
      continuing education and training 29–30
      higher education 28
      measurement 20–24
      pre-school learning 25
      primary education 25–6
      problems of the 'academic mould' 23–4
      secondary education 26–7
      technical further education 27–8
   environments 146
   information processing 86–8
   lifelong *see* lifelong learning
   multiple intelligences 81–2
   personality types 85–6
   practical application 68, 69, 73, 84–5, 97
Learning Credits 108, 180, 183 *see also* Youth
     Credits
learning cycle 84–5
   organizations 126–8
Learning for Work entitlement 60
learning frustration 121
learning organizations 20, 29, 41, 44, 57, 102,
     108, 111–12
   adult learning theory 116–18
   assessment or evaluation of learning 114, 126
      qualitative aspects 114–15
   final stages of a learning scheme 126–8
   learning episodes 119
   learning patterns 118–19
   learning stages 119–21
   managing learning processes 121–3
   organizational change 123–5

provision of training 144–5
provisional encapsulations 122–3
quantitative analysis of learning 112–14
role of the evaluator-consultant 116
   researcher-internal consultant 116
top-down approach 122, 145
work-based traineeships 150
   learning credits 183
learning outcomes 95, 97–8
learning potential
   efflorescence 71–2
   knowledge in context 72–4
   pessimism 65–6
   reform of education and training 74–6
   rejection of the genetic model 69–71
   theory of inherent limitation 66
      effect on educational system 66–9
      effect on self-concept 66
      prediction of future performance 67
learning resources 131
learning societies 22–3, 58, 108, 140
   financing 149–51
   leadership 140–2
   learning within employment 144–5
   provision of learning 145–7
   regional management of colleges 147–9
   targets 143–4
learning strategies 9–10
LEAs (Local Education Authorities) 42
   careers guidance 167–8
   16–19 provision 180
LECs (Local Enterprise Companies) 44, 180,
     184–6
Lee, Jennie 48
LeGrand, J. and Bartlett, W. 169
leisure 56–7
Leitch, A. 67
Lennerlof, L. 123
libraries *see* academic libraries
life expectancy 181
lifelong learning 12, 14, 38, 41, 94, 143
   Advisory Council for Adult and Continuing
      Education 49–51
   changing concepts of educational and career
      progression 162–4
   coherence 179–80, 188
   customer-focused education 107, 159, 171–3
   employment change 155
   entitlements 60–62
   individual empowerment 182–3, 188
   local delivery 184–6, 189
   Manpower Services Commission 36–8, 39,
      40, 51–5, 154
   national guidance strategy 164–7, 173–5
      neutrality 167–70
      quality 170–73
   national learning targets 178–9, 187–8
   national qualification system 183–4, 188–9
   Open University 47–9
   social market 180–82, 188
   spread of best practice 186–7, 189
   spreading the cost 59–60, 103–4
   support for post-initial education 54, 56
Light, P. and Butterworth, G. 73
Limb, A.G. and Cook, M. 86
limbic system 89–90
Lincoln, Y.S. and Guba, E.G. 112, 117

Index

linguistic intelligence 81
literacy 25
loans 150
local delivery: lifelong learning 184–6, 189
Local Education Authorities *see* LEAs
Local Enterprise Companies (LECs) 44, 180, 184–6
local management of schools 42
logical intelligence 81
London School of Economics 18, 19

Mager, R. 115
Maine, University of 135
Malaysia 2
management 3, 15
  professional standards 40–41
  qualifications 154
Management Charter Initiative (MCI) 41
Manpower Services Commission 36–8, 39, 40, 51–5, 154
manual workers 3
March, J.G. and Olsen, J. 124
market principles 168–9, 181
Markova, I. 72
Maslow, A.H. 105
mastery 120–21
mathematical intelligence 81
mathematics 67–8, 83
Matsushita, K. 18
mature students 44, 48, 135
Mayr, E. 70
McIntosh, N.E. and Woodley, A. 49
McIntosh, N.E. *et al.* 47
McNair, S. 167
Miller, A., Watts, A.G. and Jamieson, I. 85
Ministry of Education 97
mobile telephones 8
Modern Apprenticeships 43, 143, 185
modular assessment 144, 157, 164
Montaigne, M. de 93
Morgan, P. 24
motivation 4, 5, 15, 20, 57, 61, 89, 107, 109, 120, 158, 182
  self-concept 65, 66, 117
multi-national companies 1–2
multiple careers 8, 155, 163–4
multiple intelligences 81–2
Murphy, James 18, 24
music 80
musical intelligence 81
Myers, Isabel 85
Myers, I.B. with Myers, P.B. 80
Myers, M.S. 69
Myers-Briggs Type Indicator (MBTI) 86, 88

National Advisory Body for Local Authority Higher Education (NAB) 56
National Advisory Council for Careers and Educational Guidance 174
National Advisory Council for Education and Training Targets (NACETT) 178–9
National Commission on Education 11–12, 168
National Council for Vocational Qualifications 154
national curriculum 38
National Curriculum Council (NCC) 165
national economy 1–2

National Education and Training Targets (NETTS) 13, 19, 45, 57, 141, 143, 145, 147, 148, 177, 178, 179
National Institute of Adult Continuing Education (NIACE) 50, 51, 59
National Institute of Economic and Social Research 149
National Record of Achievement (NRA) 166, 188
NEDO (National Economic Development Office) 39, 40
networking 134, 137
neurology 88–90
Newell, A. 72
Newsam, Peter 50
Newsom report 97
Newstead, S.E. and Dennis, I. 152
niche markets 2
Nissan 4–5
norm-referenced assessment 157, 158
Northcott, J. *et al.* 13, 15, 20
nursery education 25
NVQs (National Vocational Qualifications) 6, 29–30, 40, 42, 45, 144, 148, 154, 155, 158, 166, 180, 182, 183–4
  National Education and Training Targets 13, 143, 147

O'Brien, Richard 53
OECD (Organization for Economic Cooperation and Development) 14
  UK ranking 33
Office of Standards in Education (OFSTED) 157, 186
Ohmae, K. 93
Open College 56
open learning 164
Open Tech Programme 52–3, 55
Open University 47–9
organizational change 102–9, 123–5 *see also* learning organizations

PA Cambridge Economic Consultants (PACEC) 169
Pacific Rim 20, 98–102
Paid Educational Leave 60
parental choice 42
Parsons, J.M., Graham, N. and Honess, T. 68
part-time learning 146–7, 150
part-time work 164
Pascale, R.T. and Athos, A.G. 101
pastoral/academic split 97
pastoral care 96–7
Paterson, Alasdair 137–8
Patton, M.Q. 116
Payne, Joan 22
Pedler, M., Boydell, T. and Burgoyne, J.G. 129
Peers, I. and Johnston, M. 67
periodicals 132
Perret-Clermont and Bell, N. 67
personal skills 27
personality types 85–6
Pettigrew, A.M. 124
Pettigrew, A.M., Ferlie, E. and McKee, L. 126
physical appearance 66
physical intelligence 81–2

physics 68
Piaget, Jean 88
planners 4
play 120
Plato 65
Plotkin, H.C. and Odling-Smee, F.J. 70
'poaching' employees 20, 30, 34
Policy Studies Institute (PSI) 12–13, 59
political change 93
political leadership 140–2
polytechnics 48
Porter, Michael 2, 16, 19
potential *see* learning potential
practical ability 68, 69, 73, 84–5, 97
practice 120
Prais, Sig 22
Pratt and Whitney 99
pre-school learning 11, 25
President of the Board of Trade *et al.* 61
primary education 25–6
Prior, Jim 52
prior learning 164
production industries 3, 4–5
provisional encapsulations 122–3, 125
public expenditure 181

qualifications 20, 31, 143–4, 183–4 *see also*
        vocational qualifications
    equation with competence 159
    national comparisons 33
    use in reward or funding systems 160
quality-led organizations 119, 122, 170–73

Rabelais, F. 94
radio engineering 6–7
reading 83
reform proposals 74–6
Reich, Robert 3–4, 6, 8
research, educational 24
Research and Development 99, 100
research-led teaching 131–2, 134, 136–7
research scientists 3, 6–7
Review of Vocational Qualifications 154
Richardson, K. 66, 70, 73, 88
Rivis, V. and Sadler, J. 174
Robbins report 56
Robinson, D.N. 75
robots 4, 5
Rogers, A. 114, 117, 119, 120
Rogers, C. 66
Rooker, Jeff 62
Rose, Colin 79, 80, 82
Rose, Colin and Goll, Louise 81
Rose, S. and Rose, H. 75
rote learning 96
routine production services 3, 4–5
Rover Cars 57, 83
Rover Learning Business 108
Royal Society for the Encouragement of Arts,
        Manufacture and Commerce (RSA) 58,
        91, 97, 107, 120, 152
Ruskin, John 140
Russia 140

Sacks, O. 84
safety regulations 6
sandwich courses 85

Sargant, Naomi 59, 60
Save the Children Fund 25
School Curriculum and Assessment Authority
        158
school-leavers 61, 182
schools
    links with industry 37, 38
    local management 42
Schweinhart, Lawrence J. 25
scientific advances 22
Scottish Vocational Qualifications (SVQs) 183–4
Scriven, M. 116
Sear, K. 67
secondary education 26–7
Secondary Heads Association 97
self-concept 65, 66, 89–90
self-development 5, 41
self-employment 104, 105–6
self-help groups 107
Senge, P. 102, 111
service industries 3, 5–6
set theory 67–8
Sheffield, UK 2
Sheffield University 10
Singapore 2, 100
single chance theory 82
Sixth Form Colleges 180
skill shortages 28, 105
skilled labour 2, 4, 27, 34, 38, 98, 102
Skills Choice 61, 168
skills revolution 41, 177 *see also* CBI: *Towards a
        Skills Revolution*
small businesses 8, 184
Small Firm Training Loans 61
Social and Community Planning Research 59
social cooperation 70–71, 97, 99
Social Market Foundation 181
social values 20
South Korea 2, 99–100, 187
spatial intelligence 81
spectrum engineering 6
speculative research 24
speech impediments 80
Spencer, Herbert 3
St Exupéry, Antoine de 109
Stakes, R.L. 117
standard of living 1
standards in education 94
    pastoral/academic split 97
steel production 2
Stufflebaum, D.L. 116
subcontracted labour 104
Summer Labour Force Survey 59
Sunderland, UK 4
Sweden 148
Sylva, Professor Kathy 25

Taiwan 2
taxation 181
teacher training 91
teaching methods 97
teamwork 8, 10, 99, 100
Tebbit, Norman 54
TEC National Council 169, 185
TECs *see* Training and Enterprise Councils
Technical and Vocational Educational Initiative
        (TVEI) 37, 95, 100, 107, 182

Index

technical education 27–8
technology 22, 27, 98
temporary work 164
Tenbrink, T.D. 113
Thailand 2
Thatcher, Margaret 36
Thiede, W. 117
Thurow, L. 94
Times Educational Supplement 48
training 20, 29
  Ford 57, 108
  increased investment 44
  Industry Training Board 34–6
  Manpower Services Commission 36–8
  Nissan 5
  NVQs *see* NVQs
  Pacific Rim 99
  providers 144–7
  UK shortfalls 39–40
Training Agency 22, 60
Training and Enterprise Councils (TECs) 36, 37, 43, 44, 45, 58, 60, 61, 62, 141, 147, 150, 180, 184–6
  careers guidance 168
Training Commission 51
Training, Enterprise and Education Directorate (TEED) 58, 60
Training for Work (TFW) 185
Training Opportunities Scheme (TOPS) 36–7, 54
training videos 145
transfer of learning 9, 27–8, 35
TUC (Trades Union Congress) 54
TVEI (Technical and Vocational Educational Initiative) 37, 95, 100, 107, 182

UK
  OECD ranking 33
  training shortfalls 39–40
underclass 1, 12, 106
unemployment 1, 2, 12–13, 20, 28, 36, 53
  lack of training opportunities 56, 62
UNESCO 14

UNICEF 26
Unilever 29
unit based assessment 157–8
United Nations 25
Unit for the Development of Adult Continuing Education (UDACE) 50
university education *see* higher education
University for Industry 61
University Grants Committee (UGC) 56
university libraries *see* academic libraries
University of Maine 135
University of Sheffield 10
University of the Third Age 14
USA 39, 40, 99
  new markets in higher education 135
Usher, Peter 18

value-added activities 2, 4, 20, 21, 140
video conferencing 145, 146
visual intelligence 81
vocational education 33, 39, 40, 41, 43, 44, 52, 75, 152
  employment changes 155
vocational qualifications 146, 183–4 *see also* GNVQs; NVQs
  defining standards of competence 154
  public perceptions 159
Vygotsky, L.S. 71, 72, 73, 88

Wagner, R.K. 67
Watters, K. 79
Watts, A.G. 168, 169
Weikart, David P. 25
Wille, E. 4
Work Related Further Education 182
World Bank 26

Young, David (Baron Young) 53, 54, 56
Youth Credits 41, 45, 60–61, 180, 183, 185
Youth Opportunities Scheme (YOPS) 37, 53
Youth Training Scheme (YTS) 37, 54, 150, 185

Zunz, Sir Jack 20